The CISO Journey
Life Lessons and Concepts to Accelerate Your Professional Development

Internal Audit and IT Audit

Series Editor: Dan Swanson

A Guide to the National Initiative for Cybersecurity Education (NICE) Cybersecurity Workforce Framework (2.0)
Dan Shoemaker, Anne Kohnke, and Ken Sigler
ISBN 978-1-4987-3996-2

A Practical Guide to Performing Fraud Risk Assessments
Mary Breslin
ISBN 978-1-4987-4251-1

Corporate Defense and the Value Preservation Imperative: Bulletproof Your Corporate Defense Program
Sean Lyons
ISBN 978-1-4987-4228-3

Data Analytics for Internal Auditors
Richard E. Cascarino
ISBN 978-1-4987-3714-2

Fighting Corruption in a Global Marketplace: How Culture, Geography, Language and Economics Impact Audit and Fraud Investigations around the World
Mary Breslin
ISBN 978-1-4987-3733-3

Investigations and the CAE: The Design and Maintenance of an Investigative Function within Internal Audit
Kevin L. Sisemore
ISBN 978-1-4987-4411-9

Internal Audit Practice from A to Z
Patrick Onwura Nzechukwu
ISBN 978-1-4987-4205-4

Leading the Internal Audit Function
Lynn Fountain
ISBN 978-1-4987-3042-6

Mastering the Five Tiers of Audit Competency: The Essence of Effective Auditing
Ann Butera
ISBN 978-1-4987-3849-1

Operational Assessment of IT
Steve Katzman
ISBN 978-1-4987-3768-5

Operational Auditing: Principles and Techniques for a Changing World
Hernan Murdock
ISBN 978-1-4987-4639-7

Securing an IT Organization through Governance, Risk Management, and Audit
Ken E. Sigler and James L. Rainey, III
ISBN 978-1-4987-3731-9

Security and Auditing of Smart Devices: Managing Proliferation of Confidential Data on Corporate and BYOD Devices
Sajay Rai, Philip Chukwuma, and Richard Cozart
ISBN 978-1-4987-3883-5

Software Quality Assurance: Integrating Testing, Security, and Audit
Abu Sayed Mahfuz
ISBN 978-1-4987-3553-7

The CISO Journey: Life Lessons and Concepts to Accelerate Your Professional Development
Gene Fredriksen
ISBN 978-1-138-19739-8

The Complete Guide to Cybersecurity Risks and Controls
Anne Kohnke, Dan Shoemaker, and Ken E. Sigler
ISBN 978-1-4987-4054-8

Cognitive Hack: The New Battleground in Cybersecurity ... the Human Mind
James Bone
ISBN 978-1-4987-4981-7

The CISO Journey
Life Lessons and Concepts to Accelerate Your Professional Development

Gene Fredriksen

CRC Press
Taylor & Francis Group
Boca Raton London New York

CRC Press is an imprint of the
Taylor & Francis Group, an **informa** business
AN AUERBACH BOOK

CRC Press
Taylor & Francis Group
6000 Broken Sound Parkway NW, Suite 300
Boca Raton, FL 33487-2742

First issued in paperback 2022

© 2017 by Taylor & Francis Group, LLC
CRC Press is an imprint of Taylor & Francis Group, an Informa business

No claim to original U.S. Government works

ISBN 13: 978-1-03-240221-5 (pbk)
ISBN 13: 978-1-138-19739-8 (hbk)
ISBN 13: 978-1-315-27761-5 (ebk)

DOI: 10.1201/9781315277615

Library of Congress Cataloging-in-Publication Data

Names: Fredriksen, Gene, author.
Title: The CISO journey : life lessons and concepts to accelerate your professional development / Gene Fredriksen.
Description: Boca Raton, FL : CRC Press, 2017.
Identifiers: LCCN 2016043407 | ISBN 9781138197398 (hb : alk. paper)
Subjects: LCSH: Chief information officers. | Computer security. | Computer networks--Security measures. | Data protection.
Classification: LCC HF5548.37 .F735 2017 | DDC 658.4/78--dc23
LC record available at https://lccn.loc.gov/2016043407

Visit the Taylor & Francis Web site at
http://www.taylorandfrancis.com

and the CRC Press Web site at
http://www.crcpress.com

Contents

List of Figures xi
List of Tables xiii
Prologue xv
Foreword xix
Acknowledgments xxi
Author xxiii

SECTION I INTRODUCTION AND HISTORY

1 Introduction: The Journey 3

2 Learning from History? 5

3 My First CISO Lesson: The Squirrel 9
   The Big Question: How Did I End Up in Info Security? 10

SECTION II THE RULES AND INDUSTRY DISCUSSION

4 A Weak Foundation Amplifies Risk 15
   Patching: The Critical Link. 19
   It's about More Than Patching 21
       Patching Myth One 21
       Patching Myth Two 22
       Patching Myth Three 22
       Patching Myth Four 22
   Scanning Required! 23
       Misconception One 23
       Misconception Two 24
       Misconception Three 24
       Misconception Four 24
       Misconception Five 25
       Environment Control 26
       Tracking IT Assets 26

    Risk Management 27
    Key Questions to Ask 33

5 If a Bad Guy Tricks You into Running His Code on Your Computer, It's Not Your Computer Anymore.................................39
    Worms, Trojans, and Viruses: What's in a Name? 41
        Myth One 41
        Myth Two 42
        Myth Three 42
        Myth Four 43
        Myth Five 43
        Myth Six 44
        Myth Seven 44
        Myth Eight 45
        Myth Nine 45
        Myth Ten (and My Personal Favorite) 46
    Attack Types Are Wide-Ranging 46
    Social Engineering 47

6 There's Always a Bad Guy Out There Who's Smarter, More Knowledgeable, or Better-Equipped Than You...........................49
    What about Your People? 56
    Plan for the Worst 58
    Not All Alerts Should Be Complex 61
    What about Wireless? 61
    Context-Aware Security 63
    Suggested Reading 64

7 Know the Enemy, Think Like the Enemy.................................65
    Monitoring What Leaves Your Network Is Just as Important as Monitoring What Comes In: Introducing the "Kill Chain" Methodology ...73
    Stack the Deck in Your Favor 78
    Picking the Right Penetration Test Vendor 79
    How Should Penetration Testing Be Applied? 79
    Selecting a Vendor 80

8 Know the Business, Not Just the Technology...........................83
    The Role of Risk Management within the Enterprise 84
    Separation of Duties 86
    Is There an Overlap between Legal, Compliance, and Human Resources? ... 90
    A Model Structure 91
    Risk Management/Organizational Management Interaction 92
        Executive Steering Committee 93
        Information Security Officer Committee 93

Information Security Department Staffing 94
The Compliance Arm of the CISO Office 96
Security Operations and Engineering 96
User Access and Administration 97
Advice for the New CISO..98
Tying Your Goals and Objectives to Company Goals 101
Conclusion... 102

9 Technology Is Only One-Third of Any Solution............................. 103
Let's Look at Risk Management and the People, Process,
and Technology Methodology 104
Safe Harbor Principles 106
  Prevent 109
  Detect 110
  Respond 110
  Recover 112

10 Every Organization Must Assume Some Risk...................................... 115
No Is Seldom the Answer 117
Strive for Simplicity 120
Risk Planning Is Just as Important as Project Planning 121
Dealing with Internal Audit 125
The Work.. 127

11 When Preparation Meets Opportunity, Excellence Happens 129
End-User Training and Security Awareness 130
Flashback to High School Memories… 132
Training Methods.. 132
New Hire Training 133
Awareness Seminars 135
Security Policy 143
Roles and Responsibilities... 144
  Company Board and Executives....................................... 144
  Chief Information Officer 145
  Information Technology Security Program Manager 145
  Managers.. 145
  Users 146
Formal Training 147
Brown Bag Lunches 147
Organizational Newsletters... 148
Awareness Campaigns.. 148
Tests and Quizzes 149
Funding the Security Awareness and Training Program 149
Summary 150

12 There Are Only Two Kinds of Organizations: Those That Know They've Been Compromised and Those That Don't Know Yet 155

Loss Types 158
Consequences of Loss 158
How Can DLP Help? 158
Prevention Approach 159
    PCI DSS Credit Card Guidelines 159
    Guidelines 160
    Credit Card Processing Procedures 161
Employee Loyalty Is a Factor 162
What Can You Do? 167

13 In Information Security, Just Like in Life, Evolution Is Always Preferable to Extinction 169

Security Strategic Planning 171
The Planning Cycle 172
Foundation/Strategy 172
Assessment and Measurement 172
Key Risk Identification 173
Develop the Strategic Plan 174
    Process Inputs 175
    Money, Money, Money... 179
        Capital Expenditures 179
        Operational Expenses 179

14 A Security Culture Is In Place When Talk Is Replaced with Action 181

Introduction 181
Training 183
Basics 185
Technology 187
Data Security 188
Productivity 190
Communication 192
E-mail 195
Morale 196
Metrics and Measures 197
Workplace 198
Conclusion 200

15 NEVER Trust and ALWAYS Verify 203

Trust Your Vendors: Home Depot 207
Nervous about Trusting the Cloud? 209
    Does Your System Encrypt Our Data while They Are Stored on Your Cloud? 210

Does the Provider Have a Disaster Recovery Plan for Your Data? 210
Don't Confuse Compliance with Security 211
Has the Potential Vendor Earned Certifications for Security
and Compliance That Can Provide Assurance of Their Capabilities?...211
What Physical Security Measures Are in Place at the Supplier's
Data Centers? 212
Where Are My Data Being Stored? 212
Vendor Oversight Program Basics 213
Internal Trust..213

SECTION III   SUMMARY

16   My Best Advice for New CISOs **221**
Talking to the Board...223

Appendix A: The Written Information Security Plan **225**

Appendix B: Talking to the Board **241**

Appendix C: Establishing an Incident Response Program **253**

Appendix D: Sample High-Level Risk Assessment Methodology...............**273**

Index **279**

List of Figures

Figure 1.1 Threat cycle 4

Figure 4.1 Elements versus functions 17

Figure 4.2 Support life cycle 19

Figure 4.3 Patching...20

Figure 4.4 OSI layers 25

Figure 4.5 Risk matrix 29

Figure 6.1 My dad invents "defense in depth" 50

Figure 7.1 What the bad guys want..69

Figure 7.2 Rising sophistication 70

Figure 7.3 Attack frequency 72

Figure 7.4 Kill chain 75

Figure 8.1 Balance 86

Figure 8.2 Risk versus organizational pressures................................87

Figure 8.3 Risk management organization..91

Figure 8.4 Information Security Executive Council...........................93

Figure 8.5 Information Security Officer Committee..........................94

Figure 8.6 Office of the Chief Information Security Officer 95

Figure 8.7 RACI 99

Figure 8.8 Program goals 102

Figure 9.1 People, technology, process 108

Figure 9.2 Resiliency..109

Figure 9.3 Controls versus risk areas 113

Figure 10.1 Risk versus means 117

Figure 10.2 Risk versus means (2)... 119

Figure 10.3 Keep it simple 121

Figure 11.1 Awareness poster 148

Figure 13.1 Security strategy.. 173

Figure 13.2 Security plan.. 174

Figure 13.3 Compliance program goals 176

Figure 13.4 Investment priorities 177

Figure 13.5 Impact versus effectiveness... 178

Figure A.1 Business continuity.. 237

Figure B.1 Board engagement... 247

Figure B.2 Board framework.. 248

Figure B.3 Cost of a breach... 251

Figure C.1 CSIRT organization chart... 259

Figure C.2 Notification process 261

Figure C.3 Six stages of CSIR... 264

Figure C.4 Incident RACI 270

Figure D.1 Risk assessment... 274

Figure D.2 Risk assessment matrix 277

List of Tables

Table 15.1 Trust 215

Table 15.2 Trust with value 215

Table C.1 Security level classifications 267

Table C.2 Contact information 268

Table D.1 Overall risk 278

Prologue

Gaining Wisdom along the Journey

Ask anyone in the cybersecurity industry and they'll tell you that there's a staggering shortage of talent entering the field. This is happening at a time when information security is more critical than ever before in underpinning the successful and ongoing business operations of organizations everywhere.

As we continue to experience a relentless succession of cyberattacks unleashed on both private- and public-sector organizations, government and executive leaders alike are becoming increasingly aware of just how crucial their information security postures are to their mere subsistence. Standing at the forefront of the charge to make cybersecurity initiatives a way of life for businesses everywhere are the professionals who are tasked with not only trying to thwart current or future onslaughts but also identifying a throng of vulnerabilities within their infrastructures that could lead to additional attacks or result in penalties against their companies because of noncompliance with a bevy of industry and government mandates.

These and still other problematic information security issues, such as the adoption by organizations of the newest technologies or the ever-changing ways people engage with businesses today, which are all rife with weaknesses and appealing attack surfaces, have spurred a desperate need for organizations to employ qualified information security professionals at every level—from IT security analysts and architects to risk and compliance directors to Chief Information Security Officers (CISOs). Such practitioners have far-reaching roles that must see them build, maintain, and continuously update holistic risk management and compliance strategies and day-to-day tactics that account for internal- and external-facing operations and policies.

In other words, cybersecurity and privacy needs are acutely evident to growing numbers of professional leaders and everyday citizens. Yet, the resources, budget, and qualified practitioners required to adequately address these apparent necessities remain disproportionate to the assortment of today's security challenges. Perhaps, too, the basic understanding of what now is essentially a condition of not only conducting business but also simply living day to day is still being lost on some individuals and groups who are poised to set powerful examples of how cybersecurity must be integrated into pretty much every aspect of our lives.

According to a recent study undertaken by Intel Security in partnership with the Center for Strategic and International Studies, 76% of corporate IT leaders involved in cybersecurity decision-making who participated in the research said their respective governments are failing to invest enough in building specialized talent. Based on interviews with some 900 IT decision-makers from organizations with at least 500 employees situated in a range of countries (including the United States and seven others), a meager 23% said educational programs are actually preparing students to enter the industry. More than half stated that the cybersecurity skills shortage is worse than those faced by other IT professions.

Yet the scarcity of qualified pros has become a more prominent political focal point for some in the last couple of years, prompting the likes of our own President Obama and other countries' leaders to urge greater support for the information security field and its professionals' growth and development. Even with a few promising proposals underway, however, they couldn't happen soon enough given that about 70% of the research participants said the current talent shortage is causing direct, measurable harm to their networks. In fact, one in four admitted that their businesses have lost proprietary or critical data because of the dearth of cybersecurity skills on hand within their organizations.

What's needed, they explained further, is some hearty on-the-job training, which takes precedent over a mere university degree, though individuals looking for a role in their companies must have formal educational credentials to garner any serious consideration. Also, more vigorous continuous education, engaging instructional opportunities and nontraditional methods of learning, such as hands-on exercises, hackathons, and more, likely would prove an additional boost to strengthening the talent pool.

In this regard, information security industry conferences and events—especially those boasting more varied and practical learning experiences—have become more vital and, as a result, well attended by seasoned pros and newbies alike. For Gene Fredriksen, these gatherings are a pretty decent barometer in revealing how the industry is changing and what long-time, more-seasoned leaders like him, a group he calls "the first generation of CISOs," can do to help it continue to thrive and evolve. Mentoring, as he notes in the following pages of this book, is a main component crucial to the ongoing development of this marketplace and the people in it. And this happens not only at a variety of industry events, but also is critical on the job.

"As I move further into my career, my focus is on evangelism and helping to drive the overall profession further. Part of that is helping peers explain complex issues clearly to the E-suite (executive suite)," he explained to me in an e-mail exchange last year. "It's all about passing the torch and leaving things better as the first generation of CISOs begins to retire."

He called out some signs of this metamorphosis when attending one of the longest-standing industry events, the RSA Conference, last year. As he looked around at others hitting the show, he remembered thinking: "When did they start allowing 12-year-olds on the exhibit floor? I can't believe I got my first full-time infosec job in 1989."

But it's that experience starting in the field right when it was only at the extreme early stages of any real, well-formed profession that has enabled him to pick up many a lesson along the way, study with varied and experienced mentors, make and learn from mistakes, hone and grow his technical and leadership skills, and develop and refine a robust information security philosophy. Enlisting all this know-how, he has found himself over the years establishing and managing both cybersecurity plans and departments for global organizations that often had neither when he started there. Really, as an infosec pioneer, his own vocational beginning was just as fledgling as the cybersecurity industry itself; he played an indispensable role alongside others like him to drive and mold what it meant to create, propel, and oversee an information security strategy and the teams and divisions supporting it.

After I met Gene around 2003 or so, he asked that I come to St. Petersburg, Florida, to participate in a conference he had organized at the long-standing financial services company Raymond James where he worked at the time as the company's first CISO. The roster was stellar, having other leading industry practitioners like him speaking alongside cybersecurity specialists from the likes of the FBI, DHS, and others. That I was asked to participate was an honor, especially given that our first engagement was impelled by a disagreement over some topic or another that I covered in one of my commentaries. Gene recalls contacting me with his differing thoughts.

"The following month, you put a follow-up [in another commentary] saying that Gene Fredriksen of Raymond James didn't completely agree with your views and passed them along. Shortly after that we talked and it's been a great relationship ever since," he recalls.

And it has. His professionalism, thoughtfulness, and combination of both technical prowess and business acumen saw his career blossom over the years. From Raymond James, he moved to IT industry research and analysis company Burton Group, which was acquired by Gartner in recent years, to become one of their leading industry analysts. After that, he was off to security systems giant Tyco International where he created their global cybersecurity strategy and division, thereby helping to advance the security of both internal operations and external product offerings. And, currently, he is CISO for financial services firm PSCU, which provides both traditional and online assistance to more than 800 credit unions. All the while, he has contributed columns to *SC Magazine* and *scmagazine .com*, spoken at our events—both live and online, participated on our Editorial Advisory Board, and been a cover story subject who shared his thoughts on threat intelligence gathering and kill chain processes to support information security strategies and initiatives. More than that, though, he has provided much-welcome guidance to me as my team and I navigated the industry to ensure that our brand was always improving and always meeting the needs of CISOs like him.

Mentoring—not only does he advocate it in the pages of this book, but he engages in it every single day with folks like me, his staff, colleagues, and, of course, his own kids. And he reminds us all that we should embrace opportunities to guide, educate, and welcome both new talent, whether they're just starting their careers or making transitions from others, to continue driving the overall industry, the profession itself, and ourselves ever forward.

"Much of what we do as CISOs or security professionals is based on our experiences and the lessons we have learned over the years," he states in his introduction to this book. "Mentorship is a critical part of the development of our skills."

He couldn't be more accurate. And what he provides here in *The CISO Journey* are outcomes from some of those learning moments he has experienced over his career, the challenges along the way that helped him to continue to progress professionally and personally, and the "rules of information security" that he has modified from peers or shaped and sharpened himself. Infused with a little humor along the way—because seeing the laughable side of situations is a trait that can soften even some of the hardest blows dealt to us all, Gene now presents to you all of his rules, industry best practices, and sage counsel to aid you on your own journey.

Illena Armstrong
VP, Editorial, SC Magazine

Illena Armstrong is VP, Editorial of *SC Magazine*, the leading business magazine for the information security industry, where she manages editorial staff in New York and Michigan. She is responsible for overseeing the award-winning monthly publication and its many other editorial offerings, including scmagazine.com, the *SC Magazine* Canada monthly digital editions, numerous eConferences, webcasts, newsletters, and physical events in the United States and Canada, and more. She has spoken and moderated at a number of industry events, including SC World Congress, SC Congress Canada, *SC Magazine* Roundtables, the RSA Conference, the Techno Security Conference, and others. On her watch, *SC Magazine* has won more than 20 awards, including Magazine of the Year 2009, from the American Society of Business Publication Editors (ASBPE). Before her stint at *SC Magazine*, she worked for various newspapers and magazines in New England and the southern United States.

Foreword

Security is a complex subject and an equally complicated problem to solve. Volumes have been written on the subject, much of which has a rather short half-life given the rapid change in technology and the creativity of the adversaries we face. Sir Alfred J. Ayer (1910–1989), a noted English philosopher, once said, "There never comes a point where a theory can be said to be true. The most that one can claim for any theory is that it has shared the successes of all its rivals and that it has passed at least one test which they have failed." So it is with approaches to security. There is no absolute solution, just incrementally better ones.

What Gene Fredriksen has offered us is not so much a technical discourse on security but rather a common sense approach to security based on his years of experience. He offers approaches that can lead to better solutions and enhanced security. As Gene once explained to me, "Never get into a fight without the data to back you up." This sage and simple advice has helped me throughout the years. It is common sense that many leaders of today seem to lack or have erroneously supplanted with technology. Common sense is far more enduring than technology though evidently more difficult to acquire.

What Gene presents is a sort of Ockham's Razor for security. Another way to sum it up is it reflects the KISS principle: keep it simple, stupid. Anyone who has worked with Gene knows how he avoids complexity, which has served him and the companies he has worked for well. There are no precise answers offered in this book to the myriad challenges you may face in your security role. It is more like the irrational numbers Pi or Phi that offer no precision yet present elegance in their very existence and application to real world problems.

Richard D. Lanning, Jr., PhD
Planear, LLC

Acknowledgments

With special thanks to:

Richard Lanning, PhD: His help was instrumental in the creation of this book. His ethics, analytical skills, and industry knowledge are a great asset to the company and me personally. I value his friendship and counsel.

Illena Armstrong, *SC Magazine* VP and Editor: She has been a longtime source of support and advice.

Pamela Fredriksen, my wife: Her support and love have kept me "shiny side up" during this journey. There were many late nights and long trips over the years and she has always been there for me.

Heather, Jeff, Holly, and Joe, our four children: They have kept life interesting and rewarding for me. Thanks for your support and inspiration.

Kathy Simpson: Her graphics skills are amazing. Thank you for your invaluable help.

Deborah Kobza, CEO of the Global Institute for Cyber Security and Research: A longtime friend and peer who has influenced my career.

David Bryant, Information Security Officer, PSCU: He has worked with me at many companies over the last 16 years. Thank God he is patient and long suffering.

Lori Lucas, Head of Technology Compliance for PSCU: She has also been a longtime friend and advisor.

Rini Fredette, Enterprise Risk Officer for PSCU: A great peer and an expert in the area of Enterprise Risk.

Lee Carpella: Instrumental in the editing of this book.

Larry Clinton, CEO of the Internet Security Alliance: An expert in the Cyber Security Industry and Regulatory space. Larry is a great friend and advisor.

Richard Jacek: He was my first official mentor in industry. I still use many of the skills he taught me today.

Brad Anderson: A longtime friend and associate who has helped me shape my views of technology and the world.

Chuck Fagan, CEO of PSCU: If there was a template for a Security Aware CEO, it would be Chuck.

Michael Echols, CEO of the International Association for Certified ISAOs: Mike is an exceptional resource given his broad range of private sector and government experience.

Israel Martinez, CEO of Axon: A mentor and friend for many years.

Author

Gene Fredriksen, Chief Information Security Officer at PSCU, is responsible for the company's development of information protection and technology risk programs. Gene has more than 25 years of information technology experience, with the last 20 focused in information security. In this capacity, he has been heavily involved with all areas of audit and security. Before joining PSCU, Gene held the positions of CISO for Tyco International, principal consultant for Security and Risk Management Strategies for Burton Group, vice president of Technology Risk Management and chief security officer for Raymond James Financial, and information security manager for American Family Insurance. Gene is a distinguished fellow with the Global Institute for Cyber Security and Research, located at the Kennedy Space Center. He is also the executive director of the newly formed National Credit Union Information Sharing and Analysis Organization. He was the chair of the Security and Risk Assessment Steering Committee for BITS, and served on the R&D committee for the Financial Services Sector Steering Committee of the Department of Homeland Security. Gene is a distinguished fellow for the Global Institute for Cyber Security and Research, headquartered at the Kennedy Space Center. Gene is a member of the *SC Magazine* Editorial Advisory Board and was named one of three finalists for the *SC Magazine* CISO of the Year Award in 2015. He served as chair of the St. Petersburg College Information Security Advisory Board and the Howard University Technology Advisory Board. He is a member of multiple advisory boards for universities, organizations, and security product companies. Gene attended the FBI Citizens Academy and maintains a close working relationship with both local and federal law enforcement agencies.

INTRODUCTION AND HISTORY

1

Let's get started by looking at a little history, both from a personal and an information security standpoint. In an era of unprecedented change, sometimes it takes a look backward to help chart the course forward.

My best advice? Understand where you are before you decide how to get to your goal.

Chapter 1

Introduction: The Journey

My name is Gene and I'm a long-term cybersecurity guy. In fact, I'm sneaking up on retirement in a few years. I'm not sure if I should be relieved that I've survived or sad that I will miss the daily challenge. As I reflect on my career as a CISO (Chief Information Security Officer), it dawned on me that those of us around my age are really the first generation of those to hold the CISO role. We have seen this career path morph over the last 20 or so years from a sideline buried in information technology, to a strategic and visible role. I am excited about what the future holds for those who succeed me.

I've seen all facets of information security change drastically over the years. There is an old adage from the 1930s that basically said, "Better Bank Vaults Breed Better Safe Crackers." It really is a variant on the continuous improvement cycle. As security technology becomes more robust, those creating ways to circumvent the security become more technically competent and creative (Figure 1.1). This continuing spiral means that we can't become stagnant or complacent. If we do, we will lose.

I've also seen the regulatory and governance side of the CISO job change. Let's be honest, when I accepted the first job where Information Security was part of the title, it was "Manager of Information Security and E-mail." Even the business was not sure that this new "information security thing" would be a full-time job. Even I wondered if technology might solve the whole virus and hacker problem. In the 1980s, there were few regulations about information protection, even in the financial services sector. Now, negotiating the complexity of overlapping and sometimes conflicting regulations and laws can be mind-numbing at the least.

Also, to be honest, I thought that as I approached retirement, I would be spending more time at my desk, directing a great team who would be doing the hard work. OK, now I know that was completely delusional. Today, I'm working harder than I have in my life. Whatever rules there are, change daily.

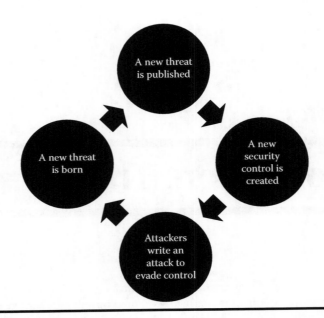

Figure 1.1 Threat cycle.

As I thought about what kind of amazing book I would write, I, like many other CISOs, came up with all sorts of technical and process topics. However, the more I thought about it, the more it became obvious to me that this was probably not the right choice.

As CISOs, we are charged with developing protection systems and processes to protect the data of a specific company. Based in a large part on our experiences, we design these systems, applying technologies to meet the needs of our business. There is never a one size fits all. Given that, I've decided to share the journey from mechanical engineer to CISO. The lessons and pearls of wisdom I've collected along the way are what have collectively made me what I am today. Let me absolutely state that I don't consider myself the model of the world's greatest CISO. God knows I've had my share of problems over the years. What I'm hoping to do is share my mistakes, experiences, and lessons. Hopefully, you will find one or two of value in this personal, slightly irreverent look at the evolution of a typical cybersecurity career. Hopefully, you will see a little of yourself in the following pages.

Chapter 2

Learning from History?

I'm often asked, "What is the most important thing about being a Chief Information Security Officer (CISO)?" Interestingly, over the years, the answer has changed, just like the field of information security.

Twenty-five years ago, I would have listed technical expertise. Most of us were one-person shops with a focus on antivirus and firewall rules. The threats were fairly slow moving, as was technology. Over the years as the job has changed, I will now unequivocally tell everyone that leadership is now the most critical attribute.

The CISO is now one role in an effective security group. Don't get a big head, I didn't say the most important, just one of the jobs.

A seasoned CISO understands the value of hiring people technically smarter than him or her. You need all sorts of tools and talent to be successful; you can't do it all yourself. Your job is to lead the program with skill, not dictate. Information security is a war of attrition, and leading your staff is like training the team to run a marathon. You can't do it by running on their heels and barking commands. You must give them something to run toward. The way you do it is by exhibiting strong leadership and having a crystal clear strategy. Be transparent and honest. You hired smart people; let them do their job. Remember, even though you undoubtedly worked hard to achieve the CISO title; don't get too wrapped up in your own self-importance. Being the leader is a job that is only needed if there is a team. Value and nurture them.

If you follow information security and stories of breaches, you'll notice as I did that every year lately is referred to as the year of the breach. We are seeing unheard of numbers of records being breached, and the reports of breaches are coming faster and faster.

As I said, we are in a war of attrition with the criminals. The professional criminals are well organized, well trained, and well compensated. When I first started, the typical hacker was a loner, or a teen with too much time on their hands. The typical attack was a nuisance attack, more of an irritant than anything. We used to refer to a large portion of them as "ankle biters." Don't worry, this will not turn into a yearning for the "good old days" discussions. The world of today is what it is. We have no control over the bad guys, we can only control how we respond and react. There is no silver bullet; if there was, we would all know about it. In fact, I propose that focusing all your efforts on searching for a technology solution will ultimately hurt your security stance.

The best security solution for a business is a balance of People, Process, and Technology controls that is tailored to the business need and mission. Throughout this book, you will see me reference the People, Process, and Technology model. Putting too much emphasis on only one segment weakens the whole model. Your job is to be the visionary that maintains the balance. There are security frameworks and control structures we can reference, but I'm sad to say there is no cookie cutter approach that guarantees security.

Much of what we do as CISOs or security professionals is based on our experiences and the lessons we have learned over the years. Mentorship is a critical part of the development of our skills. In my case, I was lucky to have an excellent mentor named Rick Jacek who taught me as much about human behavior as technology. Rick was the Technology Troubleshooter for the company. If there was a technology product headed south anywhere in the global company, Rick was sent in to fix it. It was from him that I initially learned about the importance of People, Process, and Technology, as it was never just one component that put the project at risk. He was also keenly aware of the effect of culture, particularly outside of the United States. I remember a discussion with a business unit manager in a South American company recently purchased by the firm for which we worked. Rick had to convince the manager that keeping a pile of cash in his desk drawer to "get things done" was no longer an acceptable operating model.

I also learned from various mentors that Information Technology is in place to serve the business, not the other way around. Computers are just a tool that allows us to do what we are in place to do: serve the customer. This was made clear to me in my first "Data Processing Manager" role for a manufacturing firm. My job was to run systems that supported the end goal of getting product on the shipping dock at the end of the day. If I did anything to jeopardize that goal, my job was at risk. I knew my job was less important than the people who built and shipped the product. A lesson I've kept till this day.

We have to constantly rethink our strategies and approaches. It's clear that the "build big walls" strategy of the past is not working. Technology companies would have us believe that if we buy the latest, greatest product, we will be safe, but common sense tells us that is simply not true.

We are also at a significant crossroads in the evolution of the CISO role. The image of an ass-kicking, hard-charging, and damn the torpedoes, barely legal cyber cowboy must die. While I still see many of my peers hanging on to that stereotype, it is absolutely the opposite of the C suite executive. We must become business people, able to protect the business while showing the value of what we are doing. We all remember the FUD factor: Fear, Uncertainty, and Doubt? In the past, we all used it at least a little to scare the business into making critical security investments. Well, put it away, it doesn't work in the long term anymore. You need to be a business partner, an advocate of the business, and build the critical alliances necessary to strengthen the security culture of the organization.

The other stereotype that must die is what I call the "secret police." While it is true that CISOs have many tools at their disposal that can monitor user activity, they must not be used for fishing expeditions or to instill a "big brother" mentality at a business. Ultimately, that will destroy security goodwill and culture. Watch for the security folks who like to wear fobs or toys from law enforcement. Watch for the people who say if they had to do it over again they would join the CIA or Secret Service. CISOs must investigate, but must do it within the bounds of corporate policy and culture. Like many people, I am a Dilbert fan. One of the characters that turn up from time to time is "Mordac—The Preventer of Information Services." Trust me, you never want to get pegged as that person. If people assume your answer will be no, they will look for ways around you. Your job is to say "how" to do it securely. Work with the business, be part of the solution, don't be the problem.

For most of us, we are charged with protecting the information entrusted to the company by its customers. We don't own it, and we are bound by professionalism to build and maintain a balanced security structure to protect it. It has taken me years of experiences to build an approach to security. While it is impossible to cover 30 years in a short book, I'd like to share some of the major lessons and rules I've developed. Around those lessons, I will try to inject some of my current thinking on the issues.

Have I done everything right? Hell no. The one thing I do wish is that I'd had a dedicated CISO mentor, but since that wasn't possible, I gleaned information from some great mentors over my career. My hope is that you take my experience and thinking, and find at least a couple of good ideas that will help you in your "Journey."

Spoiler Alert: Since every business is different, and the threats morph quickly, there is no silver bullet. You will have to find your way, build your alliances, and become the great CISO that the industry needs going forward.

Chapter 3

My First CISO Lesson: The Squirrel

It all started in my youth:

We all have life lessons learned as a child. Many of them are common, such as work hard, study hard, be honest, and have integrity. However, there are some in retrospect that, while we did not know it at the time, gave us long-term lessons for life.

My first lesson started with a bird feeder. As a boy, I was always messing with my father's tools, building things out of whatever I could find. One of my great achievements was a bird feeder for the yard. After careful planning, crafting, and painting, I proudly staked it out in our yard, filled it with seed, and went in the house confident that we would be overrun with colorful birds in no time.

The next morning, I jumped up, ran to the window to see the flock of birds, and much to my surprise, the feeder was empty...and no birds. The lawn around the feeder looked like a mess, strewn with seeds—those must have been some ravenous birds. I filled up the feeder one more time in the evening, confident that if I got up early, I'd see the flock of birds.

Setting my alarm early, I ran to the window, and much to my shock, I saw no birds; only a gray squirrel having breakfast...On My Bird Feeder!!!! Immediately, my mind began to formulate plans to stymie this interloper; no free food for this squirrel anymore.

Over the next few days, I tried every trick I knew; I greased the pole, I put a rubber collar on the pole, I sprayed ammonia around the pole. But every day the story was the same: the squirrel was getting fatter and my bird feeder was always empty. Not only that, but to this day, I swear that the little SOB started mocking me from his perch in the neighbor's yard. It had become personal. That little rat with a fuzzy tail was messing with me, an official Boy Scout.

The daily war continued for a couple of weeks. I was more irritated; the squirrel was fatter. Finally, one day, our neighbor, who was a retired farmer, sensed my frustration and came over with some sound advice. He said, "I see your problem, and you will never beat that squirrel!" "Why?" I asked, trying to be polite. He took a puff on his pipe, looked at me wisely and said, "You spend maybe an hour a day trying to keep that squirrel out of your feeder, but that squirrel spends 24 hours a day figuring out how to steal your bird seed. If you are not prepared to make the same effort to keep him out, you will lose."

At that time, I thought I had learned a lesson about bird feeders and squirrels. But, as I progressed in my career, I realized that it was about dealing with adversaries of any type. In the cybersecurity world, we are no longer dealing with part-time hackers, we are dealing every day with organized, well-funded, effective groups of "squirrels" intent on stealing our corporate "bird seed." These cyber criminals also communicate well and share information freely among themselves. Interestingly, this is contrary to the culture we have bred in the information security profession. We tend to keep ourselves and our organization's information locked up in a silo; we have been taught that sharing vulnerabilities and problems we have experienced is a bad thing. The actuality of the situation couldn't be further from the truth. Through this book, I will share experiences, something we must all learn to do if we are to keep pace with our adversaries. The journey from good to great is not enough. Unfortunately, our adversaries are already great at being bad.

Later in my career, I took a job where I had to live in New Jersey for a couple of years. When I shared this story at a local conference, an attendee told me that, in Jersey, they would have had a different approach to solving the squirrel story. He told me that he "knew a guy who knew a guy that could make the squirrel disappear—If you know what I mean…" Ah, what a difference cultures bring to problems. The diversity of solutions to a single problem (in this case, tongue in cheek, hopefully) shows that we must be open and ready to embrace many suggestions and solutions.

The Big Question: How Did I End Up in Info Security?

OK, I'll date myself. As a young engineer, I drew my designs on paper. You know that white flat stuff we used to use? Every morning, I stood in front of my drafting board with a new sheet of white vellum, sharp pencils, my slide rule, a company logo pocket protector, and endless possibilities. Life was good and the world was in order. My efforts were only bounded by one rule: never draw more in the morning than you can erase in the afternoon. I did everything to keep the universe in balance.

But we're not here to talk about the good old days. Let's bring it back to security. Our designs (or data) were committed to paper. Data security was basically locking the room where all the drawings were kept. If you were authorized to enter the print room, you could check out a drawing, signing a log to acknowledge your actions. All revisions or changes you made to the design were noted on the drawing, and the drawing was eventually checked back in. If needed, you could make a copy of the drawing. All critical drawings were microfilmed and the copy was kept off site in case of disaster. Simple, manual, and easy to understand. And...we always knew where the data were and if they were secure. I like to refer to this as the "good old days" from a security perspective. However, it had productivity problems, and needed to change to meet new business demands and the pace of industry in general.

Computerization came charging into engineering. As we began to explore Computer-Aided Design, we realized that even though we printed out the drawings (and locked them in the print room), we now had an electronic version of the drawings that somehow had to be secured. We started with one generic sign-on for all the engineers with no password, and slowly worked our way into each person having a unique account name and password. By the way, once we had the design on the computer, we printed it out and put it in the print room. Paper was still the official copy and archive.

As always happens, business continued to change. Production needs to build products faster and more flexibly drove the development of computer-controlled equipment, which was electronically linked to the digital designs. While the early machines kept the programs on rolls of black paper tape with ASCII format holes punched in them, it was only a matter of time until the business wanted online storage. As an engineer, one of my early projects was to connect production machines via a thick coax-based cable to a central PC-based server. Today, that is about a two-hour job to connect and format the equipment. I'm almost embarrassed to say I spent six months on the project. Now, we had connectivity from the "office" to the "factory floor." With the changes in manufacturing such as Kanban and Just-in-Time, the business also wanted the inventory levels linked real time to the manufacturing processes.

Because of the dynamic environment, we had to look at setting up a type of file level security to put a "wall" between production and designs, which were still in development. Multiple levels of folders with unique access control lists soon came around, and eventually we needed someone who specialized in this file level access. At this time, there was no Internet: Securing the electronic frontier was simply a matter of unplugging the modem we used for file transfer. There were good tools from the computer companies to manage access to files and manage user IDs. No distributed computers or PC networks, but that was all about to change.

The Internet hit us all. A project to create the first company website was a major project driven by high-priced consultants. We put in our first firewall in about 1990. It was not very sophisticated; it was simply a packet filter. Packet filters acted by inspecting the "packets" that are transferred between computers on the Internet. If a packet matches the packet filter's set of filtering rules, the packet filter dropped it. It was simple and effective, but just a beginning.

Business and academia drove continuous change. More features and functionality brought additional risks. The cycle continued to spiral. Interestingly, in the early days of my career, I thought the job would be more of an administrative function. The primary job was to design and administer access to information to protect the information from loss or accidental corruption. How wrong can one guy be?

Over the years, I developed rules of Information Security. I adopted some from peers, learned them through sometimes-hard lessons, and noticed that they were a recurring theme at every turn. They are as follows:

- A weak foundation amplifies risk.
- If a bad guy tricks you into running his code on your computer, it's not your computer anymore.
- There's always a bad guy out there who's smarter, more knowledgeable, or better-equipped than you.
- Know the enemy, think like the enemy.
- Know the business, not just the technology.
- Technology is only one-third of any solution.
- Every organization must assume some risk.
- When preparation meets opportunity, excellence happens.
- There are only two kinds of organizations: those that know they've been compromised, and those that don't know yet.
- In information security, just like in life, evolution is always preferable to extinction.
- A security culture is in place when talk is replaced with action.
- Never Trust and Always Verify.

Rather than walk through my entire life, I am going to organize the next section in line with my rules of information security. In each section, we will discuss the circumstances that prompted me to add a rule, and discuss current industry best advice on the subjects.

My hope is that I can pass on some advice, lessons learned, or stories that will strike a chord with you. Enjoy my life experiences and cyber stories. Good luck in your career!

THE RULES AND INDUSTRY DISCUSSION

This section looks at the "rules of the road" that have helped guide me over the years. Some with a little humor, most with a little pain.

I'm sure every reader will glean some nuggets of wisdom or memories of similar incidents that happened to them.

While many of them are common sense rules, I've found that in the heat of battle, common sense flies out the window. Every great football coach will tell you that the foundation of any career is built on the basics of "blocking and tackling." If you don't excel in those areas, your career options are limited.

Find your own set of common sense rules and practice them daily. That way, when you find yourself under pressure to act, the common sense part will be automatic.

Enjoy, learn, and borrow the concepts as you chart your CISO career.

Chapter 4

A Weak Foundation Amplifies Risk

I will always remember the first house we bought. It was small and crowded with four children and a dog, but it was our palace. As with any new house, I had a huge list of projects that needed to be done, so like any guy, I picked the most fun and "manly" project, which was to build a deck off the back door. Yes, the vision of grilling, picnics, and kids playing was crystal clear in my mind.

Like any young engineer, I had a great plan. I got my list together, borrowed a pickup, and headed for the lumberyard: soon I was ready to attack the project. My first task was to dig the holes for the supports that would hold up the deck. I got the first hole to the prescribed depth with minimal problems. On the second, about a foot below the surface, I hit a piece of buried concrete. Not to be defeated, I modified my layout and moved the hole about a foot. No luck—it soon became obvious to me that the piece of concrete was roughly the size of Ohio. Damn....

Needless to say, the same scenario played out on the remaining holes. Since I had no dynamite handy, I ran the posts down to the buried obstacles and decided that the support would be adequate; after all, it would have been very difficult to fix the subterranean issues. And, talking to some of my new neighbors, I found out that my new house was built on a lot with a lot of construction debris as fill. Who knows what was down there.

All was idyllic until the following spring. I noticed the deck had a definite list to the right. Sure enough, one corner had dropped about two inches as a result of the winter freeze and thaw cycles. Not to be outdone by a small problem, I jacked it up and placed some shims to level it out. Although I didn't know it at the time, I was turning into a young Don Quixote, who instead of jousting at windmills,

I was making a career out of keeping the deck level, a task that turned out to be just as futile and pointless.

Hey, I really didn't have a choice; it would have quickly gotten to a point that I could only grill flat stuff like burgers. If I tried hotdogs, they might roll off the grate and end up on the floor unless I pinned them down with toothpicks.

In the end, I really should have fixed the initial problem, which was a weak foundation. I ended up spending more time keeping the deck level than I would have spent cleaning up the legacy environment.

I'm sure all of us can relate to this lesson from my life. In technology or business, we get so busy doing new fun stuff that there is never time to fix the foundational issue. We justify it calling it everything from "legacy issues" to the one I really hate, which is "technical debt." Whatever we call it, the weak foundation and inefficiencies of the past add risk to every new project. So, we develop a new system and identify and manage the risks in the new system; however, once we place the new system on the weak foundation, any residual risk in the system is amplified due to the problems in the infrastructure.

What is "technical debt?" Missing patches and upgrades, old or non-supported applications (apps) (come on, admit that you have at least one old application that still runs on Windows XP), broken/inefficient processes, and the list can go on. There are only two ways to address it, let the bad stuff hang in until it is eventually replaced or obsolete, or fix it. The ostrich approach of burying your head in the sand and ignoring it is not a viable long-term risk management strategy.

Remember, sooner or later, your weenies will roll off the grill and it will happen at the worst possible time.

In your organization, do you have a full understanding of all the components of your foundation? You may be tempted to believe it is only built of computers and networks, but in actuality it is the full combination of people, processes, and technologies. They are all interrelated, and any one element needs the others to make the environment work robustly and smoothly. I have learned over the years that an effective foundation encompasses the three elements of People, Process, and Technology. Take away one, or have one substantially weaker than the others and you get a very unstable base. Just like a three-legged stool, if one leg is shorter or weaker than the others, there is an accident waiting to happen. Figure 4.1 looks at the three elements of People, Process, and Technology, and how they intersect with the four primary functions of any information security group. Those functions are to Prevent (bad things from happening), Detect (if they do), Respond (to limit the damage), and Recover (quickly to get the business going again).

Let's look at the components from Figure 4.1.

People: In order to adequately protect your environment, the CISO must know who is accessing the systems and why. We all have employees and customers, but many of us also must allow partners and third parties to access our systems. If you have been watching the news, you know that literally all of the major breaches have

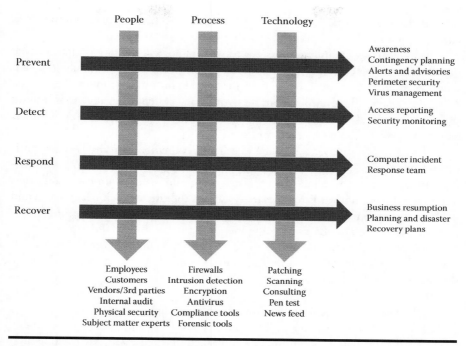

People   Process   Technology

Prevent — Awareness
Contingency planning
Alerts and advisories
Perimeter security
Virus management

Detect — Access reporting
Security monitoring

Respond — Computer incident
Response team

Recover — Business resumption
Planning and disaster
Recovery plans

Employees	Firewalls	Patching
Customers	Intrusion detection	Scanning
Vendors/3rd parties	Encryption	Consulting
Internal audit	Antivirus	Pen test
Physical security	Compliance tools	News feed
Subject matter experts	Forensic tools	

Figure 4.1   Elements versus functions.

involved a connection to a vendor or third-party partner. When you allow unfettered access from a remote location, you are extending your "risk universe" to their systems. On the positive side of the people equation, you have internal partners and peers such as internal audit, physical security, and subject matter experts. Build those relationships early and feed them through ongoing contact and team building. This will pay off in a big way when the bad stuff hits the fan and you need their help. Simply said, know your users, their functions, and your extended support resources.

Process: OK, you will hear this from me many times in this book, but a bad process is only marginally better than no process. Processes must be reliable and repeatable or they will cause more trouble than you can stand. A bad process will absolutely fail at the worst possible time. I listed a few above, patching, scanning, penetration (pen) testing.

Keep this image in mind as you read the rest of this book. Everything you do as a CISO needs to track back to these functions. This is why you were hired. Do this well and you will be successful.

So how is your foundation? Is it well maintained? Sadly, things today are not built like the Egyptian pyramids or Roman aqueducts. These have stood the test of time without the need for maintenance until recent years. The physical environment has changed much over the past 2000 years so these magnificent constructions are now in need of repairs. Unfortunately for us, the technological environment is changing at a much faster pace. So fast that most of us can't keep up.

The typical way manufacturers address technological change is through the distribution of patches, software updates, and full-scale new product releases. Considering the time and expense necessary to deploy a new product release, it is no wonder companies opt to remain on their legacy systems. Legacy tends to have different meanings to different audiences, so for our discussion purposes, legacy is any existing system in your environment.

I'm sure all of us are victims of the "Set It and Forget It" mentality. A new application goes into production and no one wants to touch it, fearing system downtime: unfortunately, this sometimes includes patching and vulnerability management. You may get away with this for the first year, but the threat clock never stops ticking. More than once in my career, I've found servers with obsolete operating systems that have literally thousands of vulnerabilities.

How do you handle the pushback from development and the business when you are facing servers with significant security issues? Start by understanding the business side of the equation.

1. What are the availability requirements for the application?
2. What is the revenue stream from the business function?
3. What information is captured or contained on the server? Are there regulatory requirements to protect the data (PCI, HIPAA, etc.)?

Now, look at the technical side and the application architecture.

4. Is there a test environment?
5. Is there a Disaster Recovery environment or hot backup?
6. Do we have a subject matter expert on the application?
7. How long would it take to rebuild the server if the worst happened?

Granted this is not a full risk assessment, but it gives you enough data to intelligently discuss the issue with management. You have an idea of the risk to the business if the application crashes as a result of patching and upgrade. From a security standpoint, you should already know the likelihood and impact of a vulnerability being exploited. Since you have asked compliance questions, you already know if there are any mandatory requirements to keep the server patched and in compliance, and the potential penalties and fines if the server is not patched.

Have a business discussion, not just a security exercise. Don't let the IT folks simply "accept the risk" of a business impact. Ensure the right people are involved in the decisions.

You can decide to stay with the current version of a system, keeping it current through patches and occasional software updates, but only for so long. Vendors don't go on providing patches forever. Eventually, they sunset their products and

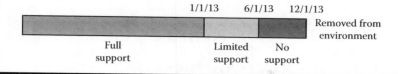

Figure 4.2   Support life cycle.

release new versions. Think of all the versions of Microsoft Internet Explorer you have used over the years or how many different Microsoft operating systems you have used. The pace at which new versions are released has accelerated over the years. Fortunately, prior versions continue to be supported, but I see that support window closing as well. Let's face it, vendors do not make a lot of money (if any) supporting older products. It ties up valuable resources.

Early in my career, I understood that just like everything, technology products have a limited time they are supported from the vendor. One of my hobbies is restoring cars; my latest is a 1957 Chevy. Chevrolet quit making parts for a 57 a long time ago. If I want parts, I have to buy them from a specialty manufacturer who builds the parts. At some point, it becomes too expensive and certainly not profitable for the vendor to continue supporting their earlier products. You need to be proactive about planning the life cycle of the critical elements in your environment. It doesn't have to be complex to start; the key is to start. Figure 4.2 shows an extremely simple method of conveying the life cycle to the rest of IT.

This lets all support functions know when they must have a component out of the environment. There will be a temptation to give exceptions and passes to the drop-dead date. However, as I've painfully learned over the years, you can dig an incredibly deep hole one shovel full at a time. Be careful and weigh any exception against the strategic direction of security and operations.

Patching: The Critical Link...

Let's face it—patching is not sexy. No one aspires to be the world's greatest patcher. Usually it is done off hours, eating into personal time. Invariably, it causes problems with applications and connectivity. Even my son, a tech manager for a college, hates the weekend patch window. Patching is much like the roll of the dice, every now and then you come up with snake eyes and all your hard work and preparations were for naught. Patching is typically "tested" by patching your development and test systems first (Figure 4.3). If they don't break, then the patch is moved into your production systems and all is well in the universe. Unfortunately, this is a very flawed strategy. As has been discovered time and time again, sometimes patches don't actually address the vulnerability they were designed for, or they introduce new vulnerabilities. You have to thoroughly test the patch against the exploit it was

001**VIRUS**01000110100
00011100101**MALWARE**
VULNERABILITY000100
01001010100011101000
0**CODEPROBLEMS**10111
1001000**UPGRADE**1000
100**BUFFEROVERFLOW**0
01101000001110 01010

Figure 4.3 Patching.

designed for as well as other potential exploits. It would be like a car manufacturer installing air bags without ever testing them. You ride along assuming they are going to work just like you assume the patch is going to work. Fortunately, the car manufacturers do extensively test their air bag designs and installations (though recent air bag recalls would seem to indicate more testing is required). You need to do the same with your patches.

I've seen it all—or so I think—but people keep surprising me. Probably the most common mistake is installing a patch that requires a reboot, and forgetting to reboot the system. So, the organization cruises along, thinking it's protected when it is not. Without a post-patch scan, you really don't know if the patch took and did what it was supposed to.

Another common mistake comes from using an automated patching tool. The tech loads up the system and assumes the system did its job. Never assume successful completion. As the old saying goes—trust but verify.

Of course, older products tie up our resources as well. Legacy software is like a car; the older it gets, the more care and support it takes to keep it humming along. You can find support for your software, just like cars, from other vendors. As time goes on, this support tends to get expensive. Recently, I worked with a major database company to buy "extended support" for an older version. The cost was an additional 20% over my current maintenance payments coming to almost $300,000 for one year.

Eventually, though, even the vendors stop supporting their own software. I recall working for a company that had an ERP (enterprise resource planning) system so old even the vendor had no one on staff that had any experience with that version of the software. There are third parties that tend to fill the void left by vendors who have abandoned their earlier products. These third parties are likewise expensive and their actual level of expertise can vary widely. In many cases, you may find you are paying these third parties to learn your software. If your software is highly customized, support from third parties can be very limited.

Once vendor support ceases, third-party support is basically focused on keeping the software functional. There is no emphasis or concern on possible security flaws within the software. The bad guys love flaws that have been identified in newer software since there is a good chance these same flaws may exist in unsupported versions of the software that still exist in the field. They have a wide-open door to your environment with no one to close it. In most cases, you won't know that security flaws exist until it's too late, and even if you do know they exist, you have limited options to address them without vendor support.

Lesson learned? Your only true and correct course of action is to make sure your legacy software is kept up to date. This does not mean you need to be on the very latest version. However, you certainly want to be on a version that you know will be supported far enough in the future to allow you to upgrade to a newer version before support ends on your current version. This is all part of software life cycle planning that is rarely done or properly budgeted for.

It's no wonder that patching falls by the wayside. There is always something more fun or more interesting. This doesn't take away from the fact that it is one of the most critical security-related maintenance tasks that take place in any organization. That one missing patch may be just the vulnerability the hacker needs to sneak through all of your elaborately placed defenses. Hackers have plenty of targets and can afford to be very specialized. A hacker may need only focus on one or two vulnerabilities, biding their time till they run across an organization that has left them an open invitation. Once they are inside your organization, and they will get in, unpatched servers provide an easy path for them to move within your organization and escalate rights.

It's about More Than Patching

Patching is just one piece necessary for the maintenance of the foundation. Other vulnerabilities that must be corrected by means other than patching exist, much like a road that has potholes and a fallen tree branch across it. One problem is solved with patching, the other with a structural change. Applications, whether internally or externally developed, are susceptible to exploit. Poor coding techniques open as may holes as any missing patch. Poor system administration and build practices can open massive holes in your infrastructure. Vulnerabilities that require actions other than patching, such as a configuration change, tend to be far less obvious and can carry far more devastating results. All the patching in the world won't protect you if you have failed to remove a system default password somewhere in your environment. As with every technology, there are a million myths about the subject of patching. Here are four that I'd like to dispel right away.

Patching Myth One

You should always wait a month before applying a new patch.

I'll admit it. At one time, I actually thought this was a wise approach. However, that was a different time. A vendor patch addressed a vulnerability, but it didn't mean that there was an actual exploit in the wild. You had time to thoughtfully evaluate the impact of a patch. Today, it is still easy to think that the organization is better off waiting for a few weeks after vendors release a patch before deploying it internally. The idea is that if you wait a month and don't hear any screaming on security mailing lists, it will be safe to apply the patch.

Great concept, but the lack of complaints from others does not mean that you won't have problems. You need to test it yourself in your own environment. If you will have problems, waiting a month will only delay the amount of time that passes until you discover the issue. Let's also remember that in today's environment, a month of being vulnerable to a serious exploit is an eternity. Today, we must patch quickly or put in compensating controls such as Web Application Firewalls to address the risk.

Patching Myth Two

If a patch doesn't break your test systems, it will not break all of your systems.

Come on: this is just testing common sense. Make sure that your test plan is representative of the environment. The plan should take into account the risk that a bad patch could bring to the organization. High risk, in-depth testing. Low risk, limited testing.

Patching Myth Three

Push the patches and forget. They install always cleanly.

So, you deploy a set of patches to your network. A week later, the compliance folks run a scan and you're told you have a ton of missing patches. Like all good computer folks, your first approach is to try and prove they are wrong. But, finally you have to give in and admit that somehow the patches didn't take. What happened? The patch required a reboot to successfully install and half the servers didn't reboot successfully. That scenario is just one of a hundred things that can go wrong with a patch deployment. The last step of a patch process is to verify; always remember that and you will avoid a ton of pain in your future.

Patching Myth Four

One size of patch management fits all.

Look, there are some basic principles that should be kept in mind when developing a patch management plan. For instance, you could take the recommendations of one of your vendors, but you have systems from multiple vendors. You could pick a package and implement the "vanilla" process in an attempt to utilize the vendor's expertise, but their processes are not representative of yours. Ultimately, you will need to tailor industry standard methods to your organization. Once you've implemented your plan, it should not be static. Regular reviews are critical to ensure that it continues to meet your organization's needs. As the organization changes, your plan must change.

Scanning Required!

Here are a few danger signs for your environment:

1. The network guys tell you that they can't produce a network diagram because the environment is too complex. Translation: I'm not really sure what is where anymore, but hell, it still works, what's your problem?
2. There are servers and apps that are too critical to be patched or scanned. The truth? If you have apps or servers that can be crashed by a passive scan, scanning is the least of your problems. These are usually business critical servers, which are so fragile that they can't be patched or scanned. Does this sound like a Business Continuity or Disaster Recovery issue? Check for backups, you may find that there is no backup of the server.
3. The vendor didn't tell me there were new patches. Who owns the application internally? Any service necessary for the business needs an owner. The maintenance of that application needs to be part of their review and raise process.
4. Finally, and always a goody: My application is patched but the underlying components are not my problem. "I just handle the code, if JBOSS or Adobe (which the application requires) have vulnerabilities, it's not my problem." IT management must understand that all vulnerabilities are their problem; no one gets to pick and choose. Ensure that someone is RESPONSIBLE.
5. Scanning for vulnerabilities besides just missing patches is crucial. Having a methodology in place to deal with the results is equally important. Devoting resources to the problem goes without saying. The only way these resources will succeed is if they are given adequate support from the top, and their efforts are recognized for the true importance they convey. If you don't reward and recognize those who are performing your vulnerability scanning and patching, it will never get the attention it needs, nor will it attract the quality talent necessary to ensure it is done correctly.

A sound vulnerability scanning program is critical to the ongoing security of your systems. Patches alone can't resolve vulnerabilities caused by the interaction of multiple systems and applications. A combination of automated and manual scanning, accompanied by a regular penetration test, is mandatory for any diligent security program. As with any program, let's look at common misconceptions and myths about vulnerability and testing programs I've encountered over my career.

Misconception One

Vulnerability scanning can identify all vulnerabilities in an organization's environment. If you do a good job at that, you can save money by not doing penetration tests.

Been there, done that—I thought that if I could do weekly vulnerability scans of the network and systems, that was better than a penetration test since I was finding issues in real time. Besides, have you seen what the Penetration Test firms get? Wow, I can certainly use that money elsewhere.

Here was the hole in my logic. The scanners are preloaded with "signatures" to detect known vulnerabilities. The vulnerabilities are simply "doors" into the company systems. No scanners are perfect, so there will always be "doors" left open. A penetration test goes beyond finding the open doors and looks at what actions an attacker could take by exploiting a given weakness. For instance, a vulnerability scanner may detect a system using a default password. A penetration tester could use that default password to see how far into the network they could get with those rights. That is a true measure of a system's weaknesses.

Misconception Two

Professional penetration testers use really expensive tools, so it's really not a good test of what a hacker could do.

True, professionals may use some custom tools, but the majority of the tools they use are freely available to the hacker community. In fact, a large number have actually been generated by the hacking community. Many of these tools are "Wizard Based," making it easy for relatively unsophisticated bad guys to compromise networks. The good things about penetration testers who use those tools is that they can simulate an attack from a malicious hacker.

Misconception Three

A penetration test was a success if the attack team couldn't get into your network.

Contrary to what you may think, if the testers couldn't get in, you probably should hire another firm. Every network has vulnerabilities that can be exploited. All systems have users that open holes. I've used some great firms over the years. At a high level, I do three tests. The first is a look from the public Internet. The second is where I give the tester access to a network jack with no user id or password. The third is where I give them the phone number of the help desk to see if they can "social engineer" their way into my system. The longest I've survived their methods is three days. That is how long it took them to get user rights (sometimes system administrator) on the network. Understanding how they got in is always invaluable. It allows you to make real changes and upgrades to your system defenses.

Misconception Four

A system compromise is only applicable to the system that was compromised.

Any penetration tester worth his salt will use one compromised system as a launch point against other systems. Once an attacker has established a foothold, they can watch for and capture user credentials to use against additional systems.

Misconception Five

Focus your penetration testing only on production networks containing sensitive data.

Many CISOs focus on production networks containing sensitive data, excluding other networks containing nonsensitive data, such as development and test environments. These are the networks most vulnerable to malware infection due to the open and fluid nature of the work performed there. The bad guys also know this and in many cases look for holes there first. It's incredibly important that they also be scanned and penetration tested as they could be launch points for production system attacks.

Take an inventory of your applications. How many are unsupported right now by the vendor? How many will be unsupported within a year? Chances are the numbers are going to be larger than you like. More troubling will be the number of applications and systems you find where no one is the owner and no one knows what they do. And don't just focus your inventory on the big name software. There is a lot of software that runs behind the scenes that is just as critical to keep current, such as Tomcat, Apache, Adobe, Java, your databases, and so on. Any in-house–developed software is most likely composed of a number of commercial third-party products. It is typically these behind the scenes–type software that makes it so difficult to keep up to date because of all the interdependencies. Upgrading one thing might break several other things.

The easiest way to explain this is to reference the seven-layer open system interconnection (OSI) model (Figure 4.4). Every application that runs in your

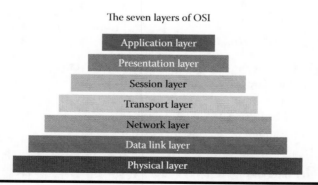

The seven layers of OSI

Application layer
Presentation layer
Session layer
Transport layer
Network layer
Data link layer
Physical layer

Figure 4.4 OSI layers.

environment is built on these seven layers, each having its own risks and vulnerabilities. True vulnerability management must look at the People, Process, and Technology vulnerabilities of all layers. The Application Layer may have vulnerabilities as the result of a coding error, and the Physical Layer may have vulnerabilities related to weak change control procedures that would allow a technician to pull or disconnect the wrong wire.

One necessary tool for tracking all these elements is an asset management system. If you don't have an asset management system, you seriously need to consider getting one. If you are a small shop and can't afford a big system, use a spreadsheet or Access database. The key point is to document, document, and document! The more you know about your environment, the better. Don't let the magnitude of a subject stop you from doing anything. I've been in many discussions that go like this:

"We all agree that we need an asset management system. If we don't know what we have, how do we know what to patch and maintain?" Everyone around the table shakes their head and agrees, but that is where the sanity gets very scarce. The production manager says, "You know these systems cost hundreds of thousands of dollars and take a couple of people to run. Unless I can collect every conceivable bit of information about the environment, we should not start." Next comes the development manager who says, "I need the tool to map all the applications running in the environment and how they relate to each other." Last country heard from is the Finance group who says "There is no way we can afford a few hundred thousand dollars for this project, let's just put it off until we can afford it." I sense many of you have been in the same meeting. We went from a simple spreadsheet to list what our equipment (better than what we had which was nothing) to a project we couldn't afford. Then because we couldn't afford the top shelf solution, we decided to do nothing. You don't have to boil the ocean. As CISO, you will sometimes make more progress by taking small steps that are lined up with a long-term objective. Here are some ideas to get started.

Environment Control

- Managing equipment life cycle and depreciation status
- Enforcing standards
- Controlling purchases
- Optimizing utilization
- Managing vendors

Tracking IT Assets

- Assigning value
- Tracking cost of ownership

Risk Management

- Tracking software licensing compliance
- Assigning and tracking ownership
- Tracking security risks

At a minimum, you should have a run book for each application in your environment. This run book should include what applications are running on what servers, when they were installed, what they do, what they interface with (especially databases), who is the subject matter expert for each, who is the business owner for each, what software language they are written in, are they public or internal facing, do they contain sensitive data, and the location of additional reference documents for each application. The more details, the better. One thing you might discover is applications installed by users and business units that have bypassed IT's normal change management processes. A configuration management tool can greatly help prevent these types of vulnerabilities entering your environment.

Lesson learned? Be sure and identify the owner for a system. Lack of assigned accountability and responsibility for a system results in legacy systems remaining in place long past their useful life. There is no one driving change for the system or accepting responsibility for the system should things go south. IT is usually left holding the bag on these systems. Yet, IT cannot speak for the business. Any attempts at changing the system are usually met with outcries from the users. In some cases, there are a very small number of users that should not realistically warrant keeping the system alive. The simplest solution for IT then becomes one of accepting the status quo even though this is not the correct decision. Why fight City Hall? Every system needs to have a business owner as well as an IT owner for the life of the system. If no one in the business feels strong enough to own a particular system, then it should be shut down.

Once you have a good inventory of your systems and run books created, you can then prioritize the systems that need attention from a security perspective based on potential risk. While every asset deserves attention from a security perspective, you simply do not have the time, resources, or money to address every server and application to the same degree. Obviously, if the system processes or stores sensitive data or is required to meet certain governmental requirements, it should be high on your list. If the loss or compromise of a system would cause business critical functions to fail, having a significant financial impact to the company, then these should sit high on your list.

How do I decide what needs to be fixed first? Each asset should be looked at from at least two perspectives when considering risk. The first is what is the likelihood that the asset can be breached? If it is behind a firewall and in a locked data center, its exposure is much less than a server sitting in the DMZ or one of your mobile assets. What is its current patch status? How many people have access to the asset? I'd like you to think in terms of a 1–10 score where 10 is the greatest likelihood that the asset could be breached. Keep that number in mind; we will use it in a couple of minutes.

The next perspective: What are the consequences to the company should this asset be breached? In other words, what is the impact to the company? Lastly, you need to consider what the probability of occurrence of a system breach is. This is similar to the risk exposure, though it focuses more on external factors, such as whether your line of business is a prime target for hackers and whether the asset in question is one a hacker would be interested in. Is it an operating system that is frequently targeted by hackers? Do you have a high degree of monitoring in place? Each of these factors can be classified as high, medium, and low or on a scale of 1 to 10. This is very subjective, but it can give you a relative idea of comparative risks.

Depending on your line of business, if you have systems that people's lives depend on, then they should go to the very top of the list. By lives depend on, I mean systems that could affect one's physical health and not some application; e-mail typically seems to be considered in this category, that people can't "live" without. I once worked at a company where they occasionally turned off the instant messaging system. The CEO strongly felt that people needed to actually talk to people, if not face to face then at least by voice. He also wanted to demonstrate that some systems aren't as critical as we might think they are.

Clearly, anything accessible from outside the company (web based or otherwise) is a higher risk to the company and needs to be given higher consideration. Age of the hardware and the applications also impacts risk. Putting old software on a new piece of hardware or vice versa does little to reduce overall risk. Just because an old system has run reliably for years without compromise is no guarantee that it will continue to do so. Older systems have most likely undergone a number of changes over the years. How thoroughly tested and documented these changes have been is a matter of concern. What were once considered minor configuration changes may have opened up large security holes that were not recognized at the time of the changes. Older systems tend to grow a multitude of interfaces over time. These tend to be poorly documented. If any of its interfaces are not secure, then it doesn't matter how secure it is itself.

If you are lucky enough to have access to the test documentation for the systems, you can learn a lot as to how secure they might be. The number and types of tests conducted will have a bearing on how secure a system is. A review will reveal additional tests that should be conducted to address new vulnerabilities that have been discovered since the system was first tested. Don't limit your review to just the test documentation. Look at all the system documentation that is available to see how security was addressed. The design may have been architected under the assumption that other things were going to be deployed in the environment that might never have occurred or have changed significantly over time.

In reviewing your systems, you need to think like a bad guy. What systems and data would they be most interested in getting access to? What ways are available to them to try and get to these systems and data? Be very creative in your thinking. The more unconventional the thinking, the more likely you are to discover potential vulnerabilities in your environment. Take advantage of your staff's extensive knowledge. Make it into a contest to see who can come up with the most ways to penetrate your environment or a particular system. If you have systems that have been breached in the past, these need special consideration. What has been done to fortify them? Are these measures still viable in today's threat environment? Is it possible that the vulnerability that permitted these systems to be breached may exist on other assets? Are these systems still needed?

Once you have identified your risks and prioritized them, you then need to concentrate on your mitigation strategies. When considering your options, more than just security concerns need to be evaluated. Business impact, resource limitations (human and system), system interfaces, technology changes, system age, functionality needs, documentation availability, subject matter expert availability, user interface, and maintenance needs come into play for the system in question and its mitigation alternatives. Like most problems, you will have to decide between several alternative solutions.

Using the previous 1–10 rating, you have a high-level view of the security risks posed by each system. By using a grid similar to Figure 4.5, you can map the scores of each vulnerability and generate an easily understood road map of what issues should be first on the "fix list." For instance, the issue identified by the bubble numbered one has a Likelihood of being exploited as a 10 and an impact of the company, if it happens, of 10. This could be a web server exposed to the Internet with an easily exploited vulnerability (10) that runs the company's e-commerce site. If it goes down, the company revenue is affected immediately (10). Plotting those

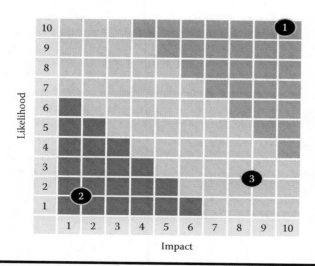

Figure 4.5   Risk matrix.

two points puts the issue in the upper right corner of the graph, meaning fix immediately. Issue two has a Likelihood of 1 and an Impact of 1, meaning that the issue is not a high priority and can be fixed at a later date. Issue three has a Likelihood of 2 and an Impact of 8. This means that while the likelihood is low, an exploit would result in a high-impact issue to the business. When you plot the issue, you can see that the 3 comes up as a Medium issue, meaning it must be fixed after the High issues are resolved.

Your firm needs to define what the colors mean. Personally, my starting point is that High issues must be resolved in two weeks, Medium in two months, and Low in six months. Don't finalize your definitions in a vacuum; form a team of business and IT leaders to develop the change windows and MONITOR the health of the program. If the process is not monitored and reported on, it will fade into oblivion, leaving the business with a false sense of security that risks are being addressed. Trust me, that is worse than never having started.

One option you always have is to do nothing. Doing nothing is usually more a matter of delaying a decision rather than a legitimate option. Opting to do nothing is usually chosen when a particular system is due to be upgraded soon or replaced. If there are real security concerns with a system, then doing nothing is never a smart strategy. We cannot ignore the inevitable. Even as a delaying tactic, doing nothing is not smart. The system is still exposed. The bad guys certainly won't be doing nothing while you procrastinate. As we all know, projects get delayed or even cancelled. If you have a security issue, it needs to be addressed now in some shape, manner, or form. Doing nothing only makes sense if the risk is small. While some may argue that the cost to mitigate may be too excessive to justify the particular option, the cost of any breach will greatly outweigh any potential solution you might ever come up with. At the very least, you need to find a way to reduce the risk if you can't eliminate it. I must caveat this in that you will never be able to completely eliminate all risk. It is an exponential curve where you eventually reach greatly diminishing returns on additional investments in risk mitigation.

Lesson learned? Not all mitigation strategies have to be costly or elaborate. Creating new policies and procedures may be a very simple and effective way to reduce the risk. Don't get caught in the techie trap where every risk needs an expensive hardware solution. Just applying additional monitoring will bring you down a bit on the risk curve. Training can always help reduce risk whether it is for your immediate staff or others. Making a few adjustments to your existing systems such as implementing a new group policy or firewall change can help reduce the risk without considerable expense.

Earlier in my career, as patching was becoming an issue, we identified a need to upgrade the web server software for an external site to address a security issue. As I talked to the developers, I found that there were a multitude of additional changes they wanted to do as long as "We were touching the code anyway." A few weeks later, I got a call from an irate product manager wanting to know why my patching requirement was going to cost about $200,000. Much to my surprise, I found out that a whole product rewrite had been included in my patching requirement.

Lesson learned? Many times, you may need to patch or fix a vulnerability in a system, especially in-house–developed systems. Be careful you are not drawn down a rabbit hole by developers and the business wishing to implement all kinds of new functionality along with the security fix. The primary motivation should be to fix the existing security flaw. Time is of the essence. Taking on new functionality not only slows down the process but may inadvertently introduce new security flaws in the rush to address the existing flaw. Developers will be more interested in working on the new functionality than the security fix. Security fixes are boring. Testing will likewise be skewed more toward the new functionality rather than the security fix. Better to just concentrate on the security fix and leave any new functionality enhancements to be addressed in a separate project.

Lesson learned? Avoid the perception of chaos. Sometimes called "Whack a Mole" management, this is where you have so many issues to be addressed that no one knows what to do first. This is compounded if you are also confused. Take responsibility, stand up a plan, and work it. Trust me, I've been in this situation many times during my career, sometimes my fault, sometimes the actions of others. Understand that you may discover new vulnerabilities or the same vulnerability scattered throughout your code. Vulnerabilities can't be ignored. Find them, list them, organize them, and kill them. Be a leader.

New vulnerabilities will always come up and must be prioritized against the degree of risk they present. To avoid scope creep and cost overruns, new vulnerabilities should be addressed and analyzed separately. If you try to do too many upgrades or patches at one time, it will only increase the chances something will be broken in the software. As you find new vulnerabilities, you need to assess where else in your environment this same code may be employed since developers often reuse code. A good software code library will help immensely in identifying where reused code is implemented.

Lesson learned? Don't alienate the Development folks. A challenge that security faces is how to properly communicate security issues to developers. Historically, the security engineers come out of network engineering, so there is a built-in "language barrier" from the start. These communication issues are not just pertinent to security, but they are definitely magnified due to the unique lingo of security professionals. Developers can more easily relate to business functions than security concepts. Your security staff needs to be adept at taking complex and obscure concepts and translating them into actionable requirements for the developers. This is not a skill that most security personnel readily possess. The employment of Use Cases can help developers more easily understand complex security requirements provided your security staff know how to develop Use Cases. Also, be aware that a developer that has worked on a project for months is proud of their achievement. Avoid calling their baby "ugly!" Tact and diplomacy are as important to a security professional as technical prowess. Build a partnership with developers, offer training, ask for input, and offer development basics training to the security staff.

Upgrading an existing system to address vulnerabilities takes lots of planning and time. Sometimes you are confronted with a decision to upgrade an existing product or move to a competitor product. My experience has been that if your existing product meets your needs and you have decent support from the vendor, then why switch? Switching is always harder and usually more costly than just upgrading. Switching should never be predicated solely on security concerns. The patching tool we were using would not support MS Server 12. Rather than upgrade the tool, a decision was made to purchase a different patching tool. We now have the new tool patching MS Server 12 assets and the legacy tool patching the rest. Getting off the old product has proven far more difficult than anticipated. Now that all assets are being patched, there is less urgency to consolidate on the one patching tool. Sadly, this scenario tends to repeat itself far too often where new systems are brought on line to replace old ones, yet in the end, both systems remain in production. What you don't want to do is throw the baby out with the bath water. While your system may be vulnerable, it may only be a small component of the system such as the database or user interface. Much like a car, you sometimes have to replace a part now and then to keep it in top running condition. Only after a fair amount of time and use does it make sense to replace the whole car. Of course, if it is just the radio that is working great, you don't necessarily want to replace everything around the radio. Designing and incorporating modular systems in your environment make this such a viable approach. Having good documentation, especially well-documented interfaces, is the key to this approach.

Lesson learned? Understand the financial impact of system support. There are a multitude of reasons why legacy systems are allowed to remain in production despite their direct impact on the foundation of your enterprise. Cost is always brought up as a key driver to stay with legacy systems. No one wants to foot the bill for an upgrade. Costs include both time and money. Plus, like the person who buys a car and drives it into the ground, there is a tendency for businesses to try and get as much as possible out of their initial investment.

The true lifetime costs of systems are rarely recognized when they are implemented. No real plans are ever presented up front that identify the end of life of the system and delineate how it will be replaced. What we have are systems that tend to never die.

In the 90s, I worked for a company that had an inventory application written in an obsolete language; eventually, the programmer retired. Every year, like clockwork, the application needed to be tweaked at inventory time, and the only person who could do it was the retired programmer. He knew he was the only resource and charged exorbitant rates to come in and do the work. Worse yet, as he got older, the company began to wonder whether he would be around for the next inventory run. After a few years, they had no choice but to rewrite the application, which should have been done years earlier. Sure, it only ran twice per year, but it calculated the inventory carrying charges passed back to the operating unit by corporate. These charges could amount to hundreds of thousands of dollars; an error was a significant financial risk to the business.

Delaying upgrades as a means to save money is not a good strategy. Older systems inherently require more personal attention to keep them running. They are more likely to result in downtime and tend to run slower over time. Users are deprived of enhanced functionality available in newer versions that could result in quicker processing and fewer errors. When vendors stop supporting their products, you need to hire specialized consultants when internal resources cannot solve a system problem. Hardware parts become harder to find and more costly. These sorts of costs tend to be overlooked.

Key Questions to Ask

- Are annual support and maintenance costs less than the system replacement costs for both hardware and software?
- If the current system support person were hit by a bus tomorrow, could you still do business?
- Can you quickly find people with the skills to maintain the hardware and/or software applications?
- Does the original manufacturer still have replacement parts for your hardware or are you using hard-to-find third-party or used resources for parts?
- Is the original vendor still in business and actively offering support for your version of the system?

If you answered "no" to some of these questions, then you probably should be on the lookout for upgrading or replacing your legacy systems before they cause serious harm to your business. If you answered "yes," to these questions, then your systems are probably fine for now, but stay alert for obsolescence by staying current on industry trends for your systems.

> I worked for a company that had a large ERP system that they stopped paying support for over 10 years earlier, yet continued to use the product on which the entire company depended. The system had to use an unsupported database as well as run on an unsupported operating system to remain functional. It finally got to the point where system failures and extremely poor response times forced the business to make a decision to upgrade it. Unfortunately, in order to upgrade, the vendor required them to pay for all of the previous years of support plus the upgrade costs. In an attempt to save money, they put the users through a lot of pain and suffering, risked potential catastrophic system failure, and exposed the business to security breaches all for naught.

People know the current system and are comfortable with it. Things currently work OK. The general sentiment is if it isn't broke why fix it? People don't like change. Upgrading a system tends to have less resistance than replacing it with something entirely different. Employees who have worked on a particular system for years do not relish having to learn a whole new system. The time and costs involved to retrain people on the new or upgraded system are certainly a factor in staying with the status quo.

Lesson learned? Challenge the assumptions regarding legacy systems. My experience is that most of the assumptions have no basis in fact. If an assumption hangs around long enough, it is assumed to be fact, and no one challenges it. For example, the U-2 spy plane piloted by Francis Gary Powers was assumed to be untouchable by Soviet anti-aircraft missiles. The strategists were confident that no missiles could reach, let alone shoot down the U-2. Yet, on May 1, 1960, the unthinkable happened; the U-2 was shot out of the sky. Ultimately, this legacy system was breached. The military was forced to recognize the risks the legacy system imposed and had to upgrade and replace its hardware. The U-2 was ultimately replaced by the Lockheed SR-71 Blackbird in 1964. Had the Air Force been able to upgrade sooner, the U-2 incident would have never happened. No SR-71 was ever shot down.

While the rest of the world marches ahead with newer technology, you may find yourself in a situation where your legacy systems cannot interface with the new stuff. Your only option may be to build very expensive customized interfaces. These will prove to be difficult to maintain. Bringing on new systems will take longer.

Keeping legacy systems around may also hurt your employees. Their skills become dated. Your good resources will leave rather than hang around to work on dinosaurs. In-house knowledge of legacy systems will quickly diminish, further confounding support of these systems. Attracting new talent will also be difficult since no one wants to work on unsupported and outdated systems. If you find yourself in a situation where you have to frequently reboot your servers, this is a very good indication that it is time to upgrade or replace. Either your in-house resources do not have the requisite skills and knowledge to find the root cause of the issues with the system or the system has reached its tipping point.

Something else to consider. Your legacy system may have gone into production three years ago, but when did coding actually begin? Now consider that developers like to reuse code and take advantage of public domain code. How old is this predeveloped code? Your software may be a lot older than you think. It's like a 20-year-old getting a heart transplant from a 60-year-old. Things may work, but what imperfections did we inherit?

Your applications are only as secure as the hardware they reside on, the operating system they utilize, and the network they interact over. Each piece has to be secure. People tend to forget how important it is to keep your hardware's firmware up to date. Most patching tools cannot address hardware firmware. Different skill sets tend to be needed to address hardware vulnerabilities.

You need to upgrade or replace. That is the only way to firm up your foundation. New software, while certainly not invulnerable, has the advantage of learning from the mistakes of the past. Like the unsinkable *Titanic* that incorporated all of the best aspects of ship design, your newly installed software is very secure against hacking until it runs into its cyber equivalent of an iceberg. And like the *Titanic*, there are a number of factors that must come into play before your software is "sunk." The Internet is a very big ocean, and your company a relatively small ship on that ocean. A technological form of global warming is setting adrift a lot more icebergs across that Internet. You may be able to travel great distances and for a long time before you come across a cyber iceberg. You have the advantage of many other corporate ships at sea with you who can help you avoid these cyber icebergs. There will be far fewer "USS Legacy" ships at sea as time goes on.

Should you decide to replace an existing legacy system, then you need to reevaluate your current security architecture. It makes no sense to put a new system in an environment with security designed around the previous system. This is an excellent opportunity to make further improvements to your security posture. In all likelihood, the decision to replace the system was not made based on security concerns but business needs. You need to ensure that security requirements are enforced before any new system goes into production. This can be a painful battle with the business. Any deviations from the security requirements must be documented and the risks signed off by the business; otherwise, you will be accountable should a breach occur in the future. Let's face it, you will be held accountable regardless but at least you have documentation that you recognized the risk. Security design reviews, code reviews, security testing, and system penetration testing must be performed before a system goes live.

There will invariably be situations where you cannot patch or upgrade in a reasonable period of time. You will have to come up with some strategy to mitigate risk. Common options available to you are segmenting off the network where the system resides, virtualization, additional firewalls and/or firewall rules, and more intensive monitoring of the system in question. Many times, alternative solutions are provided for identified vulnerabilities, so if you cannot patch or upgrade, you must resort to using these alternative solutions.

We can't forget about the other critical piece of your foundation. The one that is exposed to the elements and is at a greater risk of failing. That is your mobile assets. While PCs are an obvious risk, mobile phones and tablets are now being rightfully recognized as very serious risks to the environment. All of your mobile end points need to be password protected and the data on them need to be encrypted. Users should not have any sensitive information on their mobile devices regardless of whether they are encrypted or not. The biggest concern would be passwords that may be stored on the devices. The less your employees have on their end points, the lower your risk.

Are your end points configured so they can be automatically updated with new software versions and antivirus signature files? Do you periodically scan the end points to ensure they have the latest software installed? More importantly, are you verifying that the software installed is legitimate? Automated update processes provide an opportunity for the bad guys to usurp the process and insert their own compromised software. Your networks should be configured to prevent any end point that does not have some minimum standard of software installed from connecting. Older versions of software were obviously replaced with newer versions due to security holes in the earlier versions. Why would you want to allow older versions to connect to your environment?

In summary: You are only as secure as your foundation. Like the foundation on a home, it requires periodic inspection and attention.

The bottom line is legacy software imposes significant risks on the company. The costs to address legacy software are small compared to the costs a security breach will incur. You have to make sure your foundation is intact. One small crack can bring an entire structure down.

Is your foundation well identified or is it scattered all over your environment? For example, are your sensitive data stored in a few key locations on your network or can sensitive information be found everywhere you look? Is it in databases or is it in files? Protecting a few critical databases is far easier than trying to protect thousands of files with sensitive information sitting all over your network. You should do everything you can to minimize the storage of sensitive information in files. Once a bad guy gets access to your network, then it is generally easier for them to peruse files on the network than it is to penetrate a database. At a minimum, sensitive files should be encrypted. If you must have sensitive files, then they should also be centrally stored with restricted accesses in place.

Remember, just because things appear to be working correctly does not necessarily mean it is true. A friend of mine owns an airplane. It had a slight vibration that was certainly troubling to him. He looked for all the obvious sources for the vibration for months with no luck. In the end, it turned out that one of the three propeller blades was corroded internally, so that it did not move to take a bigger bite out of the air as he climbed in altitude like the other two blades, thus throwing things out of balance. There was no way to actually determine this without getting inside the propeller operating mechanism.

As a CISO, it is your job to understand the legacy risk being experienced by your company. To see how secure your foundation is, you may have to tear a few things apart as well. Dig deep and don't just take a surface view of things. In industry, change is constant. Change requires vigilance. Keep your eye on both the inside and outside of your foundation.

Chapter 5

If a Bad Guy Tricks You into Running His Code on Your Computer, It's Not Your Computer Anymore

---

It's tough to be the computer expert for the family and friends. As soon as the word gets out that you know your way around Windows, the calls start. Sound familiar? It's a common hazard of being an IT guy, and it isn't a bad thing as long as you can keep family and work separate.

Not too many years ago, I had a desktop technology support engineer that was in the same situation. Deb got a call from her grandma saying that her computer was miserably slow. (God knows where Granny had been surfing…) Evidently Deb stopped over, couldn't get it clean right away, so she grabbed it and promised that she would get to it very soon. The next day, Deb decided to clean up Granny's PC at lunch. She thought there may be some virus issues, so she decided to download the latest update. To get to the Internet, she plugged the PC into the company network.

The antivirus console looked like a Christmas tree—people were running up and down the aisles with their pants on fire, rumors of a Russian conspiracy were hitting a frenzy level. One

---

bonehead move brought an active piece of malware inside our network. It bypassed all perimeter controls because Deb plugged the PC into the backbone.

As background, let's talk about many of the common methods used to maliciously disrupt network communications or gain unauthorized access to network resources. One of the most common questions I'm asked is, "Why do individuals and organizations want to carry out attacks against someone else's network?" There is no doubt that there are a variety of reasons to disrupt a network. To the "script kiddies," the thrill of penetrating or disrupting a network provides an ability to brag about their prowess with common network-attacking tools. For disreputable businesses, the capability to penetrate another business' network may provide business confidential information and an ability to discredit a competitor's reputation. For countries, the ability to penetrate the networks of other countries provides a potential wealth of information about strategic, tactical, economic, and political policies that can lead to decisive victories over their adversaries. Sometimes, the only goal of a malicious attack is to render the network useless and deny the use of it to the organization's employees. With respect to home networks, protection of personal information is critical to defending against such problems as identity theft and undesired release of family and individual private information. It is easy to understand that protection of network assets is critical for all types of individual and organizational networks.

One of the primary tools of a hacker is malware. Malware is a broad category that is usually associated with computer viruses, worms, Trojan Horses, and spyware. Software that may unintentionally harm a computer user is not considered malware. Software bugs certainly fall into this category. There must be intent to do harm or act against the will of the targeted computer user. In other words, malware can do a variety of things, not all of which actually breaks a user's computer. Generally, things that don't break a computer involve spying on the computer user and collecting data from their system. Interestingly, you may find malware referred to as a computer contaminant in the legal codes of some US states, which is a pretty good description as well. Malware is definitely something you do not want on any of your computer assets.

How about a little history to impress your techie friends. So how long has malware been around? A lot longer than many of you would suspect. The origins of malware can be traced back to the late 1940s when a Hungarian-born mathematician by the name of John Von Neumann did research and lectures on what he termed "self-reproducing automata." While he was primarily focused on biological processes, he saw the potential for artificial automata. It wasn't till 1971 that a true attempt was made at creating artificial automata. Bob Thomas attempted to create a self-replicating program. He was connected to the forerunner of the Internet, the government-created ARPAnet. While his creation did not recreate itself as planned on other target machines, it did spread across the ARPAnet causing the message,

"I am the Creeper. Catch me if you can!" to appear on the command line of targeted machines. Creeper thus has been considered to be the first computer virus. In response to Creeper, we quickly had our first antivirus (AV) program called Reaper that was specifically designed to remove Creeper. While Creeper did no real harm, it did act against the will of the end users who had no control over preventing it from displaying on their command line. I suppose we could consider many of the annoying pop-ups that appear in our browsers as malware though most browsers do give us the ability to block pop-ups.

Worms, Trojans, and Viruses: What's in a Name?

What the heck is the difference between a computer worm, a Trojan Horse, and a computer virus?

A computer virus is a piece of code that attaches itself to a program or file. The vast majority attach to an executable file. A computer virus is only spread through some human action such as sending an e-mail or copying a file to some form of media. For the virus to actually infect your machine, you must also run the executable to which it is attached.

A worm is very similar to a virus and can be considered a subset of viruses. Its one very important difference is that it needs no human interaction in order to spread. A Trojan Horse is a virus that masquerades as legitimate software. Generally, a Trojan Horse does not reproduce by infecting other files, nor do they self-replicate.

Antivirus lessons: Rather than diving into a mind-numbing discussion of virus types, in the spirit of this book, let's discuss the practical side of protecting the environment against viruses. Believe me, in the last 20 years, I've heard just about every excuse for not installing or not maintaining AV protection. I'm not saying the AV systems are the security "silver bullet" that will keep us all safe. I am saying that a solid AV program is a key part of overall security architecture.

Over the past few decades, computer security has become an important concern among users. Security vendors have faced tremendous challenges dealing with complex security threats with IT experts placing more effort on educating people. Nevertheless, there are many computer security myths that exist today, and surprisingly, many people still believe them. Let's discuss a few of the most common malware myths that can put your business at risk.

Myth One

I don't need AV software to tell me when I'm infected. I'm pretty savvy.

OK, there are types of ransomware that threaten to lock your computer or report you to the FBI unless you send them 20 bucks for a custom "malware cleaner." Of late, we've seen the rise of a new type of ransomware that encrypts your data and demands a payment or "ransom" for the key to get your data back. If you have done a good job of backing up your data, you can simply restore to a date before the ransomware infected your computer. If you haven't, you have some hard decisions to make. In general, we still feel the most damaging types of malware are invisible and rely on stealth to grow and steal data.

Don't argue with your users. Have a policy supported by the executives that all computers must have AV or they are not on the company network. Faced with the alternatives of AV or no network access, most users will cave and accept.

Myth Two

I have a Mac so I don't need AV.

We have all heard this before; Windows is the only vulnerable operating system (OS). True, there are more hacks out there for Windows but Macs are also very vulnerable. I use a Mac and I wouldn't connect without AV.

You can't argue that the number of exploits that specifically target Mac users is a small fraction of what Windows users are exposed to, but that doesn't mean that there are no threats. It is generally accepted that the first virus specifically engineered for Apple computers dates back to the early 1980s. Since then, there has been a steady stream of malware specifically designed to attack Mac OS X.

The most dangerous malware targeting Macs are Trojans that hide in other programs, so be very careful what you download and always be suspicious when your computer asks you to type your Administrator password out of the blue. Your OS is just one attack vector for cybercriminals. Your web browser, Java, Adobe Flash, and other popular utilities are also constantly under attack; they provide a path to your computer as well.

From a practical standpoint, this is like arguing religion. Here's my stand; while working on a MAC connected to the company network, you will have AV, period. A single or small group of users does not have the fiscal authority to accept the risk of attack for the whole network. If they have a home machine and want to take that chance at home, go ahead, but no machine without AV should ever be allowed to connect to your company network. If you can't get that commitment and support from your CIO, it's time to go back to the drawing board.

Myth Three

(Similar to Myth Two) Linux servers do not need AV; besides, it slows my servers down.

There are many flavors of Linux. Similar to MACs, they have a reputation for being resistant to malware problems. This leads Linux admins who are largely IT professionals to resist installing AV on the systems. I've heard all the excuses. It's not necessary since Linux servers are immune to malware attacks. AV slows down my servers. There are no reliable AV packages for Linux. The list goes on.

True, it is far less common, but doesn't that lead you to believe that the attacks may be more targeted and stealthy? We have seen rootkits like the one that targeted the Security SHell Daemon (SSHD) in 2016 demonstrate that it is a real threat. Unfortunately, hindsight is 20/20. There are many Linux administrators who wished they had installed AV earlier.

If the OS is not as vulnerable, what is the big deal? Remember the picture of the OSI stack in Figure 4.4? The answer is because all malware does not attack just the OS. For an application to run, there are other components required. If the server hosts a public-facing application, there is plenty of cause for concern. An average of 18,000–26,000 URLs are compromised each day by malicious code. The malware targets vulnerable components of websites, such as content management systems like Word Press, application environments, and extensions like JBoss, and most importantly the webservers like Apache and TomCat.

Remember to check with your compliance group. Regulations like PCI-DSS may require you to install AV software on systems that store or process sensitive data.

Myth Four

E-mail attachments from my friends and coworkers are safe.

The reality couldn't be further from the truth. Every day, I see e-mails that are fraudulent. Lately, I have seen a rash of e-mails appearing to be from the CEO asking the CFO to wire money for a new program. It is a common practice for hackers to pretend to be another employee or friend to get you to open the e-mail and attachment. Most companies have some type of e-mail and spam filter. Typically, I have seen that 80% of inbound e-mail to a company is either SPAM or loaded with malware. If you think that it is always safe to open e-mail attachments sent from people you know, you should think twice because you are potentially putting yourself and your company at risk. If you get pushback on an e-mail filter from people saying that legitimate e-mail may be stopped, find an e-mail filter that allows users to review the messages that were stopped and quarantined. When the users see the type of e-mail being stopped, the objections will disappear.

Myth Five

Internet proxies and controls that stop employees from visiting porn or questionable sites are as effective as AV.

Give me a break: If it was really good, everyone would do it. Maybe it sort of worked 20 years ago, but definitely not today. Last year, a major magazine had a site for the "Thought of the Day." The site became infected with a "drive by" piece of malware, which could infect a computer simply visiting the site.

Lesson learned? The bad guys have learned they can infect more machines by compromising legitimate sites. They want to infect you from sites you trust, so your guard is down. Additionally, they will create lookalike sites, which are loaded with malware. Your foundational Internet security is not an area to be too creative or attempt to cut corners; malware protection is a perfect example.

Myth Six

All you need is security software.

"I'm safe because I use AV software," said every naïve user who placed too much hope and faith in technology. Cyberspace would be a wonderful place if good software is all it took to keep it safe. Unfortunately, software can only protect us so much. Again, I will go back to the People, Process, and Technology discussion. You may have the technology perfect, but who will respond to alerts, and what process will they use to identify the root cause of the issue? Or, even worse, how can a user circumvent your software? A CISO is expected to have broad vision and be a problem solver, not just a technician. Continue to hone your strategic and holistic skills for the benefit of your organization.

Myth Seven

Even if I get a virus, I have nothing important on my computer.

One of the metrics I track is the amount of user time lost due to a malware event. If we have to get a technician to clean and/or rebuild an infected desktop, that user is out of business for about four hours. If a virus event would infect 100 computers, that would be 400 hours or the equivalent of 10 weeks lost productivity. Moral? The damage from a virus event is seldom limited to data loss. Don't allow your users or your organization to be short-sighted.

Since I'm assuming you don't allow computers on your network without AV, let's discuss how to make your users with home computers aware. First, a malware infection can make you extremely unpopular with your friends and family. If the malware accesses your address book and sends copies of the malware to all your friends, you may quickly fall off their Christmas card list. It's not just the information on your computer, it is how it can be used to launch attacks on your computer. Second, your computer may become part of a Botnet, a group of computers under the control of a criminal that can be used for many types of attacks. Imagine your computer becoming part of a denial of service attack against a government website. Ever gotten a call from the FBI? Third, Botnets can be used to monitor your keystrokes and traffic and echo them to a command and control server overseas.

When you visit your e-banking or bill pay site, every keystroke including account number, password, credit card number, PIN, and so on could be echoed to a crimeware server.

Myth Eight

I'm as smart as the bad guys; AV just slows me down.

Wow, are these guys still around? You know the type, intelligent and overloaded with technology testosterone. Are they smarter than everyone else? While I've run into them over the years, they always eventually get a very rude awakening. Macho chest thumping and trash talking have no place in the science of information security. If you find these people, do your best to find them jobs somewhere else.

Myth Nine

I uninstalled AV on my server because it was running too slow, and uptime is most important to the organization.

Granted, there is some truth here. There are a couple of questions. First, what is the reason that AV is causing your server to run slow? Is it possible that you are having an active infection and AV is overwhelmed trying to stop it? In this case, uninstalling AV, while it may make the server run faster initially, you haven't found or corrected the root cause of the problem. The most important question is whether or not AV is important to the organization. The opinion of the system administrator will usually be slanted toward performance, but they are not in a position to make overall risk decisions for the company.

After any AV scanner has been installed in a computer, it will be loaded into the computer's memory each time the computer boots. This is done to help protect your computer at all times, from any threat. When any program loads itself into memory, including an AV program, it will consume some of the total memory available to the computer. If your computer does not have lots of memory, or is already low in memory, this can affect the overall performance of the computer.

This was more of a problem in the past, but today most computers have plenty of memory. It is more likely that a system will however slow down as the AV scanner is scanning all the files on the computer to see if they're infected.

If performance after AV has been installed is an issue, challenge the system administrator to look at all the running process and tune the performance of the server. In the case of AV, you can often determine if an AV scanner is scanning your computer, stop the scanning, and change how often and when the scanning should occur by opening the AV properties.

Ensure that the system administrator knows that AV is not optional, and impress on them that the risk of a significant malware infection can be devastating to a company. Involve their management if necessary, but trust me, this does need to be put to bed.

Myth Ten (and My Personal Favorite)

Malware is created by AV companies.

While not as prevalent as it once was, there were conspiracy theorists who said that the AV companies secretly created new viruses to maintain a demand for their product. Anyone who watches the news can tell you that the AV companies have their hands full just trying to keep up with the bad guys. There is no question that many viruses come from nation-states looking for financial or intelligence advantages.

Attack Types Are Wide-Ranging

Protection from attacks requires a combination of people, process, and technology. The right balance depends on your business model, and the risk you decide to accept. However, core defenses should include the following:

- **User training**—Educated users can become part of the solution as opposed to being part of the problem.
- **Organization security policies**—Any programs (including those utilities such as screen savers and so on) should be examined and approved by the technical support staff before installing on a computer or network device.
- **Access control lists**—Access control lists on network perimeter devices (such as routers and firewalls) can filter network traffic and block malicious traffic that uses known ports.
- **Proper access privileges**—Users of organizational computing systems should be given the least privilege needed to perform their assigned duties. If a user is not permitted, by organizational policy, to install unapproved software, system policies should be set to deny the users the ability to install software.
- **Use up-to-date AV programs and signature files**—Up-to-date AV programs will detect and block many malicious programs.
- **Auditing**—System administrators should routinely review system and security audit logs available on modern OSs. There are many system and security log auditing tools that will help administrators sort through the large auditing logs and look for specific activity. This will help spot the installation of rogue programs and establishment of new use accounts.
- **Division of duties**—In some organizations, some administrators are authorized to set up new user accounts (such as a new user account with administrator privileges) and other administrators are allowed to review and purge audit logs. No administrator should ever be allowed to perform both functions.

This means that if one administrator creates a new user account, there is at least one other administrator that will know that a new user account was created when the logs are reviewed. In that situation, it would take at least two collaborating individuals to create an unauthorized administrator account.

Social Engineering

Social engineering (SE) is the art of using human manipulation techniques, rather than technical/computer processes, to accomplish the goal of the attacker. Most individuals are raised by their parents and teachers to be helpful, polite, and considerate of others. We were raised to hold the door open for others, use proper telephone manners when talking with strangers, and look out for the needs of others. Though these teachings generally make better citizens, this training also laid the foundation for future SE attacks. SE attacks prey on a variety of human traits such as the following:

- The desire to be helpful
- Fear of not performing correctly on the job
- Frustration with complex passwords
- Lack of concern for minute details
- Tired from being overworked and stressed
- Lack of awareness of our surroundings

There are numerous organizations that have hired independent consultants to test the organization's information security level only to have the consultants gain complete access to whatever information the organization owned. A well-trained/well-prepared attacker can gain extraordinary access to organizational information otherwise believed to be secure. Many organizations have a false sense of security about how secure their organization is. The following are some of the approaches I've personally seen used to gain unauthorized access to information.

- An attacker searched the web and found organizational chart information revealing information about key individuals throughout the company. This information is used later to impersonate key individuals (managers or manager's office assistants) and illicit information from other organizational employees. Search for your company name and development tools on a site like "LinkedIn." You will quickly see how much info can be gathered quickly.
- An attacker searched the dumpster over a two-week period and found discarded technical manuals, internal telephone lists, information security policy drafts, hard drives containing organizational data and customer lists, draft network drawings including IP addressing information, invoices containing sensitive customer information, draft employee evaluation statements, a

printout of a department vacation schedule, and router and firewall configuration printouts. This information was used to technically and socially attack the organization's information assets successfully.

■ An attacker used contact information found on the Internet and called a manager's office and discovered that the manager was away on a business trip. The attacker then visited the manager's office, posed as an IT help desk administrator, and convinced the manager's assistant to give the attacker access to the manager's computer, supposedly to install updated virus software. The attacker downloaded sensitive information from the manager's computer and the organization was not aware that the information was compromised. The attacker also installed a key-logger program to later capture information that was processed on the manager's computer.

■ An attacker pretended to leave his badge at home and a thoughtful employee let the attacker tailgate through the security door. The attacker sat in the break room and overheard sensitive conversations that were later used to attack the company.

These are just a few of the attacks that have been successfully used against organizations. These should provide an idea of the scope of possibilities that an attacker can use against organizational employees. A concept not understood by many individuals is that many insignificant bits of information, when combined, provide valuable information to an attacker. Any piece of information casually provided to an attacker provides the attacker with one more piece of the information puzzle. A significant amount of SE attacks can be thwarted by policies about giving out information and physical security policies. Once developed, employees must receive initial and periodic training about SE methods.

Chapter 6

There's Always a Bad Guy Out There Who's Smarter, More Knowledgeable, or Better-Equipped Than You

I tried to bring up a few common types of attacks in use today. Attacks come in many forms, too many to cover in this book. Probably one of the more important concepts to understand is that attacks can be human based (such as social engineering or password cracking), protocol based (such as SYN flood attack), software based (such as software exploitation), and occasionally physical connection based (such as a simple man in the middle attack).

One critical concept to keep in mind is that often an organization can be more successfully attacked by social engineering methods than by technical methods. The human element is frequently the weak link in the security process. Active employee awareness training programs can greatly add to the security posture of an organization.

Use your head and keep your eyes open. Your awareness is the strongest line of defense for your organization.

I remember going to the hardware store with my dad as a child to pick up a new lock for our front door. There were no big box stores, just the local store with shelves of every nut, bolt, and home maintenance project imaginable. I remember him looking at the locks, some with deadbolts, some expensive and some cheap. After a few minutes, he picked up one of the cheapest ones and headed for the checkout. We got home, he installed it, and it really didn't look too secure. It looked as if you wiggled it enough, it would open even without a key. So, I had to ask, "Why would you buy a cheap lock to keep us safe? Why didn't you buy one that was harder to break into?" He looked at me and without hesitation told me, "Locks only keep honest people honest." In other words, if someone really wants to get in, even an expensive lock won't keep them out. Home security was more than an expensive lock. It included calling the police, yelling, and maybe even the Louisville Slugger he kept behind the bedroom door. He had layers of security in our house that got more aggressive the further in the house you got. Now we call that Defense in Depth (Figure 6.1).

The new battlefield is the Internet. In this arena, a combatant's campaign success is no longer measured by how much territory has been seized, but rather in the quantity and quality of data captured. Intelligence has replaced physical prowess as a key "soldier" attribute. Anyone with a computer can enter the war, both willingly and unwillingly. Which side of the war they are on is not so clear-cut. The enemy is now ubiquitous and highly mobile. It is an army of one and an army of many.

The bad guys have an enormous pool of allies to draw from, which is one of their greatest strengths. With such a target-rich environment and varying

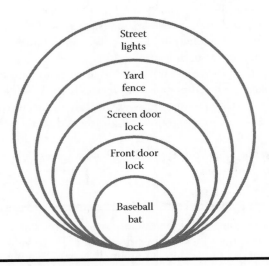

Figure 6.1 My dad invents "defense in depth."

interests, the bad guys are willing to work together to hone their skills, develop new "weapons," and share information. Because of the competitive nature of businesses, there is a general reluctance to collaborate on security matters. As recent events have shown us, breaches have occurred at major institutions that were not reported for weeks, giving the bad guys the time they needed to go after other victims.

There's Always a Bad Guy Out There: Consider what would happen if a neighborhood burglary was left unreported for weeks. People would be less sensitive to any suspicious activity. Police patrols would not be increased. Additional security measures would not be taken by any of the residents, even simple things such as leaving additional lights on at night. The perpetrators would certainly be emboldened to continue and even intensify their crime spree. The criminals would also have plenty of time to fence their plunder and capitalize on their crime, as well as cover their tracks and make a clean getaway.

Sometimes your greatest exposure is your most technical people. With top talent comes a little swagger. They know they are smart and sometimes think they can get away with more than other mere mortals can. Case in point:

When I was the CISO at a company years ago, I got a call from the Recording Industry Artist Association (RIAA), the industry watchdog that tracks the distribution of pirated recordings. The RIAA strongly opposes unauthorized sharing of its music. The association launched high-profile lawsuits against file sharing service providers. It also commenced a series of lawsuits against individuals suspected of file sharing, notably college students and parents of file sharing children. Not an organization to be taken lightly. They had tracked a server distributing unauthorized music to our network. You can imagine this was a real surprise, since we were a financial services firm.

Upon investigation, we found that one of our senior network engineers had set up an open anonymous FTP server on his desktop machine, so he could move files, and more effectively work from home. A hacker saw the open port and used it to set up an illegal music server on the engineer's machine. He was totally unaware of the existence of the server or files. They were effectively hidden.

We cleaned up the mess and explained the incident, but it could have been much worse. A privileged user effectively created a path around all the network security controls. I guess in retrospect we were lucky the bad guy was just a music lover.

Lesson learned? Anyone is at risk of being exploited. You need to particularly watch those who have advanced rights as they have the "master key" to all your most sensitive assets. Interestingly, those users are typically the ones who resist monitoring most, as they feel a lack of trust on your part. There are very good tools out there to monitor actions taken with administrative rights, both by internal and external people. Never forget the potential risk from those companies you allow to monitor and configure your systems remotely.

You get paid to monitor systems and access, not make friends. Sound tough? You don't have to be nasty, just consistent; no one gets a pass, not even your own security staff. The bad guy is not necessarily "out there," but actually may be "in here." The insider threat is very real and can wreak extreme havoc on an organization. The "insider" may not even realize that they are an active participant in a security breach. The use of social engineering is being very effectively exploited by the true bad guys. As more and more companies turn the phrase "Our employees are our most valuable asset" into a hollow slogan, the threat from disgruntled employees will increase. The use of offshore providers introduces a whole new set of challenges. Turnover tends to be very high with offshore providers. Once the data leave the building, it may be impossible to ascertain who and how they were secreted out. Depending on contractual provisions, oversight of offshore provider environments may be very limited. Likewise, penalties for breaches tied to their people or services may be contractually limited. Contracts with offshore providers, and even onshore outsourced services, are something that should be revisited by you and your legal staff. You may find your company is highly exposed. Don't assume you know all the company groups using offshore resources:

> At a previous company I worked for, it was mid-November and we are all looking forward to a little downtime during the holidays. We are always careful to set up a freeze period where no new systems are implemented, and we can do a little cleanup as necessary. I'm in the staff meeting one morning and we are discussing the upcoming network downtimes when one of the development VPs jumped up and said, "You need to be careful not to shut off my contract programmers in the Ukraine." The loud thud heard next was me falling off my chair. I knew nothing about the contractors, how they were connecting, or on what they were working. He had circumvented controls both in IT and Vendor Management, all with good intent. The company needed the application quickly and he found a firm that could deliver at a good price. This kind of action is the most dangerous since it is hard to detect, and the results can be devastating to a company.

Lesson learned? All code that is built offshore must be carefully scanned and checked for malware or control problems. Even during the development phase, carefully control all access to your systems and test data. When possible, use Virtual Desktops that only run a virtual image desktop. When the connection is terminated, there is no local residual data.

The enemy wears many faces and has many different agendas. Deciding how to prioritize your assets and where to focus your scarce resources is a bigger challenge these days. No more is it a simple matter of placing bigger locks on the doors. Financial gain alone is not necessarily the primary motive behind an attack. State-sponsored attacks are more interested in information that will assist them in pursuing political agendas. Famous Prussian general and military strategist Carl von Clausewitz has been credited with stating that war is politics pursued by other means. His words certainly apply to what is happening over the Internet.

Another concept he introduced was "the fog of war." In the Internet war, the "fog" is thick. We are faced with incomplete and sometimes even inaccurate information about our adversary's numbers, disposition, capabilities, and even their intent. Recently, there have been well publicized distributed denial of service attacks on the name servers of the Internet. Because the attack used thousands of devices infected with a BotNet, a small number of hackers executed attacks with tens of thousands of attacking endpoints. Making assumptions about enemy strength, or lack of, based on incomplete information is dangerous. We even have incomplete knowledge of the state of our very own forces and capabilities.

Where there is opportunity, you will find organized crime. Just as the 18th Amendment to the US Constitution (Prohibition) created a large criminally backed underground organization, so has the Internet. The 2014 IOCTA (International Organized Crime Threat Assessment) discusses how a service-based criminal industry that provides sophisticated products and services to other criminals is developing. These are products and services that are being used to perpetrate crimes and which are making entry into the world of cybercrime much easier.

Those who lacked the skills, tools, or resources to engage in cybercrime can now order whatever they need online.

They also now have a convenient place to market the spoils of their criminal exploits. Because these organizations operate in countries where the arm of the law cannot reach, they can operate with impunity. International law regarding the Internet is weak at best and hardly enforceable. In most cases, you won't find these criminal elements on the Internet we are most familiar with. Rather, they lurk in what has come to be known as the Darknet. It is a place hidden from standard search engines where, as stated earlier, "The enemy wears many faces and has many different agendas. Deciding how to prioritize your assets and where to focus your scarce resources is a bigger challenge these days. No more is it a simple matter of placing bigger locks on the doors." There is no lock that a bad guy cannot penetrate. Domains and protocols you find on the Darknet are not your standard fare. Anonymizers are the norm in the

Darknet. They act as a man-in-the middle, so communications appear to be coming from the anonymizing service, thus masking the actual IP address and other personal information. Connections typically are encrypted through virtual private networks (VPNs) further hiding any transactions from prying eyes.

A well-known VPN that services the Darknet is Tor, formerly known as The Onion Router. With Tor, your data are sent through several random Tor server relays. Each relay only knows the identity of the relay that sent it the data and the relay to which the data are going to be transferred.

During each relay, a new encryption key is employed. Furthermore, the relay paths are continuously and randomly generated over a short period of time. There are no server logs maintained. As you can see, secrecy is pretty much ensured. Please bear in mind that Tor has very legitimate uses. It has allowed people to communicate to, from, and within countries that repress freedom of speech.

Any time you visit a website, your general location is identified, information on the device you are using is revealed, and if you allow cookies to be placed on your computer, then your every movement over the web is now being tracked. Tor can protect your privacy. So services like Tor help the guilty as well as the innocent. Like any tool, it can be put to good or bad use.

Anonymizers don't cause crime, people do. Tor doesn't just protect those surfing the Darknet. It also allows servers to hide within the Tor network. Websites are established as Tor Hidden Services and are only accessible through the Tor network. They are not resolvable by the Internet's standard DNS servers. The Hidden Service URLs themselves are auto-generated using a public cryptographic key and consist of a 16-character string of random characters. The Darknet, though, like the legitimate Internet, is not safe from vulnerabilities and hacks. There truly is no honor among thieves. A vulnerability was identified that was sending identifying information to a central server from Darknet sites. It was also discovered that if you become an exit node for Tor, this would allow all the traffic on the Tor network to pass through your machine. In becoming an exit node, you could then perform a man-in-the-middle–type attack, secretly relaying, altering, or copying the communication. Because of this vulnerability, Tor has lost some of its attraction to the criminal element. Especially, since the man-in-the-middle could very well be the government.

The beauty of the Internet is the wealth of information it provides. The drawback to the Internet is the wealth of information it provides. Any aspiring hacker need only enter "hack" into a search engine and be provided a plethora of "how to" links on the subject. Need a tool to aid in your hacking? It's freely available for download. Not quite sure how to effect a certain hack? There is a blog a few keystrokes away that will help you through the process. A search on "learn how to hack" returned 50,900 results! There is plenty of information out there to not only get someone started down the wrong path but to keep him educated and supported on the subject. On the positive side, a search on "learn how to speak Spanish" returned nearly 9 million results. Though, without a doubt, many of these returns are commercial product offerings.

The tools out there are quite powerful, and most are free for the asking. From a CISO's perspective, it only makes sense to take advantage of these free tools and apply them to your network. You can be sure that the bad guys are using them. What better way to determine the vulnerability of your environment than by using the very same tools they are? Naturally, technology changes over time and tools come and go, so these may not be the best or still available, but they should give you an idea of areas in which to focus for similar tools.

The bad guys certainly realize that the front door is heavily guarded. Their efforts will be focused on your back doors. Back doors you might not realize exist. Back doors your own employees may have installed to make their lives easier. With the proliferation of mobile devices, the bad guys have a lot more avenues in which to gain entry to your environment. While you have some control over mobile devices inside your four walls, once these devices leave the building, your means of control rapidly diminish. In order to protect your data, the incorporation of end point encryption is absolutely necessary. But you will still need a security solution that protects laptops, tablets, and smartphones against a host of potentially serious malware threats.

Malware, short for malicious software, is a broad category of software that is designed for attack and compromise purposes. A growing trend is the use of bots that allow an attacker to take control of the infected device. If a bad guy can get a bot loaded on one of your devices, they now have a key to your kingdom. Loading a bot on a device is as easy as having a user visit a website, where software on the website looks for vulnerabilities on the device to exploit. Another common approach is to infect the device by sending the bot via an e-mail attachment. The bad guys just need to wait for an implanted bot to "phone home."

Bots can work independently, but generally they are used jointly with other bots in what is termed a botnet. The Conficker botnet was believed to consist of bots, in millions, on devices around the world. The combined resources can then be used to produce a disproportionately negative effect on other systems and users, such as creating distributed denial-of-service (DDoS) or spam attacks. The power of a botnet has made them a very attractive commodity to be sold over the Darknet.

Thus, criminal organizations don't need to be skilled hackers but simply can acquire the tools they need to carry out their harmful activities. An example of a bot is Tinba, which is short for Tiny Banker. As its name implies, its function is to steal financial information. This particular bot was commercialized and readily available for anyone willing to purchase it. The original version is also tiny in size, only about 20 kb. As with other bots, it continues to be improved and modified by the bad guys. Bots are not cheap. They are known to sell for tens of thousands of dollars, attesting to the large financial returns they can bring into the wrong hands. Again, using the example of the recent attacks against the Internet name server environment. The Bots were extremely effective and engineered to work on home devices that connect to the Internet such as DVD players and security cameras. This illustrates that not just malware, but what we consider an endpoint, must continually evolve.

What about Your People?

Even with your own employees, there should be a certain degree of compartmental-ization of information and multiple layers of access restrictions. No single employee should ever hold the entire keys to the kingdom. While implementing a two-man rule similar to the military controls surrounding nuclear weapons might be a bit of overkill, certain precautions are clearly in order. No one knows your systems better than an employee, so, from a threat perspective, they rank rather high. How much of a risk they pose is more difficult to gauge. The more controls you have in place, the lower the risk. How you treat your employees will also have a direct bearing on the risk posed.

The more controls you have in place, the lower the risk. Satisfied, well-compensated employees constitute a lower risk. Work with Human Resources to ensure that your key employees are paid well, commensurate with the job market, and are appropriately titled. This will also control the poaching of your critical employees by rival companies. Keep job descriptions up to date and work with your employees in crafting them. You might learn things about their job responsibilities you were not aware of that could impact security if the resource was to leave and these functions were not identified and appropriately filled by their replacement.

As we continue to harden our infrastructure to attacks, the hackers have to find a new weak link in our defenses. That weak link is the people. The use of social engineering is proving to be very effective in giving the bad guys the access they need. While the techniques of spy lore (such as blackmail, or outright buying of the information from those willing to betray their companies) are effective, it is cheaper and easier to trick the users into doing things that give the bad guys what they need. Getting the user to visit a compromised website or a website that appears legitimate when in fact it is not can be quite effective in retrieving sensitive information from an unsuspecting Internet surfer. Getting the user to download something from these sites makes it even easier for the bad guys. The bad guys can also call your users directly and attempt to trick them into providing them with the information they need to compromise your environment. And don't forget about your myriad of partners. How many have access into your environment? How many have domain access? With the rush to offshore IT services, you now have people with full access to your environment that you have very little control over. If the bad guys can't break through your defenses, they may certainly go after your partners. How secure do you think your partners' environments are, especially your offshore partners? While you may have contracts in place to "protect" you, you might want to take a real close look at the fine print. Chances are, the monetary damages they will be liable for are very small compared to the actual damages that would occur. Your contracts with your partners should permit an independent third-party audit and penetration test of their environments each year. Your partners are like folks with passports. As long as the passport is in the right person's hands, there is no problem letting them pass through the gate. Unfortunately, a hacker can steal a partner's credentials, and like an unreported stolen passport, just walk right through the gate into your domain.

The bad guys know they can effectively prey on unsuspecting users during times of uncertainty. Consider an announcement by a major retailer that their systems were breached, resulting in millions of credit card numbers being released. A bad guy could piggyback on this opportunity to contact individuals, telling them their card has been compromised and needs to be replaced. They then proceed to extract as much personal information as possible from the person in what appears to be an effort to help the customer resolve a problem. Customers, concerned over their personal information, unwittingly release the very information they are trying to protect. Knowing the e-mail addresses of a few IT folks can also be exploited by the bad guys during a real incident by creating e-mails with forged sender addresses, which is very simple to do and is known as spoofing. The bad guy then simply interjects himself into the troubleshooting dialogue, appearing as a fellow employee, and begins extracting information from others in the e-mail threads.

Getting the user to visit a compromised website or a website that appears legitimate when in fact it is not can be quite effective in retrieving sensitive information from an unsuspecting Internet surfer. Getting the user to download something from these sites makes it even easier for the bad guys. The bad guys can also call your users directly and attempt to trick them into providing them with the information they need to compromise your environment.

While maintaining a blacklist can eliminate a large number of the bad sites from access by your users, these sites are being generated faster than blacklists can be developed. Whitelisting is more effective, but the size of the Internet and the number of legitimate sites make it hard to maintain such lists without affecting your users. Educating your users is your best defense, but as the saying goes, "There is a sucker born every minute." No matter how well you educate your users, there will be that one that clicks on the pop-up that says, "You've Won One Million Dollars!" or some other nonsense. Regrettably, it only takes one user to bring down your environment.

Where you have even less control is the myriad of social network sites that exist. While you may be able to control access to such sites from within your environment, your employees do whatever they want from the privacy of their home using their own assets. Monitoring what your employees are placing for public view on these social network sites is a monumental task. Unfortunately, social networks are now frequently mined by the bad guys for information through botnets. People place an incredible amount of personal information on these social network sites that can be used against the very person that posted the information or to extract information from close associates by impersonating the poster. What is more troubling is the amount of company-sensitive information that employees place on these social network sites. Having both personal and company information can help a bad buy to appear very legitimate, easily tricking others into revealing sensitive information. This process is known as phishing and is highly effective. Receiving a well-crafted phishing e-mail message from what you erroneously believe to be a mutual acquaintance may cause even those savvy about security to let down their guard.

And don't forget about your myriad of partners. How many have access into your environment? How many have domain access? With the rush to offshore IT services, you now have people with full access to your environment that you have very little control over. If the bad buys can't break through your defenses, they may certainly go after your partners. How secure do you think the environments are of your partners, especially your offshore partners? While you may have contracts in place to "protect" you, you might want to take a real close look at the fine print. Chances are, the monetary damages they will be liable for are very small compared to the actual damages that would occur. Your contracts with your partners should permit an independent third-party audit and penetration test of their environments each year. Your partners are like folks with passports. As long as the passports are in the right person's hands, there is no problem letting them pass through the gate. Unfortunately, a hacker can steal a partner's credentials, and, like an unreported stolen passport, just walk right through the gate into your domain.

In order to get to your data, the bad guys are after your source code. If you don't think so, just conduct an Internet search on source code leaked to see how much proprietary code has been stolen. Having access to your source code allows the hackers to closely scrutinize it for security exploits. This is part of the debate over open source software. Some feel it is more secure since everyone can analyze the code and provide feedback. Proprietary code does not get the same level of scrutiny, though any flaws found are also more quickly exploited in open source software. Microsoft suffered a leak of its Windows 2000 and NT4.0 operating systems. Considering these systems were used on millions of computers worldwide, the importance of this source code to the bad guys is immeasurable. Of course, besides identifying exploits in the code, access to the code would give a competitive edge to any Microsoft rivals. Source code can be just as valuable as data, so it requires similar protections.

Plan for the Worst

So what do you do if you suspect the bad guys have already penetrated your perimeter? While prayer is always an option, there are a number of other immediate steps you need to take. The first and foremost thing you need to do is sever the communication ties. This will probably be the most difficult decision you have to make. This will naturally have a huge impact on the business. It is neither a decision that can be taken lightly, nor one that can be delayed for long. The longer you delay, the more damage you may incur. Having a predefined set of rules and conditions that would prompt the isolation of your business, and that have been signed off by all of the senior level executives in advance, will go a long way in making the decision easier.

If you don't already have one in place, you need to create an incident response team. This should consist of your top talent. It will need representation from the business side to assist in damage assessment and communicating with the business. It also needs senior-level people with good communication skills who can keep public affairs/corporate communications and senior level management abreast of what is transpiring. The incident response team should also consist of people with basic forensics skills. They should know what data are important and how to preserve them for further forensics analysis. Forensics analysis should not occur until after the situation is stabilized, but you need people involved that will prevent valuable information from getting lost or destroyed in the recovery actions. Just as every police officer is trained how to not contaminate a crime scene, so should your incident response team be trained as to how to handle the forensic elements of a cyber-attack. The incident response team needs to be activated at the first indication of a problem. With today's technology, they do not necessarily need to be on site unless, of course, the decision has been made to sever communication links. If you have multiple sites, then you need people that can physically get to each of these sites in a reasonable period of time. You should also have backup communications in place, since corporate communication systems may not be available. The primary responsibility of the incident response team is to accurately assess the situation and secure the environment as necessary.

Once the situation is contained, they can relax a bit and focus on other aspects of the incident. One important task is to document all actions that were taken. This will help in event reconstruction, as well as help with any subsequent legal proceedings. After containment, you can then begin the arduous task of assessing the extent of the damage and begin recovery procedures. Communication will be key during a crisis of this nature. Your public affairs/corporate communications office needs to be brought into the situation. Ideally, they should have a crisis plan already in place for events such as this. Customers and partners need to be informed. The infection might very well have originated from one of your partners, and depending on your business, you may run the risk of infecting your customers. At the very least, if business operations are affected or customer data are involved, your customers need to be told something. IT should never deal with the public or press directly. Prearrange a communication plan with the marketing or public relations departments. They will help wordsmith the message and avoid any missteps with the public.

Bringing in law enforcement right away will help ensure that important forensic data are not lost in the turmoil. You should have contracts in place with businesses that specialize in forensic analysis and they should be brought in right away. Secrecy seems to be the normal approach in the wake of a cyber-attack, but being frank and open will lead to better preparedness for not only your business but others as well. Legal concerns, though, tend to stifle the free flow of valuable information.

Usually in situations like this, it is better to rebuild systems from scratch rather than try to remove the malware. Care must be taken in using backups of the systems since these backups may very well include the malware. The systems are far less important than the data themselves, which are most likely what the bad guys were after. It may be difficult to determine exactly how much of those data have fallen into the hands of the bad guys. This is especially difficult if they had unlimited access over an extended period of time. Data are rarely actually taken; they are simply copied; so there is no gaping hole to tell you what is missing.

You need to obtain all of your log files. The quantity and quality of logging that you do will have a direct bearing on how much you can reconstruct of what has transpired. Since the bad guys can be in your environment for months, if not years, before detection you may not have logs back far enough to fully reconstruct the chain of events. If the bad guys are really good, they will have altered your logs as well. Log files need a high degree of security on them just like the systems and data themselves.

Monitoring any unusual changes to log files may be your first indication that you have a problem in your environment. Obviously, you hope you never have to call out the incident response team. Having a multilayered defense will reduce your risks of a penetration. The more obstacles you put in the bad guys' way, the more likely they will give up and go elsewhere or do something that will alert you to their presence before they can actually do any harm. Of course, there are those who like a challenge, so there will always be the risk your defenses might attract a few bad guys wanting to prove how good they really are. In the cyber underworld, there is a pecking order and those looking for increased bragging rights. Just as in any profession, there is a desire to be the best. In the hacker world, much of how good you are is demonstrated by successful hacks or data thefts. Many groups like "Anonymous" post messages after hacks claiming responsibility to demonstrate their prowess and power.

Not all protection layers need to be concentric. You can provide a multilayered defense around your most critical data that lies within another multilayered defense around your network. All things do not have to be protected to the same degree. In most cases, the data are where your greatest defenses should be focused. And depending on the constitution of the data, you may need different layers of defense for the data themselves.

Ridding your environment of outdated and one-off systems will reduce your risks. These systems never get the full attention they need. They are either old or little used technologies, so they are not fun to work on and add little to the resume. Most likely, the vendor has long since ceased support, or it is marginal at best, since they may be from small companies or technologies that have subsequently replaced support. Your biggest risk may come from the free shareware someone was able to download into your environment.

Setting up around-the-clock monitoring is one of your best defenses. Having systems to do the monitoring is not sufficient. You need people that can understand the data and react promptly to what they see. The volume of data can be staggering, so developing baselines from which to draw comparisons will help facilitate identifying anomalies in your environment. Security Information and Event

Management tools can greatly assist in this endeavor. Again, though, you need people to actually interpret and respond to the data provided.

Not All Alerts Should Be Complex

This is one reason gauges have been replaced with "idiot" lights in cars. People tended not to look at the data until after things began to break. The flashing red lights, while typically a precursor to things breaking, at least get the driver's attention and hopefully get them to take immediate action to avoid a major breakdown. Had they been monitoring the temperature gauge or oil pressure gauge, they might have seen the rise in temperature or decreasing pressure sooner, giving them more options. Airplanes tend not to have idiot lights. Pilots are trained to monitor their gauges as a matter of routine. Options are limited for pilots, so the sooner they can detect a problem, the better the final outcome will be.

Lesson learned? Alerts should be tailored to the audience. A 10-page analysis may be good for an engineer, but a red/green light is more effective for an end user.

While we focus on the core network, our extended network cannot be ignored. Client side software is becoming increasingly the target of choice for the bad guys. This certainly makes sense. There are far more targets of opportunities with client side software. It used to just be personal computers; now, we have tablets, cell phones, and anything connected by Bluetooth, as a possible penetration source. The degree of protection extended over these assets is usually far less than that covering your servers in the data center. Having physical access to a personal device can allow a bad guy to install a variety of things that may go undetected, yet provide the information they need to fully penetrate the device and ultimately your network.

The amount of data devices now contain, compared to just five years ago, is staggering. So even if the bad guys can't penetrate your network, they may get a mother lode of data from just one portable computer. You really have to rein in this extended network. You also need to limit the data that are out there, and what is out there has to be encrypted.

What about Wireless?

Few corporations do not have a wireless network. How often is the security of this entry point to the network actually tested and to what degree? There are a variety of tools available such as AirCrack and Wifite to help in this regard. In order to see what is actually flowing over the network, tools like Wireshark should be employed. These will identify whether outdated network protocols are being used over your network. They can also graphically show where encryption is needed.

Deploying an application without validating its security status is, regrettably, rather commonplace. It is better to find the holes in your applications before they are deployed. There are a number of tools to help you in this area such as Zap and Vega. Since no corporation can run without databases, these should be an area of concern. Tools like OpenVAS and SCUBA can help you determine how secure your databases actually are. If you are developing mobile applications, you can be sure vulnerabilities exist in these applications. The technology is still evolving, developers are gradually gaining experience in this area, and when it comes to Androids, the number of variations introduces a high degree of complexity. A tool such as Drozer can help with Android development. For iOS, you might want to consider AppScan.

You can even buy a tablet device specifically designed and configured to penetrate wired and wireless networks. PWN Pad is one such commercial-grade tool. It is small and lightweight. A hacker could sit outside your building with such a device and use your wireless network to gain access. It has six different covert channels to tunnel through application-aware firewalls and intrusion prevention systems. The increased use of mobile devices not only makes it more challenging to protect systems and data, but devices such as PWN Pad make it easier for the bad guys to break in. It should be noted that this device was listed as temporarily sold out. Question is who is predominately buying it, the good guys or the bad guys? Every day, the technology becomes more powerful, smaller, and has new features to make it easier to use. At the same time, your wireless network is becoming more powerful and feature rich to enhance the user experience, potentially opening the door for new attacks. Carefully engineer and control the risks when you implement new technology, particularly those that allow greater network access.

Of course, there are ethical hackers, the so-called white hats, and obviously they need a means to learn their craft. The white hats are essential in our battle against the bad guys. There are plenty of commercially available courses for this. Though just like learning how to shoot a gun, there is no way to know whether the knowledge will be used for good or evil.

If you don't like the war analogy when discussing the cyber threat, then there should be no argument that we are all in a race. As we continue to evolve and improve our defenses against attacks, the hackers and cyber thieves are likewise evolving their techniques. Most breaches have been found to have used varying modus operandi to gain access and compromise systems. The bad guy need only focus his talents and resources in a particular direction much like a racer focuses on a particular race such as cross-country, 100-yard dash, or hurdles. For example, a particular bad guy may be looking for weaknesses in your wireless network to gain access to Linux systems. We, on the other hand, are running multiple races at the same time against a very large field of other talented racers.

There may be other races we are not even aware of that we should be participating in. Modems have become somewhat passé, yet there has been more than one case where a modem has been found connected to some obscure server in the data center. Hard to protect against things you are not aware of yet some bad guy might have this modem sitting at the finish line of their race.

The fact the bad guys can specialize means their knowledge level and skills are quite honed. We do not have the resources or the time to become so specialized. The bad guys can and likely are specialized down to a particular make and model of hardware and/or version of software. Such expert knowledge allows them to find and exploit vulnerabilities before they become public knowledge. Besides preparing for new types of attacks, companies also need to continue to deal with and defend against older types of attacks. As sophisticated as the technology and techniques get, we still can't ignore the fact someone can break down the door and steal the hard drives. Is it a likely scenario? Probably not. Is it still possible? Most definitely yes. Do you have to consider it? Without question! So while someone breaking down the door is not likely, a hard drive leaving the environment is not that far-fetched. Especially, as you retire old systems and the size of these devices continue to shrink. One lesson here is that even the most improbable of scenarios can produce very feasible situations affecting security.

Lesson learned? Are you aware that every multifunction office machine has a hard drive? Are you aware that thousands of the last documents printed or scanned are resident on the device? What happened to the last copier you traded in? Did you keep the drive? ALWAYS retain and destroy the drive. Write it into the lease contract when you procure the equipment.

Context-Aware Security

A new approach to security that is gaining a lot of followers is context-aware security. Context-aware security is the use of situational information to include such things as identity, location, time of day, applications accessed, or type of end point device to improve information security decisions. Analyzing a combination of these factors can help determine if something is amiss. For example, you find a user VPNing into your network at 2 a.m. when this user historically only VPNs into the network between 8 p.m. and 11 p.m. While it may be innocent, it certainly bears a further look. Now, if they are normally located on the East Coast but your data show them on the West Coast, then this may be more plausible as a security event. Context-aware security is not new. Credit card companies have been using this for years. The challenge is collecting and storing a sufficient amount of data from which to develop a reasonable baseline of information needed to make intelligent context-based decisions.

And let's not forget about the ubiquitous Cloud. Unless you put tight controls in place, your users will be uploading anything and everything to Cloud-based providers. While these providers may not have any malicious intent, you have no say or insight into the security they have placed on their environment to protect your data. What becomes more troublesome are the Hybrid Clouds. While they offer advantages of efficiency and availability, they pose a very real risk of exposing sensitive information into the public cloud space. While cloud security has certainly improved, it is still an area that deserves your attention and specialized tools.

The bad guys are out there. They are getting smarter and better at what they do. They are also getting more particular about who they go after. No one is safe. No one can rest on their laurels. This is a battle that goes on all day, every day. There are no holidays, no breaks, and no truces. In this battle, there are no real winners, only losers. Today's cyber battles are reminiscent of World War I trench warfare. Each side deeply dug in, yet constantly trying to penetrate the other's lines. Each side introduces new technology that is quickly countered by even newer technology. In the end, a lot of time, money, and resources have been expended with little to show for it except the ability to fight another day.

Suggested Reading

Cyber Resilience Review (CRR): The CRR is a no-cost, voluntary, nontechnical assessment to evaluate an organization's operational resilience and cybersecurity practices. The CRR may be conducted as a self-assessment or as an on-site assessment facilitated by DHS cybersecurity professionals. The CRR assesses enterprise programs and practices across a range of 10 domains including risk management, incident management, service continuity, and others. The assessment is designed to measure existing organizational resilience, as well as provide a gap analysis for improvement based on recognized best practices.

Chapter 7

Know the Enemy,
Think Like the Enemy

What do you have that the enemy would like to steal? If you were the bad guy, how would you steal it? It's not always motivated by theft. If you were the enemy, how would you disrupt your business and why? Case in point:

One of the companies in my past provided global products and services. Most of these services were highly competitive and service driven. Not a lot of profit per item, but incredible volumes. In my normal reports, I received a notice that an engineering office had been broken into in the United States, and the local assessment that it was a routine theft, a break-in where the thieves grabbed a few laptops left on desks. Local management and law enforcement were sure that the laptops would end up in a local pawnshop, and no client data were on the machines, just some engineering files. My first mistake: believing the local assessment.

A couple of months later, I got a panic call from one of our foreign locations that a key piece of high-volume production equipment was behaving strangely and ultimately shutting itself down. They would reboot the PC controlling the machine; it would start again, but ultimately slow down and shut itself down again. It had been behaving like this for a couple of weeks and the technicians had tried everything. If we couldn't get this resolved, we would start missing customer commitments, and probably start to lose contracts. There were other suppliers in line just waiting for us to crash and burn. The local engineers had reloaded the programs and it didn't make a difference. Something would continue to eat CPU cycles until the controller crashed and shut the machine down. It sure began to sound like malware, but how would it get on the system, after all we were guaranteed that the system was isolated on the network with no external connectivity. So, one of my security guys grabbed his go bag and hopped on a flight.

So, here is what we found on investigation; there was a custom piece of malware on the system, not incredibly sophisticated, but very effective. It attacked the memory locations critical to the operating program, slowly eating the system resources until there were not enough resources to keep the PC running. It ran at a slow speed to not show up as a runaway process and flag its existence. Once identified, we were able to isolate and clean the PC and the registry settings to ensure the code would not reactivate.

Now the big question. How did it get on the machine in the factory? The machine ran three shifts a day, seven days a week, meaning that the operator of the system was there for some long midnight hours. Even though we had been told it was completely isolated, we found that a well-meaning network engineer set up the machine for Internet access so the operator could surf the web during the boring hours. It was done as a favor, so there was no change request or oversight: hey, what could it hurt? It was behind a firewall, and we were running antivirus. All good logic except the operator was also using web mail to keep up with his friends.

Lots of unanswered questions: How did the attackers know how to write the code to attack specific memory locations? How did it get on the machine? What was the motivation? How did they know how to find and attack a specific system in the middle of a foreign country?

So, we got the talented people together, filled the coffee pot, ordered in pizza and set up a war room. Nobody was leaving until we got some answers. The first key piece of the puzzle was the discovery that this business was an acquisition about a year prior, and like many actions, there were layoffs in the engineering ranks. Also, there was a ton of bad feelings toward the company as the office was really tight knit, with many friends and family working there. Any guess where the engineering office was? You're right; it was the location that had the break-in and laptop theft months before. When we interviewed the people in the office, we found a key piece of missing information. The thieves had walked through the main office (with many laptops in plain sight), entered a back office, and stole only two laptops. Interestingly, the owners of the laptops were working on the machine control project.

On the compromise side, we were able to locate and reverse engineer the attack code. It actually contained some code identical to the operating code developed thousands of miles away. Further investigation showed that the code had come in via an e-mail attachment opened by the operator that looked much like a legitimate e-mail. So, we know the how but what about the why?

Simply, it was revenge and competitive loss. If the company could not keep up with production commitments due to malware problems, they would lose huge, high-volume contracts to competitors.

As an aside, to show that if anything can go wrong it will, the engineering group was in the process of building another machine to bolster production when this problem came to light. Any guess where they got the disk image to load on the new machine being built? Of course, they had requested the technical folks in the factory to burn a disk image of the existing production machine and they loaded it on the new machine. Luckily, we intercepted the problem and cleaned it or there could have been a vicious cycle of infection and reinfection.

So, what did I learn? First, nothing is ever as simple as it first seems, particularly to the distributed management and users making the call. Second, traditional data breach for profit, while very prevalent, is not the only answer—never become comfortable, always challenge your assumptions. You don't get paid to take the easy answer; you are one of the last lines of defense for the company; if you don't challenge and dig deep into issues, who will? Third, when you identify a threat vector, learn to think like the enemy. If you were going to shut down production equipment for revenge, or for competitive gain, how would you do it? If you were going to steal your company's data, how would you do it? If you were going to interrupt key production of engineering processes, how would you do it? Here's a real-life example:

In the mid-1990s, there was a system administrator who worked at a manufacturing company that stored all its programs that ran its computer-controlled machining centers on a central, networked disk. The administrator started to feel like his job may be in jeopardy, so he wrote a program that would delete all the program files, including the backups, if he didn't reset the program counter every day. He felt that if the company fired him, they would pay a heavy price the next day. As it turns out, he was right about getting fired. The company walked him out the door, and a day later, all the program files were gone and the company was at a standstill without the information to run its machines. Fortunately for the company, the process that deleted the files was still on the system, and it was easily tracked back to the fired administrator. He was charged and served time, but the company was still on the hook for lost business, time to reengineer the program files, and so on.

Moral of the story: If you give the keys to the kingdom to an employee, be sure you know who they really are and that they can be trusted (Figure 7.1). Also, when the managers of that employee started the process to get rid of him, why didn't they take a close look at the damage he could do and take steps early to mitigate that damage?

I often draw on history to evaluate the problems I face every day. Do that often enough and you will find that while the technology may change, the fundamental motivation and methods remain the same. Case in point: We've all heard of the story of the Trojan Horse. How different would the story be if the guy who tiptoed out of the horse that night was not able to open the door to let his friends in? It probably would be more of a folly about how some idiots thought they could defeat a fortified city with a wooden horse. Think like an attacker and develop defensive strategies. Most networks today focus on keeping bad stuff out, but let information freely flow from the inside out. Why don't you lock down your outbound traffic? Why don't you lock the door so the guy crawling out of the Trojan Horse can't easily open the doors and let your corporate jewels flow out to the Internet?

Also, looking a little further, how long do you think that the guys inside the wooden horse could have stayed there undetected? If they wanted, they could have stayed inside days, collecting intelligence about the city and its inside defenses. That is, because the city did not think a bad guy could get inside, they ignored the possibility of that threat. Is this sounding familiar? How about the number of highly public breaches where, when the details were released, the investigators found out that the bad guys had been resident on the victim's network for months without detection?

It is time for a paradigm change. CISOs can no longer assume their "wall" is impenetrable (Figure 7.2). Get serious; put the same effort in protecting the interior as the exterior.

Why do they want control over our system?

They want to steal our data, and use our
system to attack others

Figure 7.1   What the bad guys want.

What are the lessons for today?

1. As dedicated as we are to protect our data, there may be hackers more dedicated to steal it.
2. Since our focus must be enterprise wide, a focused cybercriminal will almost always have the upper hand because they can be persistent, and focused on a specific target.
3. The criminals will always attack a weak link in the defensive chain. Typically, that is the human element. We need to understand where our "targets of opportunity" exist.

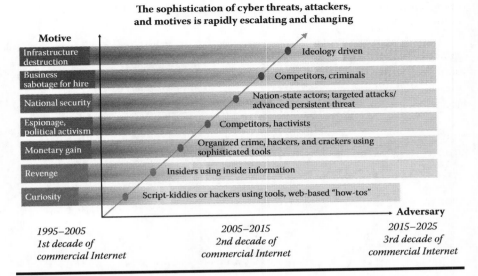

Figure 7.2   Rising sophistication.

Given the complexity of modern software and network environments, if an attacker looks hard enough, or waits long enough, a weakness will become apparent that can allow the attacker to compromise the target. Because of this, common sense tells us today that there are only two types of organizations—ones that have been penetrated and ones that do not yet know that they've been penetrated. Focusing solely on keeping attackers out of a network is no longer the best strategy to protect an organization from cybersecurity threats.

If an attacker is successful in establishing a foothold on the network and hiding their presence, they will have unlimited time to probe and snoop around the company infrastructure. During that time, they may use reconnaissance to find where the company jewels are really kept. When we hear about massive breaches, we also typically hear that the attacker existed on the network for months or even years.

Many companies—mistakenly—believe that they are perfectly safe behind a firewall. The fact is quite the opposite: if you can get out of your network, someone else can get in. Attackers often seek to compromise the weakest link in a network and then use that access to attack the network from the inside. The most common cause behind the presence of vulnerable applications is failing to stay on top of security updates. Perhaps, because of a lack of time and resources, an administrative policy is written for less frequent updates. More commonly, patching is withheld due to concerns over breaking custom programs/applications. It seems that throughout my career, patching always appears to take a back seat. Not for a lack of concern, but because with limited staff and resources, something has to wait. After a period of neglect, the "technical debt" can be stacked up by an organization and become insurmountable and yield a fertile target for all types of public attacks.

Keeping up to date on patches and security updates is a good start toward protecting your network. There is no hard and fast way to achieve and/or maintain perfect security on any network. The goal of any security controls and counter-measures should be to defend your network while maintaining ease of use and accessibility.

Today, just like the squirrel of my youth, hackers are winning on sheer speed and determination. Is there any way we can swing the odds in our favor? Can we affect the time frames of an attack cycle?

Here's how.

Over the past few years, attackers have proven to be adept at compromising even the most secure organizations. A common theme in successful attacks is per-sistence. Given the complexity of modern software and network environments, if an attacker looks hard enough, or waits long enough, a weakness will become apparent that can allow the attacker to compromise the target. Remember, the attacker has an army of allies who take great pleasure in discovering vulnerabilities and sharing their discoveries. It is like a badge of honor to be the first to crack some line of defense. One need only look at the frequency that Microsoft publishes new security updates to get a sense of how much attention is being spent by the attackers on Microsoft alone looking for vulnerabilities. More troubling is these are only the vulnerabilities Microsoft has become cognizant of. Undoubtedly, others exist that are known only to the attackers. Consequently, focusing solely on keeping attack-ers out of a network is no longer the best strategy to protect an organization from cybersecurity threats.

The history is self-evident from Figure 7.3. In the 1990s, the time from a vulner-ability being announced to an active attack in the wild was months. In the 2000s, the number began to shrink; until today, we see attacks before we know there is a vulnerability or problem. When speaking to groups, I equate the 1990s to an impending hurricane. You have days of warning to prepare or evacuate. Today, it is more like a tornado touchdown, which, in many cases, occurs without warning. The losses are sometimes greater in that people did not have time to prepare.

The numbers speak volumes: It only takes minutes from the initiation of an attack for an attacker to compromise a system. Once access has been achieved, data can be extracted quickly. Within organizations, it takes on the order of months to discover the compromise, and weeks for the breach to be resolved. Clearly, attackers have the upper hand. The task of defending networks is becoming more difficult, rather than easier, as perimeters continue to expand through the use of external cloud systems, mobile devices especially the phenomena of Bring Your Own Device (BYOD), and integrated services with external third parties.

Unfortunately, we cannot turn back the clock and return to more innocent and less complex days. As attackers become more skilled and systems become more complex, it is next to impossible to keep systems completely free from compromise.

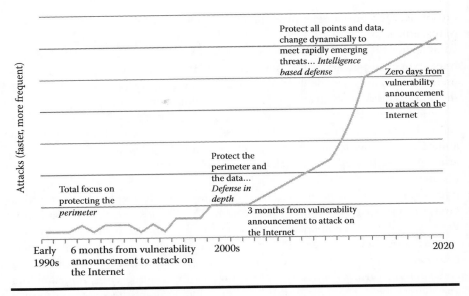

Figure 7.3 Attack frequency.

I'm not saying that we should give up. In fact, I strongly believe that it is still possible to prevent most attacks and—even when an attack is successful—it is possible to identify and remediate the breach before harm is incurred. The key is to shift the time frames of an attack, so that the odds are stacked in the defender's (not the attacker's) favor. In warfare, defenses are built to slow down the enemy. By slowing them down, you have a chance to adjust your plans and successfully defend against an attack; Cyber warfare is the same. Use the tools you have such as network segmentation, firewalls, honeypots, and other systems to slow up the attacker, giving you more notice to stop the attacker before serious damage occurs.

It's also important to understand that cybercrime is an economic crime. In my experience, there are very few attackers that look for complex targets to "test their skills." That is easy fodder for movies and TV shows, makes for great stories, but it is not reality. The average attacker is looking for an easy target. If an attacker finds that a target is too expensive in terms of time, effort, and resources to breach, the attacker will switch attention to an easier target that offers the same rewards at a lower cost. For example, segregating networks so that the attacker cannot easily gain access to confidential information means that attackers have to work harder before they can extract valuable data. The harder and longer the attackers have to work, the better the chances they will leave traces that can be identified.

Network vigilance is another factor that can reduce the time frame from compromise to detection. It is during idle periods that attackers are able to explore networks and steal resources without hindrance. By identifying abnormal network activity and distinguishing it from normal day-to-day activity, incursions can be detected before they cause harm. Modern Security Information and Event Management (SIEM) systems allow logging data from Intrusion Prevention System (IPS) devices, firewalls, file servers, and domain servers to be aggregated and analyzed. Not every attacker will generate alerts from the IPS system, but alerts such as users attempting to access files outside of their job role, or at odd times of the day, should prompt security teams to investigate further.

Prioritizing network security alerts requires procedures and practice. A typical set of security tools can generate gigs of logs every day. The CISO must look at how to prioritize the alerts. Drinking out of a fire hose is never easy; you must learn to drink without drowning. Minor alerts should be ignored so that response teams can focus on important issues. Despite the headlines, major breaches are rare events. Security teams may only be faced with such an incident once a decade. However, when an organization is faced with such a scenario, security teams need to be able to respond quickly, effectively, and confidently. This can only happen if people are trained and practiced in responding to such incidents. Working through theoretical exercises to decide how to respond, and practicing responses to simulated attacks, should be standard practice in incident planning. By reviewing the results of such practices, improvements can be implemented so that when a major incident does happen, teams know exactly how to respond and react. Now for the real key:

Monitoring What Leaves Your Network Is Just as Important as Monitoring What Comes In: Introducing the "Kill Chain" Methodology

A kill chain is defined as a systematic process to target and engage an adversary to create desired effects. This terminology has its roots in the US military. They refer to this as a targeting doctrine, defining the steps of the process as find, fix, track, target, engage, assess: find adversary targets suitable for engagement; fix their location; track and observe; target with suitable weapon or asset to create desired effects; engage adversary; assess effects (US Department of Defense 2007). This is an integrated, end-to-end process described as a "chain" because any one deficiency will interrupt the entire process. The strategy for us is to interrupt the chain as early as possible to limit any damage by a hacker to the potential target.

The essence of an intrusion is that the aggressor must develop a payload to breach a trusted boundary, establish a presence inside a trusted environment, and from that presence, take actions toward their objectives, be they moving laterally inside the environment or violating the confidentiality, integrity, or availability of a system in the environment. The intrusion kill chain is defined as reconnaissance, weaponization, delivery, exploitation, installation, command and control, and actions on objectives.

With respect to computer network attack or computer network espionage, the definitions for these kill chain phases are as follows:

1. Reconnaissance—Research, identification, and selection of targets, often represented as crawling Internet websites such as conference proceedings and mailing lists for e-mail addresses, social relationships, or information on specific technologies.
2. Weaponization—Coupling a remote access trojan with an exploit into a deliverable payload, typically by means of an automated tool (weaponizer). Increasingly, client application data files such as Adobe Portable Document Format (PDF) or Microsoft Office documents serve as the weaponized deliverable.
3. Delivery—Transmission of the weapon to the targeted environment. The three most prevalent delivery vectors for weaponized payloads by Advanced Persistent Threat (APT) actors are e-mail attachments, websites, and USB removable media.
4. Exploitation—After the weapon is delivered to the victim host, exploitation triggers intruders' code. Most often, exploitation targets an application or operating system vulnerability, but it could also more simply exploit the users themselves or leverage an operating system feature that auto-executes code.
5. Installation—Installation of a remote access trojan or backdoor on the victim system allows the adversary to maintain persistence inside the environment.
6. Command and Control—Typically, compromised hosts must beacon outbound to an Internet controller server to establish a channel. APT malware especially requires manual interaction rather than conduct activity automatically. Once the channel establishes, intruders have "hands on the keyboard" access inside the target environment.
7. Actions on Objectives—Only now, after progressing through the first six phases, can intruders take actions to achieve their original objectives. Typically, this objective is data exfiltration, which involves collecting, encrypting, and extracting information from the victim environment; violations of data integrity or availability are potential objectives as well. Alternatively, the intruders may only desire access to the initial victim box for use as a hop point to compromise additional systems and move laterally inside the network.

A kill chain is a process for finding and taking action on a target (Figure 7.4). This integrated, end-to-end process is described as a "Chain" because any one deficiency will interrupt the entire process.

- At each step, the malware must "phone home" for more instructions. If we interrupt any one communication, we win.
- Rather than focusing all cyber protection efforts at one point (i.e., the perimeter), network and information defenses must be designed to interrupt the "kill chain" at multiple layers in the system. This yields a much more robust security infrastructure than traditional methods.

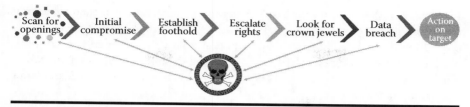

Figure 7.4   Kill chain.

In the real world, we have to face the fact that, despite our best efforts, we are not going to be able to defend against every attack all of the time. This does not mean that information security is ineffective. On the contrary, security managers are on the front line fighting against the world's most sophisticated adversaries. But to succeed, we need to stack the odds in our favor through better planning, defense strategies that frustrate attackers, and faster spotting, response, and recovery efforts. We can build the biggest castle with the largest moat to protect us, but the sentry in the parapets is our most effective early warning system. We shouldn't wait till the siege engine has brought down the walls to react. As General George S. Patton, famous World War II General most noted for his actions at the Battle of the Bulge, so eloquently said, "Nobody ever defended anything successfully, there is only attack and attack and attack some more."

While we in industry can't really go on the offensive, though the idea is interesting, we must realize that, as a corporation, we tend to be a somewhat large, static object. Nothing is easier to target than something that is not moving or, in the case of industry, remains unchanging. We cannot rest on our laurels and must be constantly varying the target landscape that we present to the hackers. We need to be proactive in what we do and not reactive. Sort of like the *Star Trek* series where they adjust the shield modulation to thwart the enemies' ability to penetrate their defensive perimeter around the star ship *Enterprise*. Also, another huge lesson from *Star Trek* is: Never be the landing party crewman in the red shirt—it means you will be the one to die. (Fashion tip for your next board meeting update.)

Another example comes to mind. I don't know if you remember those little biospheres they used to sell and still may. They were self-contained ecological systems and were completely sealed. They would have a few tiny shrimp, a small twig more for show, and some plant life of some sort. There would be an air bubble at the top. The plants and shrimp were symbiotic. Without the one, the other would not survive. I suppose in a way security folks and hackers have a somewhat symbiotic relationship. Without hackers, there would be no need for security folks at least in any great manner. Without security folks, hackers wouldn't be needed since there would not be any security to overcome. I remember reading an article where an owner of one of these biospheres described how it appeared to be dying. His solution was to shake the biosphere vigorously a few times each week. According to the article, the biosphere came back to life. In essence, that is what we have to do with our environments and our people. We need to shake them up a bit.

George S. Patton also said that if everyone is thinking alike, then somebody isn't thinking. To effectively counter the bad guys, we need to think outside of the box. Using the same defense strategies and tools that every other corporation uses just makes the job easier for the bad guys. We need to be creative in our approaches. They know how we think, act, and respond. We need to start thinking, acting, and responding like them.

Facebook had and may still have an interesting approach to improving their security. They offer a minimum of $500 rewards to White Hats for uncovering vulnerabilities in their software. Facebook's White Hat Responsible Disclosure Policy reads:

> If you believe you've found a security vulnerability on Facebook, we encourage you to let us know right away. If you give us a reasonable time to respond to your report before making any information public and make a good faith effort to avoid privacy violations, destruction of data and interruption or degradation of our service during your research, we will not bring any lawsuit against you or ask law enforcement to investigate you.

If you don't know the link to Facebook's White Hat Responsible Disclosure Policy, you might have a hard time finding the page. But I suppose if you are a White Hat, finding the page would not be a problem. While this approach may not be appropriate for everyone, it does show some thinking-out-of-the-box–type mentality. Considering the costs of a breach, this is a very cheap insurance policy. Some people just like challenges, so essentially Facebook is getting a lot of very low cost testing of their applications. The White Hats may spend weeks or even months trying to find vulnerabilities. Using full-time resources for this type of effort would be extremely expensive. Of course, Facebook has no idea who or how many people are actually looking for vulnerabilities at any one time. This also provides the bad guys with an opportunity to practice their trade with new tools and techniques on a real production system without fear of prosecution as long as they abide by Facebook's Responsible Disclosure Policy.

I would not recommend offering rewards to your own employees for discovering vulnerabilities. You would be incentivizing poor coding and architectural designs. Rather, you should do the opposite. There are a number of tools and services out there that can be used to scan your software and environments for vulnerabilities. Establish various thresholds and reward your staff for keeping software and systems under them. The downside to Facebook's policy is it runs the risk of an insider intentionally incorporating vulnerabilities in the environment and then colluding with a White Hat to share in the rewards.

Sun Tzu, a Chinese military general and strategist from around 500 BC, stated that if you know the enemy and know yourself, you need not fear the results of a hundred battles. Winning the war against the hackers will require us to know them in great detail. The best way to know them is to act like them. Our tools are less important than our human resources. Tools cannot interpret the data presented. Tools cannot make judgment calls. Tools cannot think. They are indispensable tools in the fight, but they cannot replace the human element. George Patton, famous World War II US General most noted for the Battle of the Bulge, realized this and stated that wars may be fought with weapons but they are won by men. I am a firm believer that our people are our most valuable assets. We need to continually invest in their skills.

Carl von Clausewitz, Prussian military thinker, said that many intelligence reports in war are contradictory; even more are false, and most are uncertain. The same is true of the data we receive from our many tools. False positives are an expected outcome of any tool. It takes smart, dedicated people to decipher what is real and what is false. False positives can be just as disruptive to a business as true positives. They consume valuable time and resources, diverting them from other pressing tasks. Security folks are combination detective and weatherman; we sift through the clues to develop a picture of what has happened and then evaluate the data to forecast what might occur. Just like detectives and weathermen, this takes training.

The best training is that which gets everyone to start thinking like a hacker. To truly master the tools and techniques of a hacker, you have to basically become one. This is the premise behind the Certified Ethical Hacker training and certification. We have to understand that the tools we use in industry are not what are being used by the hackers. Getting the tools that the hackers use into the hands of your staff along with proper training will give them a whole new perspective on how the bad guys operate. It will certainly heighten their awareness of things to look for in the environment that are out of the ordinary.

Sun Tzu sums things up pretty nicely when he said the opportunity to secure ourselves against defeat lies in our own hands, but the opportunity of defeating the enemy is provided by the enemy himself. Understanding the tools and techniques of the hackers allows us to discover and exploit their weaknesses. Just as they spend countless hours studying our defenses and analyzing our weaknesses, so must we study theirs. Every good hunter knows their quarry. Knowing the enemy attacks the castle with archers, we raise our shields over our heads. Should we know they will attempt to breach the walls of the castle, boiling oil will be waiting for their arrival. Should we know in advance the enemy employs siege engines we build our castle with a moat or concentric walls, the first layered defense so to speak.

There are lessons to be learned from the early concentric castle builders. Such defenses were extremely expensive to put in place. Today's network technologies are likewise not cheap. The time required to implement these defenses consumed a lot of time and resources. Implementing any new technology in our environments requires lots of testing and training. These were not a defense mechanism to address an immediate threat but rather one envisioned for the distant future. By the time they were put in place, they were either not needed or overcome by newer technology. When a zero day attack occurs, it is too late to put up new barriers. As we well know, the effectiveness of our current defenses quickly erodes over time. Lastly, they were so effective that rather than break into the castle, the attackers would simply sit outside and try to starve the occupants out. Here, we have the classic denial of service attack.

Knowing how the hacker will respond to each form of defense we put in place gives us the advantage of being able to respond quicker to their countermoves. Carl von Clausewitz said it is better to act quickly and err than to hesitate until the time of action is past. We do not have the luxury of time on our sides. Knowing our enemy allows us to respond somewhat quicker. And respond we must, to sit by idly will accomplish nothing other than pass advantage over to the hackers.

We all should have a pretty good idea of where the crown jewels lie in our environment. These are what the hackers are after. If you do not know where the crown jewels reside or even worse what crown jewels even exist, then you are in trouble. The immediate first step that you must accomplish in conjunction with the business is isolating the crown jewels. Most people don't alarm the bathroom or place cameras there. At least, I sincerely hope no one does the latter. Nor should we spend excessive time and money trying to defend areas of little or no interest to the hackers. This is somewhat analogous to Sun Tzu's philosophy that he who knows when he can fight and when he cannot, will be victorious. In our case, we need to know what we can defend and what we cannot.

Identifying the crown jewels is no easy task. It takes time and effort to separate out the rubies, diamonds, and emeralds from the amethyst, amber, and pyrite. They all look shiny and pretty, but they have vastly different intrinsic values. The business typically views everything as highly valuable. After careful consideration and analysis, what was once thought to be gold turns out to be nothing more than pyrite (fool's gold). Once the crown jewels are identified, it is then easier to aggregate them in one place that is more easily defendable rather than spread all over the environment. Of course, there are risks in putting all your eggs in one basket, but it is more easily defended, and the costs are far more manageable. Clearly, the federal government believes this is true in keeping our gold reserves in basically two places, Fort Knox and the Federal Reserve Bank of New York. A sort of primary and backup for continuity of government just as our crown jewels should have a primary and backup site for business continuity.

Stack the Deck in Your Favor

Make sure that you hire skilled people to run attacks and simulations on your environment. My favorite approach is to hire a nationally known firm and give them three challenges. First, give them lobby access to look at wireless vulnerabilities. See what they can find out and if they can discover any unsecured access points or break into an approved device. Second, they are allowed to have a network connection inside the firewall, but no network credentials, user accounts, or any inside info about the network layout. This is what someone who talked their way into your office would see if they found a vacant office and jacked into the network. Third, they are to look at your organization from the Internet for holes and vulnerabilities.

Picking the Right Penetration Test Vendor

Penetration tests can be excellent tools in determining your network's security—when they are done correctly. Handled badly, they can put sensitive data in the wrong hands, cause production system delays, or, worse, corrupt critical production data. Since there is nothing to guarantee that the testing firm is a fully competent provider, let's look at some key points to consider when picking your supplier.

I once heard that in security testing, there is actually an inverse Golden Rule: "Do unto yourself before others do unto you." In other words, the only way to be sure that a hacker can't penetrate your defenses is to hire someone to test your defenses in a controlled, trusted manner. A competent partner will try to identify and exploit vulnerabilities in systems and networks by mounting attacks from outside systems. Personally, I also ask them to tell me what an inside user with questionable ethics could do. As the old saying goes, you don't want to focus on the "hard crunchy, exterior while ignoring the 'soft gooey' interior." A bad actor with even basic inside access rights can do immense harm to an organization.

Personally, I only use reputable firms avoiding hiring reformed hackers to conduct penetration tests. There are plenty of incredibly talented, reputable firms. Hiring a firm rather than an individual can provide additional practical and legal protections for your organization. No organization should voluntarily expose itself to attack—which is what penetration testing does—without protecting itself from possible fallout. At a bare minimum, no organization should hire anyone to conduct penetration testing without imposing legal protection from nondisclosure or confidentiality agreements to safeguard what's learned during such testing from public disclosure or misuse in the wrong hands. Reputable firms routinely procure indemnity insurance to demonstrate their seriousness about keeping sensitive information private and confidential. To be most effective, penetration testing must be repeated at regular intervals and when systems or networks are changed or updated.

How Should Penetration Testing Be Applied?

Typically, penetration testing is used to validate defenses of an organization. It can, however, be used in other ways including the testing of response plans, and the capabilities of internal response teams. A surprise penetration test is a good way of measuring the detection and response capabilities of any organization.

Inside or outside resources? Penetration testing can certainly be performed using internal resources. There are pro and con positions for each decision. Most CISOs will lean toward an external resource simply because they don't know legacy details about the environment. Internal people may automatically gloss over a vulnerability because "that's the way it has to be."

When you hire outsiders, the results

■ Will provide a double-check against in-house security audits and self-checks
■ Can be cited as "objective proof" of security for regulatory and customer audits
■ Will provide an objective evaluation of the IT security posture, policies, practices, and procedures

Selecting a Vendor

Here are the criteria that you should use to select a suitable penetration-testing vendor:

■ **Name recognition:** If you are going to use the results of the test as proof of your capability, you will want to engage a well-known name. That will add credibility to your report.
■ **Confidentiality:** Make sure the vendor explicitly states it will preserve and protect the information it develops during testing. Understand how the report will be delivered and if it will be encrypted during transmission.
■ **Insurance:** What if the tester loses your information? What if they shut down or corrupt critical production systems as the result of their testing? Does the vendor carry sufficient liability insurance or bonding? You must make sure they are adequately covered.
■ **Reporting results:** It's important to agree in writing what reports and recommendations will be in the final deliverable. You should request copies of all logs, reports, and other raw data collected during testing. The vendor should also provide best practice documents and assistance for remediation of identified issues. Finally, ensure that you have a chance to review a draft of the final report to correct any bad assumptions or errors on the part of the testers.

Beyond these items, vendors should be bound to a specific contract with terms and conditions that specify a statement of work, causes for termination, confidentiality and liability, indemnification, and so forth.

Here's the key, if the firm you hired to test you is not able to penetrate you and gain advanced access, you did not pick the right firm. You don't run a penetration test to prove how good you are, you run it to find new holes and paths to the corporate jewels that you do not know about. This is not about pride; this is about protecting the company. Leave your ego at the door.

Chapter 8

Know the Business, Not Just the Technology

A few years ago, I got a call from a CISO at an insurance company. He was new to the role, just having retired from the Army as a Colonel. After 30+ years in the military, he was ready to make his mark in the civilian world. His background was impeccable, having been in the cybersecurity world for over 10 years. He was well educated and well spoken: basically the whole package.

However, he called me completely frustrated with his new role. It seemed that while he had published a whole new policy set, he couldn't get the general company population to comply. He was always finding people who were violating a policy, but could not get support from the offender's management or even HR for disciplinary action. He lamented, "I long for the good old days when I could send someone to jail for not obeying an order (policy). Don't these people know that security is important? It's like they just don't get it!"

There are the five words that set off all kinds of alarms for me. I can't tell you the number of times I've heard those words uttered: They Just Don't Get It. I've learned over the years that companies are in business to make money. It's much better for them to be secure, but they don't exist to comply with your security edicts, they are in business to provide goods and services. You need to understand how your security controls reinforce the business goals and objectives. Let's look at some basic risk management principles. At the end of the chapter, I'll have a suggestion on how to map security to business objectives.

The Role of Risk Management within the Enterprise

Please notice that I said Risk Management, not audit, and so on. As I said earlier, I started my career in manufacturing around the time that process control and quality processes were undergoing major changes.

American Industry finally figured out that the only way to improve quality was to integrate it into the manufacturing process, not try to inspect it in at the end.

That integration of quality was incredibly successful and gradually made its way into other industries. Unfortunately, in technology risk management areas, we have not totally made the transition. Recently, I heard a senior manager refer to the mission of Internal Audit with the simple phrase "Checkers Check." I must admit, I'd rather have heard it phrased "Checkers Don't Just Check." Checkers can add value by becoming a part of the continuous improvement process. True, we will always have a mandate for traditional audits, but let's not lock away the considerable expertise of the audit staff when they are not auditing. We need to move toward a model of process control, where monitoring and evidence is integral to the process, yielding a snapshot of compliance in real time.

In my early days as a young engineer, I worked with a cranky old German plant manager. Honest to God, he was a captured U-Boat Commander who stayed in the United States after he was released from a POW camp. Got a good mental image of him and his management style? I can vividly remember him walking though the plant and scolding the workers saying, "Work is not a place for laughing, pay attention!" Anyway, I digress: He had another mantra that I carry to this day. It simply said, **"If you are not going to add value, don't pick it up."**

He was focused on keeping people on the factory floor from picking up parts and work in process if they couldn't contribute positively to the final product. It also applies to technology processes. If you do not intend to make a process, program, or technology better, don't touch it. That also goes for audit of a process. Unless you intend to add value by suggesting actionable, value-added suggestions, move along. Checking just for checking's sake is an intrusive, risky practice to embrace. Always, always focus on adding value!

Rework is the most expensive way to produce a quality product. We had a "Rule of Tens" when I was an engineer. It said that if you found and corrected a problem at the subassembly level, it could cost a dollar to fix. If you had to correct it at the final assembly level, it would cost 10 dollars. If you had to correct it when assembled into a product, it could cost 100 dollars, and if you had to travel to a customer site to repair it, that could cost a minimum of 1000 dollars.

Risk Management is about preventing future problems by looking at existing processes. Find and correct issues before they get expensive.

No discussion of risk management would be complete without talking about where this function should rest within the enterprise. It is an important subject and will have a significant impact on how the enterprise views the risk function. In this chapter, we will discuss an optimal approach to the organization. The truth is that there is no absolute answer for how the management structure should be organized. The correct design is one that will integrate with the current management structure while providing adequate visibility and separation of duties.

The appropriate level of visibility is one that provides senior management with a clear, unobstructed view of risk issues within the organization. If the risk organization is placed too low in the organization, risk issues will be potentially distorted through multiple levels of interpretation. It is seldom malicious. Remember the grade school game where one person whispered a statement into the ear of their neighbor, and that person did the same with their neighbor? At the end of the line, the message was seldom what it was when started. In the areas of risk, it is more complex in that risk must be conveyed in a specific context with a certain level of importance. Often, in many organizations, the Chief Risk Officer maintains a working relationship with the Audit Committee of the Board of Directors. This enables the CRO to convey risk concerns directly to the highest level within the company.

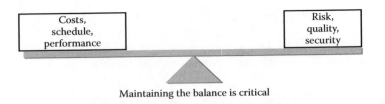

Figure 8.1 Balance.

An appropriate organizational separation of duties is one that avoids a conflict of interest between the risk duties and other duties a manager may perform (Figure 8.1). For instance, let's look at the following example:

> Tom is the CIO of a large medical record processing firm. The auditing firm used by the company has suggested that a formal group be formed to monitor the risk metrics of the company related to technology. Tom pulled together a group of analysts and gave them the job of creating audit reports relating to access and the creation of user and system accounts. Monthly, the group created a report detailing all the violations found during the month and sent it to the CIO for review. All the users showing up on the violation reports were in the IT organization and ultimately also reported to the CIO. The analysts were also responsible for recommending risk controls for IT projects. In the event of a difference of opinion between the risk analysts and the development department, the CIO made the final decision.

Separation of Duties

This concept, while simple, is difficult to articulate within the context of an organization. Simply stated, it is the idea that one person should not be in a position to perpetrate fraud or abuse against the organization by himself or herself, or in the case of management, to exert undue influence on staff, which could result in fraud or abuse.

The simplest example of separation of duties has been around for decades. It is the basic accounting control, which says that the person in an organization who creates checks should not be the person to sign them. This old fashioned separation of duties ensured that one person could not fraudulently create a check that could be turned into cash. While simple, this provides a clear model of what is required.

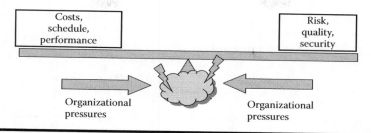

Figure 8.2   Risk versus organizational pressures.

In today's electronic age, signatures have been replaced with electronic approval, but the concept remains the same.

Whenever risk and operational priorities collide, there is potential conflict (Figure 8.2). Normally, these issues can be resolved through organizational controls.

An example more applicable to most of today's organizations relates to who creates and reviews audit reports. Let's take a look.

Holly, the manager of the computer operations department, just got hit with a finding from the external auditors. She carefully reviewed the finding—it seems that during the audit, the examiner found several dozen powerful system accounts existed that had not been used for over a year. Additionally, several of them had full system administrator access.

"Swell: don't the auditors understand the pressure I'm under to get these accounts set up for production? My people work their tails off just to keep their head above water on most days. Besides, shouldn't someone else have told me to remove these accounts when the applications were retired?" Obviously, these powerful accounts had been created to support applications and initiatives, but when the systems were retired, the IDs were never removed. Holly continued to review the audit report and came across the comment regarding the assignment of too many accounts with full domain access. "I guess they do not understand about setting up accounts, particularly for system development. If I don't give these accounts full access, the developers will be back here every 10 minutes asking for the rights to be changed. What will that do to productivity?"

As a response to the finding, the CIO created a policy requiring daily review and sign off of accounts set up by the operations department, and directed Holly to get the reports set up and to do the daily review herself. She would be held personally responsible to make sure that this finding was not repeated and that only properly set up accounts would be created and maintained.

Holly created a new role within her department whose task it was to create the daily audit reports and forward them to her for review. She would be responsible for following up with any of her subordinates that were not properly administering access.

This is an interesting study from a few perspectives.

1. Clearly, Holly is responsible for the performance of her subordinates, and the daily audit report will be a good tool for monitoring their activities.
2. The fact that the analyst responsible for creating and following up on the daily reports works for Holly may put the analyst in an uncomfortable position. The analyst gets reviews and raises from Holly, so they have a vested interest in making their boss look good.
3. In the above example, the audit reports never leave Holly's department, meaning that noncompliance with the new oversight policy may be concealed from upper management.
4. Holly is also under considerable pressure to grant expanded access to these system accounts to make sure there are no production or development problems. What about the expectations of her customers? Does that undue pressure expose risk to the organization?

When discussing these issues, remember it is about discussing the scope of the position, not the individual in the role at the time. There is no doubt that Holly is a trusted individual in the organization, but will Holly always be there? Keep personalities out of the discussion. When it becomes personal, risk controls will usually take a back seat.

Let's look at potential controls to address the four points above that could help overcome the potential for conflict of interest.

1. The use of the reports as a control to gauge employee conformance to policy is a positive step. This will help monitor system administrator activities of both experienced and novice associates. It may also provide a history to weed out associates who are not adequately protecting the company from this risk.
2. The analyst responsible for creating and following up on the reports could and probably should report to another department. This will remove any future inference of conflict of interest.
3. A simple control in this example could be the distribution of reports to the organization's Internal Audit department or another administrative department in IT. A second set of eyes on a report that are not in the same immediate reporting chain is an effective compensating control.

4. There are two potential controls that could be used to address these points. First, it appears that the departments creating the requirements are not fully detailing the rights necessary for the applications to work properly. Holly's area is compensating for this lack of detail by granting excessive rights to the accounts. The creation of a procedure to detail required accesses and mandating the information as part of the set up process will address this issue. Secondly, Holly may want to limit the ability to create super-user accounts to only one or two of her people. This will require the administrators to get the needed detail for appropriate account setup.

In the finest tradition of the separation of duties concept, keep in mind who your risk management group reports to. In some companies, this role is contained within IT; in others, it might be Legal or Compliance, just to name a few. While some case can be made that Compliance is an appropriate group to be part of, the autonomy of the risk group should be maintained as much as possible. The IT areas are typically one of the groups that are monitored the most and it doesn't make for good working relationships or effective reporting of risk issues when both groups report to the same person. This also serves to put that individual (usually the CIO) in the bad position of having to referee issues between the risk and security groups and the operational areas. Most folks in this position would welcome the ability to point the finger at an outside group and say that they are responsible for the new policy or change.

However, it is also important that decisions be made with representation from IT as well as other areas. Do not make policy or risk decisions without involving those that need to know. You must include their input when evaluating a risk posture.

It had been a long day of meetings and everyone just wanted to go home. We were down to discussing a few final risk areas involving potential financial impact if things went wrong. The team agreed that the potential financial impact of the risk was approximately one hundred thousand dollars, and the risk of the event happening was low. Paul, a supervisor, stood up and said, I'll accept that risk, where do I sign? Looking at him, I asked, "What is the largest invoice you can approve without your manager's approval?" Paul quickly replied "Ten thousand dollars, what does that have to do with anything?"

Paul didn't get it, but the company had set his limit of approving financial transactions at a specific limit. He didn't understand that he couldn't simply assume a hundred-thousand-dollar risk for the company.

Lesson learned? Always make sure that those accepting risk have the authority and signoff to do it. Put the risk acceptance in writing and have them sign it. These decisions are too critical to execute with a handshake. People have a very short memory when the crap hits the fan. Protect yourself, your people, and the company at all times.

This will also ensure that the decisions that come down already have the support they need and will pass easily. In the event that an impasse is reached, it will be necessary to elevate the issue to those who have overall responsibility for the program. This would mean a communication with the Board of Directors if senior management cannot agree. It makes everything better if there is an already established reporting relationship. The purpose is to let them make the final decision since they would have responsibility to the ultimate boss, and the shareholders. In the instance that there is no Board of Directors, the CEO or company president would be the appropriate party.

Is There an Overlap between Legal, Compliance, and Human Resources?

Risk Management, Legal, Human Resources, and Compliance sometimes have similar functions. This should be viewed as a consumer relationship in most instances. Risk Management will provide information to Legal, Human Resources, and Compliance areas and act as a consultant in matters of risk. Audit will also factor into this and may use risk assessment tools as a source for auditing compliance with approved company policy. Having a good working relationship with these areas is very important, and understanding their needs will go a long way to insuring your risk program is viewed as necessary and important to the health of the organization.

Questions to ask about the structure:

Does this structure place a conflict of interest on the CIO in that he may not report all incidents to Executive management that was reported to him?

Does this structure place pressure on the analysts reporting policy violations to keep their manager out of trouble?

Does this structure, which lets the head of IT make decisions regarding technology risk, place him in a potential conflict of interest when faced with pressures to deliver systems quickly and cheaply?

What compensating controls could be put in place to ensure that any issues relating to conflict of interest are resolved and discovered?

Appropriate levels of control as well as appropriate levels of management and organization placement are the key factors of success. There are no magic bullets for organizational structure. Each organization must evaluate the trade-offs between organizational efficiency and risk avoidance. Many times, the controls are simple. In the above example, a control that states that all policy violation reports also get sent to internal audit would ensure that management outside of IT is getting a view of the risks in the organization.

Typically, most technology risk functions will start out within an IT structure. In some cases, this makes sense. But the conflict of interest between the needs of IT and the needs of risk management will eventually begin to show. Many companies find the CSO and the managers in charge of IT operations in the CIO's office in conflict over patch deployment priorities, head counts, operational functions, and any number of other issues. This can adversely affect the needs of the business and slow necessary control deployments.

A Model Structure

Let's start first with a general description of the Risk Management organization chart (Figure 8.3).

Keep in mind that this should be a simple structure by its very nature. There should be very clearly defined roles for each person that is well understood

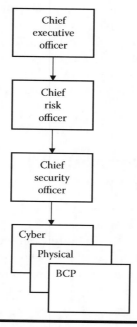

Figure 8.3 Risk management organization.

throughout the organization. This structure provides a clear path to executive management.

Chief Executive Officer	Responsible for leading a highly ethical organization that treats its customers, employees, partners, and shareholders with respect and stewardship. The CEO and board must be deeply engaged in managing the organization's operating risk in a way that delivers maximum value in a safe and secure environment.
Chief Risk Officer	Simply defined, this person is responsible for the oversight of all risk management activities for the company including information, financial, and operational.
CSO	Ultimately responsible for all aspects of the information risk program. Sets the tone for risk and security programs for the entire organization. Interfaces directly with the senior-level corporate executives as well as the Board of Directors (if applicable) and presents high-level metrics on a regular basis. Sets policy with executive approvals.

Many organizations today are combining the information security, business continuity, and physical security departments under the office of the CSO. This structure enables the creation of an overarching strategy for all security and integrity operations in an organization. It is based on the recognition that you cannot have good cybersecurity without good physical security. You cannot have a good emergency response plan without the involvement of physical and information security.

Risk Management/Organizational Management Interaction

Transparency refers to the clear exposure of risk issues to the organization's management. In order for the operating management of an organization to make informed decisions, it is critical that they understand any information risk issues that exist in the business- or technology-related systems. A good way to facilitate the necessary communication is the creation of two operating committees in the organization. They are the Executive Steering Committee and the Information Security Officer Committee.

Executive Steering Committee

As previously stated, a strong relationship between business goals and objectives and risk management activities is critical. Buy-in and support of Integrated Risk Management (IRM) strategies is a key element to the success of risk management programs. The Executive Steering Committee is composed of executives from the organization whose mission it is to review the key strategies of the Information Risk Department and provide direction and guidance as required (Figure 8.4). This group is also the body that will ultimately approve organizational-level risk policies.

Membership of this committee should remain at the strategic level to ensure that the group does not get mired down in detail-level tasks.

Information Security Officer Committee

As important as executive buy-in of IRM initiatives is the clear understanding and support of initiatives from the operational units of the organization. This group provides input and guidance to the IRM group at an operational level. This committee

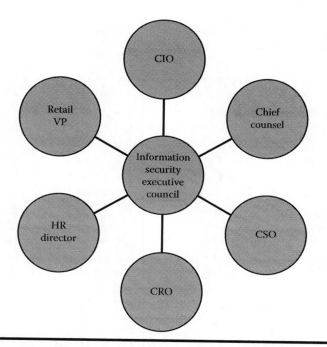

Figure 8.4   Information Security Executive Council.

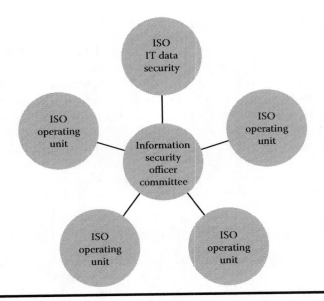

Figure 8.5 Information Security Officer Committee.

is composed of individuals appointed as Information Security Officers from the operating units of the organization (Figure 8.5).

This group, chaired by the Organization's Information Security Officer, is responsible for creating and maintaining the IRM Operational plan, providing updates to management regarding progress against the plan, and reviewing any IRM initiatives for impact to the operating units of the organization.

The Unit Information Risk Officers (IROs) should be selected by the head of the operating unit. A face-to-face discussion with the unit chief to talk about duties, focus, and time commitment of the individual is critical. The Unit IRO should also be of senior organizational level to make sure he or she can speak for the unit in matters relating to risk. The individual is also responsible for the dissemination of information to and the administration of risk programs that are applicable to the operating unit.

This committee should meet monthly at a minimum and maintain a complete history of decisions and discussions for future reference. A sound historical record is important for the ongoing development of new initiatives and discussions with auditors and management regarding past initiatives.

Information Security Department Staffing

Figure 8.6 looks at the three basic components of the Office of the Chief Information Security Officer. In my experience, this organization works well to address risks and

Office of the chief information security officer		
Compliance	Security ops and engineering	User access and administration
⋏ ITS liaison to ERO, HR, Legal, IA, Cus	⋏ Execute defensive strategies	⋏ Provision/ de-provision users
⋏ Coordinate ITS response to findings	⋏ Maintain and engineer network security solutions	⋏ Create/own roles and authorization and entitlement process
⋏ Maintain regulatory calendar, manage compliance programs	⋏ Maintain security architecture and SLAs	⋏ Implement new IDM functionality

Figure 8.6   Office of the Chief Information Security Officer.

maintain an adequate separation of duties within the group. The number of analysts in each group will vary based on the size of the organization. If the organization is small enough, the same person may perform both duties. An important element of this equation is that the positions of the people in the reporting structure as it relates to the dotted line relationships should be equal. As it occurs in most companies, security may be thought of as a hindrance or simply a necessary evil. If a junior-level person is trying to communicate security or risk needs to a vice president, it is too easy to have those needs ignored. In some areas, position plays an important part in the weight of the arguments and it is easier to communicate as equals.

If the organization is large or geographically diverse, you may want to implement a strategy of Information Security Officers responsible for a specific business unit or geographic area. As the CISO of a large international company, I implemented an ISO for each of the major business units as well as an ISO for each major geographical unit. This gave me an effective tool for coordinating information security projects and getting important information disseminated. We had a weekly call taking care to rotate the times to make sure our team members in Asia weren't always on a call at 9 or 10 p.m. The following were the basic duties of the ISO and their supporting information security analysts.

Information Security Officer	Responsible for working with Line of Business leaders and communications with the business owners. Ensures new or changed policies are distributed and understood. Coordinates incident response duties with Line of Business leaders and may work with appointed Information Security Officers within those units. Reports Key Performance Indicator metrics to business. Coordinates overall risk assessment activities and consults for risk mitigation activities.

Analyst	Responsible for coordinating technical controls and monitoring elements of risk assessment activities under direction from ISO. Works with operational departments on tactical security operations and is involved in daily security monitoring activities. Implements and controls content for security and risk awareness programs.

The Compliance Arm of the CISO Office

You can sum up the goal for the compliance group very simply as "NO SURPRISES." Have you ever seen compliance people running down the aisle with their pants on fire trying to get an audit report signed before a deadline? It's not pretty, nor is it good for the organization. Great compliance people coordinate and track the IT responses to Audit and Regulatory Findings. Remember the "No Surprises" goal? Nothing is worse for the credibility of an Information Technology group to the Board than missed audit corrective actions. Any audit-related misses will probably be reported to the Audit Committee of the Board.

Don't let audits happen to you, manage them. The Internal Audit department should maintain an audit calendar, so you know what audits are coming. You also should know that regulatory exams are coming, so BE PREPARED! This group should also maintain regulatory calendars and manage compliance programs.

Security Operations and Engineering

While the risk role should be outside the IT infrastructure, there will remain a standard operational component that still needs to be handled. Typically, this will fit best within the areas that already understand how to perform to this standard. IT processes are geared toward making the best use of people and resources in an operational mode. Things like IDS/IPS, firewalls, VPN, antivirus, and other strict technology controls should be under security operations control. How they use these systems should stem from the Risk Management policy; but the daily care and feeding should come from the operational groups. The major duties of this group can be summarized as follows:

■ They execute defensive strategies. This is different from tools; a strategy is a combination of multiple tools and processes working in concert to protect the organization.
■ They maintain and engineer network security solutions. These are the tools and systems that must be put in place to provide point protections.
■ They are responsible for maintaining the security architecture and Service-Level Agreements (SLAs). The architecture is the set of guiding principles

by which information is protected. This can include build sheets for equipment, coding standards for programmers, and the tools to guide the decisions related to the protection of information.

■ They develop SLAs. SLAs must be realistic and published. Also on an ongoing basis, the performance against those SLAs must be published. The SLAs can be as simple as the uptime of critical security systems, or throughput measures to make sure the tools are not adversely affecting network traffic.

User Access and Administration

This area is highly operational and one of the most critical for stopping breaches and loss of information. Over my years, I can't count the number of times I've heard of a terminated user who discovered their remote access hadn't been turned off come in and steal information or just cause havoc.

BIG LESSON: Pay particular attention to terminated users with Administrative Rights. Understand that they may have created multiple user accounts, so just turning off their domain user name is not adequate. Have the domain admins look for other accounts attributed to the user, but be careful, some of those accounts may have been created as process IDs and simply turning them off may crash a production system. Sounds confusing? Hell, if it was easy, anyone could do it. So, here are their major functions:

■ Provision/De-provision users. Provisioning should have an SLA. From the time HR puts a user in the system, no more than a day should pass before the user id is set up. Measure and publish conformance to the SLAs. Also make sure you have a contingency plan for bubbles of work. For instance, if your company acquires another firm and you have hundreds of users to process. Or if your organization regularly runs training programs, how will you set up a class of 30 users in one week in addition to the normal workload?

■ This group must Create and Own roles and the authorization and entitlement process. Roles are the key to effective security. Setting up each user individually or "the same as Bob" is insanity and is a ticking time bomb for a breach or regulatory issue. When I go to a new organization, I always ask how many groups or entitlements make up my access rights. The worst I ever found was 96. How in the world could you effectively manage the rights of thousands of users with that kind of system? Drive a Roles process. Start with the basic role of "What does every employee get?" Then build by department. A side benefit is that you will find users that have access to everything because over the years they have worked in every department and no rights were ever taken away.

■ Implement new Identity Management Tools and Functionality. No one person can maintain the complex business requirements and entitlements required today. It takes tools. There are many great choices for everything from single sign-on to role-based access. If you don't have a tool, establish a scripted bake-off and make the potential vendors perform in your environment. The evaluation team should include folks from the business as well as IT operations. Since some of what your tools will do may replace some of the work by the domain administrators, you need their involvement and support.

Lesson learned? Include the Audit and Compliance folks. When the audits show up, they will be looking for proof that your systems are operating and controlling risk. Identify and create those reports as part of the initial process. Today, a common requirement for many audits is that the managers attest that their subordinate's access is correct on a quarterly basis. You can develop an automated system with workflow or do it with e-mailed spreadsheets and manual effort. If you choose the latter, be ready to join the witness protection program as there will be people looking for your blood.

This discussion is not meant to be all-inclusive for the purpose of planning for your department. Rather, it is in place to make sure that the thought process of separation of responsibilities and conflict of interest issues are addressed up front. It is very difficult to fix these problems after the process is in place. Sure, there will be organizational battles in the beginning while defining the structure, but it is better to fight them now and keep the autonomy that is required than try to fix it later after it has been established.

Advice for the New CISO

Think in terms of your new role as one of a manufacturer of widgets. A successful manufacturer clearly understands what raw materials or subcomponents he buys and clearly understands what he sells. His suppliers know the quantity, quality, and delivery expectations for the raw materials they sell to him. Conversely, his customers know what he sells, and have an expectation of quality and delivery performance.

The CSO "buys" data from many sources related to risk. It is critical that the suppliers of those data clearly understand your expectations regarding quality and deliver according to your expectations. All sources of risk information should be governed by an SLA with the supplier. For instance, if your risk analysis processes include a weekly review of the firewall logs, you should have a clear agreement as to when the logs will be available for your use. If you neglect to formalize your expectations, the suppliers will eventually find other activities that have a higher priority for them, and your data source will dry up.

What you "sell" is information or risk intelligence derived from the data sources. Set clear expectations with the consumers of the information regarding format and delivery.

	Network operations	Info risk mgmnt	IT operations	IT documentation
Export firewall logs	R	A	I	I
Review firewall logs	C	R	I	I
Archive results	I	C	R	I
Distribute weekly report	I	C	R	I

Figure 8.7   RACI.

Another useful tool is a responsibility matrix. Since the security of any organization is reliant on the activities of many people, a clear understanding of who is responsible, accountable, consulted, or informed for each primary activity is required. This tool, commonly called a RACI matrix (Figure 8.7), is an invaluable part of the risk analysis process. It can aid in the quick identification of areas where responsibilities for risk related activities are cloudy.

The RACI chart is designed to help people define and understand who is Responsible, Accountable, Consulted, and Informed for the various tasks or decisions required either by individuals or teams. By completing the RACI, the manager or project leader clarifies what is expected and by whom. It's very important to first identify the various tasks in that process and then identify the roles (people or groups or departments) and finally their responsibilities for a given task. Typically, we associate a task with at least one role or, in some cases, multiple roles.

So basically, the RACI matrix is a responsibility assignment matrix. Let's go through each association type in detail below:

■ Responsible

This is the person or position required to complete a task. Each task must have a responsible person or position assigned to it to ensure that the task or decision receives due attention. Typically, only one person or position is assigned responsibility for completing a task. In other words, he or she is the "doer" of the task or activity. The person who is "Responsible" need not be accountable for that task, even though in some cases the same person can be "Responsible" and "Accountable." The degree of "Responsibility" can vary and multiple roles can share the responsibility of a single task. Also, one role can delegate the responsibility to another role. Using the RACI matrix, we can see if a role has too many or too few responsibilities and try to adjust the workload.

■ Accountable

The person or position accountable for a task is responsible for insuring that it is completed on time and in a manner that meets all expectations for it. The Accountable (A) person or position does not have to physically do the task. Accountability must be assigned to each task. In Figure 8.7, IRM is accountable to monitor the Export firewall logs process, assuring the log files are received on time. "Accountable" is the person or role who has the final authority and accountability to a given task. For any given task, there is only one role/person accountable. We **can't delegate** this accountability to other roles or individuals or entities.

■ Consulted

The person or position assigned consulting status for a task must be consulted by the Responsible (R) person or party before performing a task. "Consulted" are the people or roles that we consult and get advice from before and during the performance of the task. When there are many people who have "Consulted" roles, the time taken to accomplish the task increases. On the other hand, too few or no "Consulted" roles assigned to a task means that task has the risk of underperforming. Any task with a consulting position assigned to it must be consulted with before the task is performed. Because of the delay caused by consultations, their use should be minimized. The responsible party should be empowered to do the required task with very few exceptions. In the above example, if IT Operations had a project to redesign how and where the logs were archived, they would get the input of the IRM group.

■ Informed

The person or position assigned informed status for a task is required to be informed that a task has been completed. The person or position with the "I" can be informed before or after the fact. The Informed (I) person or position is not being informed for permission or approval. In Figure 8.7, you can see that the group responsible for exporting the firewall logs is Network Operations. Since the review is a Risk Management function, Information Risk Management is Accountable to ensure it gets done by monitoring the review process. Both IT operations and IT Documentation are informed if the process changes or breaks down. You need to make sure the right people/ roles are informed after we perform a task successfully. If too many roles are informed after a task, we need to see if it's necessary to do so and minimize on that.

Why do we need RACI?

■ RACI is a good communication tool. Without RACI, projects risk having poor communication and poor handoffs.
■ RACI makes sure each and every task has an owner (a role who owns the task).

- People tend to think they are the ones who are responsible and/or accountable whereas they might actually be in "Consulted' or "Supported" roles. Assigning wrong roles results in duplication of effort and misunderstanding and even fighting in some cases.
- RACI allows the right people to be assigned to the role of consulted.

The RACI chart should initially be completed by a small working group and then shared with employees or team members. The RACI is a living document that changes over time as people become more and more accountable for their results. In a team environment, the RACI is typically reviewed at the same time the team charter is being updated with new goals.

Tying Your Goals and Objectives to Company Goals

Let's assume you have a set of six goals and objectives for Info Security. They are as follows:

- Prevent hacker- and threat-related downtime due to attack or compromise.
- Improve performance and security of the ecosystem.
- Provide a unified offering of threat alerting to all locations.
- Protect the environment from attack while legacy apps are decommissioned.
- Security issues prevented, analyzed in advance.
- Achieve all Regulatory and Recertification Goals.

At the same time, the company has a set of high-level goals:

- Grow the company.
- Increase customer satisfaction.
- Deploy Salesforce.com CRM.
- Reduce operating costs by 5%.
- Establish sales presence in Europe.

It is your responsibility to ensure that your actions support the business. The first step is to map out where yours match the company's. An easy way to explain the relationship to management is through a simple table (Figure 8.8).

Establish a relationship and be able to, in simple terms, explain the connection. The final step is to relate your granular projects to your security goals and objectives, again using the table method.

While simplistic examples, if you follow an approach similar to show the business that you can connect an identity management project to the corporate goal of growing the company, you will have greater success. Keep It Simple. We are all technologists and as such have an irritating habit of trying to geek things up. Take

Information security and compliance program goals	Identity management	Intrusion prevention	Incident correlation	Legacy sensitive file clean-up	Static code analysis	Forensic server	Botnet intercept	Network access control	Encryption implement	Cloud architecture	Training sales department	Training awareness	Training response	Staff development
Prevent hacker- and threat-related downtime due to attack or compromise	✓	✓	✓	✓		✓	✓	✓	✓	✓	✓	✓	✓	✓
Improve performance and security of the ecosystem				✓	✓	✓	✓	✓	✓	✓	✓	✓	✓	✓
Provide a unified offering of threat alerting to all locations		✓	✓			✓					✓			✓
Protect the environment from attack while legacy apps are decommissioned	✓	✓	✓	✓	✓		✓	✓	✓		✓	✓	✓	✓
Security issues prevented, analyzed in advance	✓	✓	✓	✓	✓							✓		
Achieve all regulatory and recertification goals		✓	✓	✓		✓	✓	✓	✓		✓	✓	✓	✓

Figure 8.8   Program goals.

it from me, nothing irritates or alienates executives and the Board faster than you trying to show how smart you are. Business is their domain. If you are going to talk to them, show the simple respect of learning their language and explaining your contribution in terms that add value to their goals. If you do, I'm sure they will "GET IT!"

Conclusion

Organization, separation of duties, and responsibility definition are never an easy process. Certainly, the approaches outlined above are one of a number of methods that may be appropriate for your organization and structure.

In all cases, documentation and analysis are key factors. Leave nothing undefined or cloudy, particularly with your major initiatives.

The work up front will pay huge dividends downstream. As always, make sure all involved or interested parties are engaged and have the opportunity to provide input. Remember, transparency of risk issues to the business and being inclusive in your approach to analysis are critical to your long-term success in any organization.

Chapter 9

Technology Is Only One-Third of Any Solution

I finally moved from engineering to become the Information Systems manager at a manufacturing company. I had a lot to learn and was totally in love with the cool technology.

Our corporate auditors came for a visit and asked me to tell them about our backup procedures. Let's take a quick reality check: no WAN, no Internet, all backup included lugging around disk packs or tapes. "No problem," I said. "Bob comes in early once a week and copies the production disk packs to our backup packs." We walked in the computer room and I showed the drives and the disk packs we used for rotation. "Once Bob finishes copying, he takes the packs to his car and takes them to the bank, just like our policy says." I pulled the procedure sheet from the wall and gave it to them to show that I wasn't just another pretty face. I, the Supreme MIS Manager, had this puppy under control! I continued, "At the bank, Bob puts the packs on a shelf in the vault and brings the last week backup packs back here for rotation."

The auditor reviewed the paper, made a couple of notes, and said, "OK, let's go to the bank!" Sounded good, since I'd read the policy but never visited the vault myself. In retrospect, the vultures circling overhead should have tipped me off that my day was about to get really ugly.

We walked into the bank; I introduced myself and told the bank manager that I was there to see the backup disk packs in the vault. "Sure," he said, "Haven't really seen anyone from your company here in a while." Strange, I thought, Bob comes every week. He took us back and inside the vault on a shelf were four disk packs. Breathing a sigh of relief, I said, "Here they are—just like they are supposed to be."

The auditor pulled a pack, looked at the label and asked, "Why is the date on this pack almost a year old?" I grabbed the pack and sure enough he was right. The backup I had in my hands was almost a year old!

Fast forward to me getting ready to throttle my buddy Bob! I called him to my office and told him that we had visited the vault and there were no current backups there. "No problem," Bob said, "Taking the packs to the vault every week is a real hassle. The real intent of the backup process is to get the backups off site. That is what I do." "So," I said not really wanting to hear the answer, "Where the hell is 'offsite' these days?" He thought for a minute about if he really wanted to tell me and finally said, "The trunk of my car."

When I had a few deep breaths and regained my composure, I asked him to show me. We walked out to the parking lot, went to his car, and sure as hell, there were my freaking current backup packs in his trunk beside a 50-pound bag of calf feed. (Did I mention that Bob had a hobby farm?) I later found out that instead of driving to the bank, he was meeting his friends for breakfast at the local diner.

I'll skip the gory details that followed, but what did I learn that day that I'll always remember? Everything that we do has a people, process, and technology component. If we don't pay attention to all three, we and the business are set up for failure. In this case, a lazy employee could have brought down the business if we needed to recover the data and he was out of town. A car accident could have destroyed our business backups, or a sliding bag of feed could have damaged or covered the disk packs with dirt and dust. The technology worked, it created the backups: unfortunately the rest sucked.

Let's Look at Risk Management and the People, Process, and Technology Methodology

Risk management for technology systems is not a new subject. It has, however, changed in scope and importance as our information systems become larger and more interconnected. The Internet has grown from a few nodes to billions. Our corporate networks have gone from a few networked computers to global Wide Area Networks. Looking at these numbers only as trends, and factoring in the complexities of our own business models, you can see the challenges to effective risk management emerging.

In 1990, a risk assessment process was fairly contained and vertical. The primary consideration was to make sure that the security of the system was maintained. Interconnectivity of systems was usually on the same platform or within the same facility. The user base of any system was known, with most of them being employees or associates. Any remote office connectivity was usually over leased lines, which had low risk.

As the Internet became a prevalent medium for interconnectivity, many of the stable controls we took for granted began to fade. New threats and exposures had to be factored into the risk of doing business in the Internet age. Risk assessment moved to more of a project-by-project analysis that took into account the multiple variables that affected a project.

This age also ushered in some of the very visible cases of computer abuse, fraud, and crime. Major financial institutions became the victim of computer crime. White-collar crime rose to new levels as the technology level of the "bad guy" increased. Very visible cases of corporate malfeasance also came to light, which adversely affected the financial markets and investor confidence. Because of these factors, state and federal government started to develop new rules and legislation in an attempt to implement basic levels of risk management controls for companies. The first of these was the Gramm–Leach–Bliley Act, or as it is commonly known, GLBA.

The GLBA has its roots in the financial failures of the Great Depression. Congress passed the Glass–Steagall Act in 1933, which prohibited national and state banks from affiliating with securities companies. The sentiment was that this separation of banking, securities, and insurance functions would make the financial infrastructure of the United States more robust. With some revisions, this maintained as status quo until 1999 when the GLBA repealed sections of these acts and allowed financial services companies to expand their services once again.

However, one overriding concern from this expansion of services was the protection of client data. It wasn't always theft of data that bothered regulators. Many institutions treated client data as property or an asset that could be bought, sold, or traded. Very visible cases became known where some financial institutions were selling customer information to marketers. Voter sentiment ran high, demanding some basic protections to their identity data.

This sentiment was also evident on the international front where, in 1995, the EU passed the Data Protection Directive, which required that international data exchanges that used EU citizens' personal data be afforded the same level of protection that their home country would afford them. The immediate impact to US institutions that did business in Europe meant that the controls over an EU citizen's data had to meet the standards set forward by the EU, not just the US standards. US companies were now faced with a barrier to do business in the European Union. What emerged from these challenges was a Safe Harbor process. The EU Protection Directive is an example of a safe harbor law. It sets comparatively strict privacy protections for EU citizens. It prohibits European firms from transferring personal data to overseas jurisdictions with weaker privacy laws but creates exceptions where the foreign recipients have voluntarily agreed to meet EU standards under the Directive's Safe Harbor Principles. The European Union has, for many years, had a formalized system of Privacy legislation, which is regarded as more rigorous than that found in many other areas of the world. Companies operating in the European Union are not allowed to send personal data to countries outside the European Economic Area unless there is a guarantee that it will receive adequate levels of protection.

Such protection can either be at a country level (if the country's laws are considered to offer equal protection) or at an organizational level (where a multinational organization produces and documents its internal controls on personal data).

The Safe Harbor Privacy Principles allows US companies to register their certification if they meet the European Union requirements. After opting in, an organization must recertify every 12 months. It can either perform a self-assessment to verify that it complies with these principles or hire a third party to perform the assessment. There are also requirements for ensuring that appropriate employee training and an effective dispute mechanism are in place.

Safe Harbor Principles

These principles must provide the following:

- **Notice**—Individuals must be informed that their data are being collected and about how it will be used.
- **Choice**—Individuals must have the option to opt out of the collection and forwarding/transfer of the data to third parties.
- **Onward Transfer**—Transfers of data to third parties may only occur to other organizations that follow adequate data protection principles.
- **Security**—Reasonable efforts must be made to prevent loss of collected information.
- **Data Integrity**—Data must be relevant and reliable for the purpose it was collected for.
- **Access**—Individuals must be able to access information held about them, and correct or delete it if it is inaccurate.
- **Enforcement**—There must be effective means of enforcing these rules.

The initial privacy protections only regulated financial institutions; however, they have become a catalyst for baseline security standards. These laws directed the regulatory bodies to develop specific standards and examination criteria related to the security and privacy of customer information. The resulting regulatory guidance mandated that the security program identified and prepared by the organization be based on a risk assessment of the organization.

Risk management, without question, is the biggest challenge faced by Technology Executives today and is how we must manage the increasingly complex and interconnected information systems we use today to support our business. Every organization has a mission and purpose. Invariably, these organizations use people, processes, and technology to process the information that supports their business needs. Risk management plays a critical role in protecting an organization's information assets, and therefore its mission, from risk.

The primary objective of risk management activities is to be an enabler to the organization in its efforts to meet its business goals and objectives. This enabling process contributes by

1. Ensuring appropriate security of the technology systems that store, process, or transmit information
2. Enabling management to make well-informed risk management decisions to justify the expenditures that are part of an IT budget
3. Assisting management in having confidence in critical IT systems based on the supporting documentation resulting from the risk management process

Many times, risk management discussions center only around technology. While an effective risk management process is an important component of a successful IT security program, it is important to remember that the principal goal of an organization's risk management process should be to protect the *organization and its ability to perform its function*, not just its computer-based information assets. It is important that the risk management function be not just viewed as a technical function, but as an essential management function of the organization.

As we previously discussed, each organization uses people, processes, and technologies to perform its functions. Even in systems that we think of as being primarily technology based, the three components exist. And each of these components introduces a degree of risk to the organization. Looking at the example of a typical nightly batch run in a data center, there is a people component in the computer operators or coders who programmed the system. There is a process component in the order in which the jobs run and the interrelationship between them. For instance, one stream of programs can provide the input for subsequent processing, and the technology component, which includes the hardware, software, and networks over which the whole system communicates. Analyzing only one facet of the system would not give the organization a clear picture of risk. Figure 9.1 depicts the three factors to be analyzed during the process.

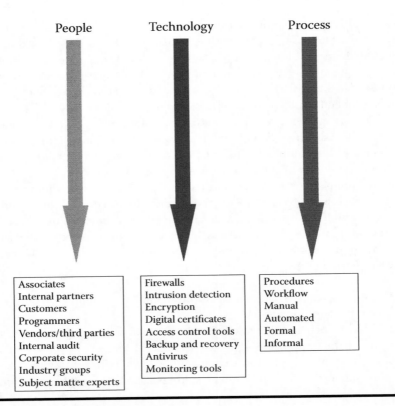

Figure 9.1 People, technology, process.

In our "backups gone wrong" story, the technology was in place; we had a great written procedure of how things were supposed to work, but we completely missed on the people part. I should have had a detective control to make sure that the packs actually got to the bank. I could have rotated the duties; I could have required the bank to verify the delivery to the vault. There is no single right answer. You need to define the controls that work for your organization.

Since we have identified the three types of risk, we can now discuss the activities that make up the continuous cycle, which helps us control or mitigate the risk. The four activities are Prevent, Detect, Respond, and Recover. To bring these activities into focus, let us look at a standard corporate virus protection program.

Standard antivirus protection is the classic risk management exercise. Tools and processes have been installed to defend the company against viruses. Should a virus get past the perimeter protection, it should be caught at the desktop, and a message should be generated if user intervention to remove the virus is required. Finally, new definition files are regularly downloaded to continuously improve and update the defense.

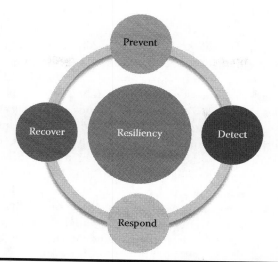

Figure 9.2   Resiliency.

In the terms of Risk Management, those activities are called **Prevent, Detect, Respond, and Recover.** Figure 9.2 is commonly used to show their relationship. Note that the middle is Resiliency. This reflects the business's ability to continue to function despite adverse events and activity. Overall, a business with high resiliency has better risk controls than one without.

Prevent

The first of these activities is "Prevention." In other words, let us stop the incident from happening in the first place. If we use the example of virus protection, no one would argue that the best virus is the one that *did not* infect your systems. Organizations spend a significant amount of money to install systems, which keep viruses out. Prevention, in risk management terms, is a "Preventative Control." In the case of virus protection, it is a technology control. There are many other types of preventative controls. For example, a key people-based preventative control is employee badging. This control helps *prevent* unauthorized individuals from entering your facilities. A common preventative control on the process side is "separation of duties." In this control method, processes are designed in a way to ensure that no one person has all the rights to compromise a system. An example of this would be separating the responsibility of maintaining an organization's firewalls from those who maintain the routers and network devices. If the process and responsibilities are properly designed, it will "prevent" one person from completely opening up the organization's network to attack.

Detect

The second activity is "Detection." In other words, if the primary preventative control fails, what controls are in place to detect that an incident has happened? If we look at the example of virus protection again, if the Preventative Control of screening incoming e-mails fails and a computer system becomes infected, an alert from the system notifies a technician that the system needs a virus cleaned. This type of *detective* or "after the fact control" must be designed to provide timely notification of the incident depending on how much of an impact the incident may have on the organization. The greater the impact, the quicker the notification should take place. Just as with preventative controls, there are also detective controls for people and processes. A people-based detective control may be something like periodic background checks. Many companies check the background of people in a critical position before hire, but few require yearly background reviews of those same critical people. Ongoing checks detect whether the individual has had legal or financial troubles over the last year, which may affect his or her work.

Respond

Responding to an incident is a critical phase of the process. Given the fact that any threat or vulnerability may come to fruition despite our best efforts, the ability to respond in a timely and effective manner is critical. It reinforces the old adage, "The right time to look for the fire extinguisher is before your pants are on fire." Prior planning is critical.

Utilizing the virus protection example, let's look at a scenario:

Tom was on the way out the door to work when his daughter told him that her laptop was running hopelessly slow, and she really needs it tomorrow for a class assignment. Could he please take a look at it before then? He grabbed it, stuffed it in his briefcase, planning to take a look at it during lunch.

As lunch rolled around, Tom thought that it probably just needed a file re-org. As long as he was at it, he should probably make sure she has all the latest operating system patches. Heaven knows that is the last thing on her priority list. He flipped open the laptop, turned it on, grabbed the network cable from his desktop unit and plugged it in.

We probably do not need to take the story much further. This is a common occurrence at many organizations. Tom's daughter's laptop was infected with a load of malware, which tried to propagate across the company network. By plugging this laptop in, he circumvented the perimeter protections for viruses.

It's not always so obvious that the action is wrong. At one of my jobs, I noted some outbound connections that didn't look right. We started looking and traced the connections back to a desktop in one of our customer support areas. Nothing had popped up on antivirus, the user wasn't surfing risky sites, but the traffic was definitely originating from her machine.

After a couple of days of testing and pulling our hair out, we traced the source back to a search engine tool bar meant to optimize coupon sites. As it turned out, Mary was an avid coupon clipper. She had taken her laptop home to do some work, and along the way stumbled on a site that offered this cool tool. She downloaded it, installed it, and started reaping the benefits. The only problem is that the toolbar leveraged a zero-day vulnerability, allowing it to get in our network undetected.

AND... Sometimes it is a false alarm.

It was month end Friday afternoon, and just before we left for the weekend, an alert popped up that we were seeing outbound traffic for Vietnam. Unique for our business at that time since we were solely a US financial services firm, we had never seen this destination before as part of normal business traffic. Compound the suspicious nature that it was week and month end with lots of financial transactions flowing.

But we all resisted the urge to become "cyber cowboys" (remember the intro of this book?) and took a measured approach. We tracked down the user through the IP and took a walk to the department. As it turned out, in addition to month and week end, it was also the beginning of Vietnamese New Year, and the clerk was searching for and downloading recipes and artwork for her family dinner.

Lesson learned? Never miss an opportunity to make a user friend. A cyber cowboy may have shut off her machine or demanded that it be reimaged. This right approach was to talk about safe surfing and appropriate use. This helped reinforce the culture of security we all want to build.

Also, be sure you have the correct machine before crashing in and grabbing it. I can't count the number of times that I've seen a well-meaning network administrator fail to recognize that the IP they are seeing is the VPN gateway and grab the last user machine to access via VPN. In 99% of the cases, it will be the wrong machine and you have embarrassed a user needlessly.

Response controls include plans and tools to find a problem system in an acceptable time, based on the severity of the risk to the company.

Recover

Once the notification that a system on the network is attempting to spread viruses on the organization's network, and the offending systems is identified, the recovery processes begin.

From a technology standpoint, the action would be to immediately disconnect the system from the network. There may also be a process to clean other infected PCs on the network if any infection attempt was successful. Regardless of the exposure, it is important that effective recovery plans exist before the incident happens. This critical phase is often overlooked in the risk measurement process but is critical in the return of critical systems to a usable state. Additionally, from a people standpoint, there is obviously a need for continuing education of Tom from the earlier example on acceptable computer behavior.

If we take the four control activities discussed above and overlay them on the People, Process, and Technologies illustration, we will arrive at the diagram shown in Figure 9.3.

The intersection of each arrow is a point at which a discussion of threats, vulnerabilities, probability, and controls should take place. This graphic is extremely useful when consulting with business partners or development organizations to discuss the different types of risk a system may encounter.

The basis of any risk management process is a standard frame of reference, or a common language you and the organization speak. Take the time to articulate and document what each of the lines on the above graphic mean to your organization. Remember that the People, Processes, and Technologies are the resources that the

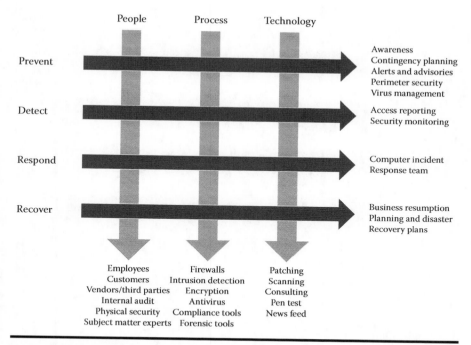

Figure 9.3   Controls versus risk areas.

organization uses. The Prevent, Detect, Respond, and Recover are services that your company uses. An example used in this chapter is virus protection. The antivirus software is a technology; the antivirus program management is a preventative service.

What are your stories or life lessons? What would your "rule" look like for this chapter? How would this framework have helped you detect, prevent, respond, and recover?

In future chapters, we will refer back to this model as we explore the specifics of an effective risk management program. In conclusion, a truly holistic risk management program looks at all facets of risk and establishes a common framework to which the organization can refer. The use of the methods discussed in this chapter will assist you in establishing the foundations of both.

Chapter 10

Every Organization Must Assume Some Risk

When discussing risk, I often think about the story of the two blind airline pilots. There were always a lot of questions when the passengers saw the Captains with their white canes feel their way into the cockpit, but they thought it was a joke, after all how would they know what to do? Besides, the company would not put the passengers at risk, correct?

So the airplane is at the end of the runway and the pilots push the throttle forward. The engines roar and the plane starts down the runway, rapidly gathering speed. The plane went faster and faster, closer and closer to the end of the runway. Soon the passengers begin to panic and begin to scream, "We're going to die!!" On hearing that, the pilots pulled back on the yoke and the plane leapt into the air. Once the plane leveled out and things calmed down, the one pilot said to the other, "You know, one of these days the people aren't going to scream and we will be in real trouble."

What's your approach to risk management? Is it the blind pilot approach where you roll along until the business screams? You'd be surprised how many companies have no plans for a crisis. It's human nature to assume bad things only happen to other people, right? Hopefully, you have a plan and a strategy to mitigate risks before they become a crisis. No sugarcoating: the business relies on you to maintain effective risk management controls. If one day they wake up and find themselves speeding toward the end of the runway, you did not do your job. And unlike the story of the pilots, you will probably not get another chance to fly with the company.

Let's face it, in our personal life, just as in business, we assume risk every day. As a matter of course in our daily lives, most of those decisions to accept risk are unconscious. When we drive to work, we assume the risk of having an accident. When we walk across a street, we assume the risk of getting hit by a car. When we climb a flight of stairs, we assume that we will not fall and break a leg.

In our personal lives, we would not dream of being so risk averse that we would not drive, cross a street, take the stairs, or leave our house. We have built-in compensating controls to reduce the risk. We look both ways, we drive defensively, we use the handrail on the stairs, and if those controls fail, we have auto and health insurance to cover the downside risks. Interestingly, the desire to think through potential risks comes with experience and maturity. I remember being 18 and immortal. The thought of any adverse outcomes were overcome by enthusiasm and naivety. Being a risk manager is the same; with experience comes a mature ability to analyze risk and design controls to mitigate that risk.

In security, many inexperienced leaders are risk averse. It's easy to just say no to anything new and justify the position by saying it is too risky. Case in point:

In my younger days, I actively campaigned against buying desktop computers with writeable CD drives in them, saying that a user could copy massive amounts of data and easily walk out the door. Sound familiar? Rather than looking for compensating controls, I forced a restriction on the business. Eventually, it was pointed out to me that buying PCs without the standard drive was actually making every order a special order, driving up cost and lead time. In my haste to reduce my narrow view of risk, I actually ended up costing the company money and time. I found that with appropriate controls, we could monitor for inappropriate activity and allow the desktop group to function efficiently. This is a lesson that has stuck with me over the years. Security and risk decisions have far-reaching implications: think them through. Understand what you can change and what is inevitable. If it is inevitable, then accept that fact and work on the design of People, Process, and Technology controls to protect company assets.

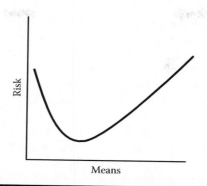

Figure 10.1   Risk versus means.

No Is Seldom the Answer

There are many definitions of risk. In simplistic terms, risk is the conflict between (ends) the desired outcome and means (resources) (Figure 10.1). While we tend to view risk as being generated from a lack of means, excessive means can also increase risk.

Applying too many resources (means) to a problem results in resources being drawn from other areas, thus transferring risk to these areas. A classic example of this is the common belief that by throwing more and newer technology at a problem, this will solve an existing problem. What typically happens is you have the new technology in place but not the resources, training, or experience to effectively operate the new technology. A false sense of security is created. The greatest system in the world is useless if you don't know how to use it or interpret the data it presents. Here's a classic example:

> In the early days of layered security, we used multiple systems to cover various threat vectors. Firewalls, intrusion detection, antivirus, and so on. The problem we faced related to a lack of a way to connect the dots. Each system passed alerts and it was up to me and my staff to manually connect and analyze events. Then one day, the thing we had all waited for (wait for it), the Security Event Information Management system became available. It even sounded incredibly cool. At last, here was the technology that was going to give us a step up on the bad guys. It was very expensive but seemed worth it, if it delivered as promised.

Fast forward ahead a few months, the system is in and we begin testing. Immediately, the security inbox begins to fill with thousands of messages and alerts. Technology had allowed us to move quickly from too little to too much data. It quickly dawned on me that we hadn't reduced risk, we had actually done the opposite by hiding meaningful alerts in a mountain of data. Talk about the needle in the haystack.

Now we got to deal with a new process called "tuning." We had to train the systems to ignore the false positives and bring the critical alerts to our attention. Honestly, in the early days of SEIM, we didn't really get the bang for the buck we expected. While the industry has significantly matured over the years, it is still a problem to be overcome.

There are many ways that analyzing data and alerts can go wrong. The risks of too many alerts, not recognizing a new alert as a real threat, or not knowing what to do when the alert is real. As with any problem, all we have to do is look to history for an example.

During the early morning hours of December 7, 1941, radar picked up two blips approaching Oahu, Hawaii. These were very large blips that the operators had never seen before. Their first inclination was a system error and they began troubleshooting. When it became apparent that the radar was operating properly, the radar findings were passed up the chain of command. At first, no one was available to take the information. Eventually, someone was contacted who incorrectly surmised the blips were B-17s or Navy planes. The radar operators were told to ignore their findings. The rest, as they say, is history.

Achieving the proper results must be done at an acceptable cost. While risk is at a minimum at point A in Figure 10.2, this does not mean the costs are acceptable at that point. Most of us have to operate somewhere to the left of point A. How far to the left is the critical question. A security department does not run on an unlimited budget.

Risk is proportional to the amount of uncertainty. I've always said that I love "boring." Uncertainty always increases risk. The risk curve in the graph tends to flatten out as we reduce uncertainty. Training also reduces uncertainty as system operators become more adept at operating their systems and understanding the data collected. These very data are what tends to push us to the right of point A.

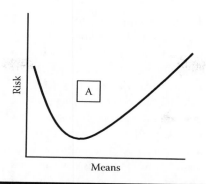

Figure 10.2   Risk versus means (2).

We have so much data we cannot process all of them. Data are useless unless they can be converted into information. Information is critical to reducing uncertainty.

Information is available both internally and externally. Staying on top of the latest threat assessments will help keep the curve flat. There are many publicly available sources of threat information as well as paid services. Most vendors of security-related products have a wealth of information they freely provide to their clients. The challenge is absorbing, filtering, and processing the information. Analyzing data tends to be a secondary responsibility, if it is done at all, when it should be a primary role. Just like each military branch has its dedicated group of intelligence specialists, each business should likewise invest in dedicated intelligence analysts and not just system administrators. Whether you recognize it or not, there is a war going on and industry is the target. Good methodical and careful analysis is the best defense against becoming overconfident and careless in how much risk you are willing to bear.

As the saying goes, it is not the destination that matters but the journey. While we know where we want to be (the ends), and we have the resources (the means), we are still left with execution (the ways). For every problem, there is generally more than one solution. The journey though can be unduly influenced by the means. The resources at hand may take you down the wrong path, the proverbial "tail wagging the dog." Current investments in people and technology may not necessarily be the right fit for future needs. While it is hard and expensive to separate oneself of prior decisions, such painful decisions sometimes need to be made. Anyone who has gone through a divorce or leaving a job for a new one can relate. Failure to make a decision in dealing with a status quo that is clearly ineffective only increases risk. Since multiple paths lead to the same destination, one should not place your entire faith and confidence in one direction. The threat environment is constantly changing and adapting. One must always have options to thwart an opponent that has identified your strategy and countered it. In security, the greatest risk is one of planning for certitude. As Wilbur Wright stated in 1901, "Carelessness and overconfidence are usually more dangerous than deliberately accepted risks."

There is no perfect defense to reduce risk to zero. A 100% solution to any problem is unrealistic. The Maginot line was deemed to be impenetrable. (How did that work out?) The Germans simply went around it, because the line was built to reflect the current threats and was not modified to reflect changes in threat, in this case, how wars were being fought. Creativity and technology will eventually defeat any form of defense. As we define our objectives, develop our strategies, allocate our resources, and implement our tactics, the opposition is likewise doing the same. Complicating the equation is the fact that we are dealing with multiple external adversaries and to a lesser degree internal ones as well. Though we can't discount the very real and potentially far more serious risk internal threats pose.

Security is the corporation's insurance policy. And like any insurance policy, it has lots of exclusions. Each explicit and implicit exclusion is a potential risk. It is critical that the exclusions be well documented and communicated. The business, just like your average insurance policy holder, is totally unaware of the fine print and assumes everything is covered. Such assumptions have led to the downfall of many a CISO. Wilbur Wright in a letter to his father back in 1901 summed it up well, "The man who wishes to keep at the problem long enough to really learn something positively must not take dangerous risks."

Strive for Simplicity

There is always a temptation to make things unduly complex. We've all heard of KISS. Sure it is an old saying, we've all said it. KISS is an acronym for "**Keep it simple, stupid**" as a design principle noted by the Navy in 1960. The KISS principle states that most systems work best if they are kept simple rather than made complicated; therefore, simplicity should be a key goal in design and unnecessary complexity should be avoided. Variations on the phrase include "keep it short and simple" and "keep it simple and straightforward" but they all mean the same thing: Avoid unnecessary complexity.

Lesson learned? As I said, in my younger days, I was an engineer who designed automated assembly machines. I learned from a mentor that "The Best Automation Is No Automation." In other words, before you look at building a million-dollar machine to automate something, first try to eliminate the need for the machine by redesigning the process or product. Take that same approach when looking at technology problems. First, try to eliminate the need; if you can't, make sure you implement the most simple solution.

People, Process, and Technology are the three variables in any risk equation. Making any one overly complex has a detrimental effect on the other two. If we look at the illustration in Figure 10.3, we can see that if we keep the people, process, and controls simple, we have a much lower risk of an adverse event. While we know it is not always possible to avoid complexity, always remember the KISS principle.

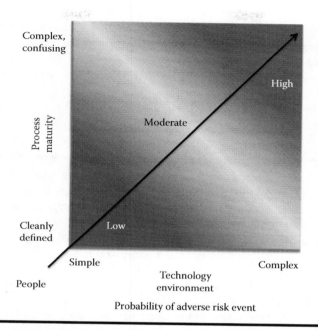

Figure 10.3   Keep it simple.

Risk Planning Is Just as Important as Project Planning

Success is predicated on getting the entire organization to support the level of acceptable risk proposed. In order to plan for risk, one must identify it. Identifying and quantifying the risk is the challenge. There are multiple techniques available to do a risk assessment. While these may provide quantitative results, in reality, risk assessment is more an art than a science. It is dependent on a number of subjective considerations. One's perspective of things is certainly influenced by where they sit in an organization. Self-assessing is fraught with danger. Human nature naturally tends to make you reluctant to reveal inadequacies in your areas of direct responsibility. Third-party assessments provide a much more realistic evaluation of the actual risk. There are a number of key factors that any risk assessment should consider to include; the immediacy of the threat, likelihood of the threat, economic impacts, data privacy, bearing on company reputation, legal implications, and competitive impacts to name a few. The results of a risk assessment are certainly dynamic, changing over time and circumstances. Thus, it needs to be a frequently employed process and not something pulled off the shelf at budget time. Using a consistent and systematic approach will produce more reliable results and certainly be more defendable.

You must be able to regularly defend your current security position and only advance your position at the right opportunities. The key to success is recognizing those opportunities. Advancing too soon will only create internal political enemies to contend with in addition to the very real external threats. A security wizard will have contingencies in place to deal with a changing threat environment and not only be able to recognize when the threat environment has actually changed but be able to implement the contingencies in a timely fashion. With a dynamically changing threat environment composed of a myriad of threats and actors, coupled with internal restrictions, and having no clear vision of potential effects of actions taken to address a threat defines the challenge and risk that comes with being a CISO.

When I was in school near Denver, Colorado, I and some of my friends decided it was the perfect time to learn to ski. After all, how hard could it be? It turned out to be less about skiing, and now in retrospect, more of a major lesson in risk and risk management.

We loaded up, drove to a nearby ski resort, rented some skis, and charged toward the ski slopes. Lessons? Ha! It was similar to the line from the old western "Lessons? We don't need no stinking lessons!" Of course, we bypassed the bunny slope (Oh-Puh-Lease) and headed directly for the chair lift. As it turned out, the lessons were just starting.

Lesson one: When you see the sign on the top of the chairlift that says "Stand Up," get your butt off the lift chair. This was followed quickly by lesson two, which is "It is very hard to look cool when you are lying on your back with the chairs spinning around over your head." In retrospect, I see parallels to basic risk management. First I charged toward a bad decision about where to ski, and second, I didn't act when I saw an obvious warning sign at the end of the chair lift ride. Taking pause to act on either would have made my day at the slopes much better.

My friends and I survived our first day with only a few bumps, bruises, twisted ankles, and damaged pride. The pain we experienced that day taught us to do things differently to mitigate the risk of future pain and embarrassment. For me, I bought some reasonably priced goggles that didn't fog up since it helps to see where you are going. Eventually, I swallowed my pride and actually took a lesson or two and found it made our outings much more pleasant.

So, what's to be learned? Assess risk before you head down the steep hill. Take a lesson or two, or talk to your peers so you can learn from their experiences. Once you learn a painful lesson, don't forget it: learn from your experiences. Lastly, you don't need a hundred-dollar pair of goggles to see clearly, particularly if you don't know that you will want to make skiing a serious hobby. You should start with reasonable controls and technology to control risk. A million-dollar solution is not always better than a thousand-dollar solution. Common sense? Yes, but these are the things that will make you a better CISO in the long run.

What about the following trips? The more I skied, the better I became. After the days on the slopes, my friends and I would share stories about things we had learned. I became convinced that for at least the foreseeable future, skiing would be a great activity.

As our organizations mature and our products and services develop, it is important to review our risk approaches to people, process, and technologies. With an eye to market penetration and volume, is a simple firewall enough, what about intrusion detection? Is the business interested in developing a customer facing public website for e-commerce? The message is that Risk, just like Business, is never static. Business needs must drive the risk methodology and controls, but security must evolve with the business.

Bear with me as I stretch this story to one more point. As I began to enjoy winter sports, I learned that despite trying to save money, the equipment for downhill skiing didn't work for cross-country skiing. Aside from the obvious choice of skis, I found that the goggles I used for downhill didn't work at all for cross country. While they both kept wind and snow out of my eyes, I found a good pair of sunglasses that worked best for cross-country.

In dealing with risk, you only have the ends, the ways, and the means to adjust and be flexible. One size does not fit all, and while a solution may "keep the snow out of your eyes," it may not be a fit for the business. If you try to force flexibility on every solution, you will find that you may compromise the security of the whole solution. You will need to be creative as you look at risk and security issues. Don't restrict your creativity exercise to just money and people; think in terms of resources in general. There are many ways to improve efficiencies and reduce costs without reducing headcount or changing tools. Look at ways to reduce the waste of inefficient or redundant processes. Go back to the drawing board and take a fresh look at where the business is and where it is going. Be a business partner instead of a "risk cop."

> My wife to be (at that time) had a similar first ski trip experience, with a different lesson learned. Since we are very much alike, when she jumped off the bus, she headed directly for the bigger slopes. After a few false starts, she managed to negotiate the tow rope to the top, pointed the skis downhill and pushed off. In what can only be described as a slow motion train wreck, she made her way down the hill and found herself headed for the ski lodge. It then occurred to her that the one thing lessons would have taught her was how to stop. Seeing no other way out, she fell and skidded to a stop. Much like me, she eventually swallowed her pride and headed for the bunny slope and lessons (including how to stop).

In technology, we tend to put things in gear without considering all aspects of the risks facing us. For a few years I worked at a company that had a great disaster recovery plan to fail over to a remote data center. The secret was that no one had any idea if we could ever fail back to the main data center once we moved production to the backup site. Evaluating risk requires us to think through possible conclusions and resultant risks to the company.

Flexibility applies across the board. When the costs to achieve the ends become too prohibitive, the ends may need to be adjusted to more realistic objectives. While a retinal eye scanner may increase physical security, having one at every entrance may not be realistic. Limiting their use to high-security areas may be a more acceptable solution. Or rather than a retinal scanner, will a hand scanner suffice at a lower cost? Or you may want to change your allocation of resources to meet a potential risk. You have a set number of end point encryption licenses. Rather than blindly deploy them to an entire department or division, allocate them based on potential risk across the entire company. How likely is a desktop PC to walk out of the building as opposed to a laptop? Is the receptionist's PC as great a risk as that of a company financial analyst? As previously mentioned, the number of ways needs to be considered and alternatives need to be kept in reserve. Rather than encrypt the desktops, what about physically securing them to a desk?

One of the best ways to reduce your risk can be summed up in the words of Sun Tzu, a Chinese military general and author of *The Art of War*: "To know your Enemy, you must become your Enemy." While most of our focus is on assuming a defensive posture, training for an offensive role can provide much insight into how a security breach manifests itself. Many of the beginning signs of a potential security breach go unrecognized. Having never seen such a breach nor understanding its mechanics, it is understandable how potential breaches become successful breaches. If your staff thinks like a hacker and practices the techniques of a hacker using the tools they have readily available, they will become far more attuned and sensitive to changes in the environment that portend a breach. Directly engaging the enemy is not a viable tactic. Such actions would only invite a much greater onslaught since this would be viewed as a challenge by the hackers. You would have far more to lose than the hackers. Unlike football, it is better to intimately know the offense rather than actually having a good offense. Having a good defense, though, is still an imperative.

So the bottom line is you will always have risk in your environment. How much and where it resides is your job to help the business decide what is acceptable. Security should never make the final determination as to what should be protected or to what degree. Security's role is to identify the risks, offer potential solutions, implement the appropriate controls to reduce those risks, and then monitor for how well the controls are performing. Explaining the risks to the business requires diplomacy, tact, and the ability to take complex and abstract concepts and reduce them to simple terms that are meaningful to the business. Saying this server is vulnerable and we might lose some data has far less meaning and impact than saying this server contains sensitive data that are at risk of being stolen, which could give a competitor a significant insight into our customer base. The real challenge is getting the business to prioritize their data assets. Unfortunately, when dealing with the business, everything tends to be critically important. Placing a dollar figure on what it would cost to protect each piece of data helps the business to more accurately prioritize its business assets. Having a charge back model is the best way to ensure that the business knows what is protected and what is not. This also makes it clear that if you aren't paying for it, it isn't protected!

Dealing with Internal Audit

Internal Audit performs a valuable process and can be a powerful ally. They check the controls to make sure they are effective, and more importantly that we are doing what we say we are doing. While information security controls are proactive, the audit function is reflective, looking at evidence that we have protected the environment, as we should. This is a classic example of separation of duties. If the control designers audit themselves, it is not possible to get an objective analysis for the business leaders. So auditors should never design and implement controls, and information security should never audit.

Audit has changed over the years. Those of us that have been around a while remember the classic audit department. Many of the auditors focused on "catching you do something wrong."

New to the company, I laid plans to start my initial risk assessment to identify the problems. Trying to build a relationship with the Audit group, I decided to invite Ed the audit manager to be part of the team.

For the next four weeks, we worked as a team to identify the gaps and document plans to move forward. Looked like a good teaming exercise, at least on the surface. Little did I know that Ed prescribed to the 1950s school of being an audit curmudgeon.

Imagine my surprise when I received a formal list of audit findings on my desk that looked suspiciously like every item we had discussed in the team. Not only did he write up the issues, but he also got kudos from his management for doing such a complete assessment of IT risk.

Lesson learned? I go back to one of the core behaviors: You can't control others' behavior, you can only control how you respond. You might think a normal response would be to never cooperate freely with audit again, but that will make you look bad, maybe even having something to hide. Instead, my lesson was to set expectations and ground rules before inviting audit into a project. Document in e-mail. When properly done, you will find that Audit can be a tremendous partner. Once you have an agreement with Audit, you will find they are a powerful ally in the risk management process. For instance:

- They can help you design effective controls in a consistent manner.
- They can help you design controls that are easily audited, particularly valuable when the external auditors come to town.
- Audit can be an advocate to senior management when discussing business risk.
- If you involve them early, there will be fewer surprises and arguments when the first audit rolls around. It is hard for them to argue with processes they helped to design.

Nobody likes surprises when being audited. An audit is just like any other process or project, it must be managed. You must involve the business and IT managers of the audited systems early. Don't just look at the scope, look also at the rules of engagement. Things such as the auditor's access to data and information must be defined early.

A few years ago, we were going to have an audit of our perimeter controls. All of our administrators and engineers were on notice. The audit team showed up the first day and requested a system login and copies of all the firewall rules for review.

Being good administrators, the IT staff flatly refused the request, thinking it was a test. The auditors demanded, the administrators dug in their heels, and the issue quickly spiraled out of control. By the time I stepped in, feelings were on edge, and the tone of the upcoming audit was negative.

Lesson learned? Set the ground rules in advance:

If there are restrictions, such as on access requests or windows of system access and testing methods to limit impact on production systems, they must be specified in advance. Make sure the auditors conform to your policy on handling sensitive information. *There was a recent case where a financial services examiner carried sensitive information out of the bank for further review. On the way back to the office, the examiner lost the thumb drive and the bank had to notify its customers of a potential breach.* If the organization has restrictions on e-mailing data or encryption requirements, those rules and policies must be discussed and documented in advance.

If the auditors will conduct a penetration test, notify all parties in advance including your network provider. There is no sense in alarming your partners for scheduled testing. It's also a great idea to make sure any penetration testing is done off normal production hours. A test is important, but don't let it affect your customer's access and response time.

As I've said before, an audit is just another project that needs to be managed. I've learned over the years to not let audits "happen to me." Focus as much on the prep work as the actual audit. Find out what the auditors can reasonably expect you to provide such as the basic data and documentation they might need to navigate and analyze your systems. This typically includes the following:

- Copies of policies and procedures. Policies may include end-user policies (password expiration, virus scanning, acceptable use), privacy (for internal users and client data), privileged access (sysadmins), and incident handling. Procedures will be more operationally based on the audit.
- A list of servers, components, and so on.
- Network topology, specifying target IP ranges.
- External security devices (firewall software, IDS).
- List of application software.

The Work

The process of testing your system's security should be part of the overall plan. **A key takeaway:** Keep track of the IT hours expended in support of audits. This is a critical piece of information that will be valuable when budget time rolls around. The time spent in support of audit is significant but is usually overlooked. Make sure the auditor details this plan up front and then follows through without it becoming a fishing expedition. Again, you are not trying to hide details; you need to manage your resources and scope of the "Audit Project."

The auditor will review the relevant policies to determine the acceptable risks. The auditor will confirm that the environment matches management's description of the systems. For example, the documentation may talk only about Linux servers, but a review shows some Microsoft servers. Auditors often use security checklists to review known security issues and guidelines for particular platforms. Those are fine, but they're just guides. They're no substitute for expertise, and you may have to contribute some technical help.

Many auditors will want to run a vulnerability scanner to check the systems. Personally, I recommend against any non-IT person running a tool that may damage the infrastructure. Propose that the Auditors observe a security analyst running the scanner, and take the results directly from the analyst. Discovering security vulnerabilities on a production system is one thing; testing them is another.

Final thoughts—Above all, remember that there is a risk to taking an adversarial approach to risk management. True risk management is an inclusive process to benefit the business. Avoid empire building, oppressive controls, and complex procedures. Ensure that the end result of the process is a safer, more productive business environment.

Good for your career, great for the company.

Chapter 11

When Preparation
Meets Opportunity,
Excellence Happens

A few years ago, I had the opportunity to meet a staff photographer for National Geographic Magazine. I watched his presentation of spectacular photographs in awe; I could only imagine the thrill of capturing some of those images.

When he was wrapping up, he remarked that many people ask him if "being in the right place at the right time" is the key to amazing photography. He told us that simply having the opportunity is only a small part of the equation. The instant that he snaps the picture, he needs to be completely focused on the action and composition, not the setting on his camera and where the buttons and adjustments are. That is the preparation, breath control, and muscle memory that is the result of taking thousands of pictures over the years. He stated that it is the magic that happens when preparation meets opportunity.

So what does that mean to us? Simply put, if we expect our users to practice safe computing, we need to prepare and train them so they make the right choices automatically. For us, that's all about training and testing our users.

End-User Training and Security Awareness

The purpose of awareness training is simply to focus attention on security. Awareness presentations are intended to allow individuals to recognize information security concerns and respond accordingly when faced with an information security issue. Awareness relies on reaching broad audiences with effective training methods. Effective IT security awareness presentations must be designed with the recognition that people tend to tune out a repetitive message. Because of this, awareness presentations must be ongoing, creative, and motivational, with the objective of focusing the learner's attention so that the learning will be incorporated into conscious decision-making.

Behaviors learned through a single session tend to be short term and specific. Ask my wife, changing my irritating behavior is a nonstop job for her. Constant messages and ongoing reinforcement are the only way to change behavior. An ongoing program of training is critical to create actual organizational change. The fundamental value of IT security awareness programs is that they bring about a change in attitudes, which changes the organizational culture. The cultural change is the realization that IT security is critical because a security failure may have adverse consequences for everyone. When this cultural change takes root in an organization, all users will realize that Information Security is everyone's job. This chapter explores various subjects included in awareness training as well as different methods of delivering training and tracking progress.

I have a saying that I use often in presentations: "You will know that you have instilled a culture of security when action replaces rhetoric." In fact, it is one of my primary means of determining how serious security is taken by management and the employees. Just seeing and hearing people talking about security is an indicator of awareness; doing something about security such as integrating it into your daily actions is a sign of true cultural change.

Let's look at an incident that happened about 15 years ago.

Cathy had a problem. She is the supervisor of a claims processing department for an insurance company. She has received reports that Neal, one of her new employees, has been spending way too much time on the Internet. The few times that she has walked over to see what he is doing, he quickly minimized the open window before she can get a good look at the screen. Cathy eventually took her concerns to Human Resources who asked for a report to be run on Neal's activities. The report came back that although Neal was not spending excessive time on the Internet, he had been accessing porn sites. Cathy called Neal in and, with the help of HR, dismissed Neal from his job for cause. He had violated the acceptable use policy.

Neal appealed the firing. He claimed that the company had not told him that this conduct was unacceptable, and since he was completing his assigned work without complaint, the company was not justified in its actions. Because the company could not produce any proof that Neal had been briefed or trained regarding the company standard on acceptable use, the court agreed and awarded damages.

Essentially, the courts are saying that unless both parties understand the contract, there is no contract. Does this sound familiar? Has something like this happened in your organization? The answer is most likely a yes. This scenario happens all too frequently in organizations today. Because information security–related issues are still relatively new to many organizations, the thought of effective training and tracking of security awareness issues has not reached maturity. Traditional issues such as human resources policies, business ethics, and workplace acceptable behaviors have been thought out and adequately covered for years, because the risks and potential financial losses have a historical basis. In fact, most employees will understand the vacation or dress policy better than their responsibilities to secure data. It will take a significant effort to bring information security issues into the same sharp organizational focus.

I've tried for years to emphasize that for an information security group to be successful in an organization, the culture of an organization must support the security initiatives.

No one by nature knows his or her responsibilities for information security activities. It must be a learned activity. Culture is slow to change and requires constant reinforcement before it becomes a part of organizational daily behavior. Awareness training is the most cost-effective means of reducing the information security–related risks faced by any organization. Educated users are less likely to misuse company resources or fall victim to common exploits targeted at end users such as social engineering– and e-mail–borne viruses.

Flashback to High School Memories...

Everyone has two memories of high school: the teacher and classes they loved, and the teachers and classes they hated. What made the difference? It's the understanding that even a great subject can be made into pure torture by poor presentation. Mine was Carl. He has a soft-spoken voice and a bland presentation that was guaranteed to put you to sleep. And somehow, I always got his class right after lunch. I still can feel my head bouncing off the desk... Been there? Not everyone is a good presenter; there is nothing wrong with that. Don't be afraid to use those individuals who can light up a class, even with a dull subject.

Security awareness has the potential to easily fall into the torture category. It's mandatory and can be boring. Let's face it; most people don't perceive the value. How do we communicate the value?

Awareness training is the most important component in any information security initiative. Awareness training is a mechanism, which educates employees on the following key security issues. If an organization has been successful, any individual in the organization should be able to easily answer the following questions:

- Is the action I am about to take right or wrong?
- Would I choose to report a wrong action?
- Would I know how to report the wrong action?

An effective awareness program teaches the importance of information security–related issues, not just the rules. It fosters a climate that supports information security activities and helps management implement mechanisms to reinforce the security culture. Make it personal. An awareness program should begin before the user has access to company computer resources. It must be easily accessible by both internal users and those from outside the organization that use computing resources. It must be easily understood and it must be kept fresh and in front of everyone. Awareness training is not a one-time event; it must be a continuous process.

Training Methods

Should formal training be "Big Blast" once a year or quarterly? There are as many acceptable awareness-training methods as there are opportunities. Blended awareness programs are a critical piece of effective programs. Remember, security is a learned behavior, and the only method to ensure that a learned behavior stays with the student is to stay in front of the student. Constant refreshers are very important. Posters, stress balls, calendars, and t-shirts are very effective training tools. You don't have to lock the user to the computer-based training.

- How about a Bug Bounty—cash for process or code bugs?
- How about a Security Art contest?
- How about a Security Slogan contest?
- Make it fun, be the great teacher, not Carl.
- Lunch and Learn with free pizza.

New Hire Training

Here is a scenario from my past. It was Deborah's first day at Big Networks, Inc. She has been told that her first day will be nonstop training and benefits sign up. Not exceptionally thrilling but nonetheless necessary. This is not her first job, so she knows pretty well what to expect. Later in the afternoon, an analyst from the Information Security Department came down to give a 10-minute presentation. He discussed a few key points, but two really stuck with Deborah. The first was that she was responsible for all actions taken with her login credentials, and the second was that she should protect her password from disclosure. She'd never really thought of that concept before, but it made a lot of sense.

The next day, she actually started in her new department. Shortly after she got situated at her desk, the department PC Liaison came up to her and introduced herself. She explained that she was there to help with any issues that may come up, sort of a departmental tech support person. Along with that, she told Deborah that part of the PC Liaison's job was to maintain a listing of everyone's user ID and password in the department, in case someone forgot, or was on vacation one day when information was needed from her PC. Wait a minute: now she was confused. She was being told two different things. Deborah referred the issue to her new supervisor, saying that she had been told in her first day of training to never share her account password with anyone. She referred her supervisor to the info sec department to clear up the confusion.

As it turns out, the practice was a long-standing "service first" initiative in the department. Everyone had always taken it as sound practice, and never questioned it. It was part of the traditional culture. The Security Trainer helped the department understand how to go through acceptable processes if access to information was needed. Because of a 10-minute training session, a serious security exposure to the organization came to light and was corrected.

An awareness and training program is crucial in that it is *the* vehicle for disseminating information that users, including managers, need in order to do their jobs. In the case of an IT security program, it is *the* vehicle to be used to communicate security requirements across the enterprise.

An effective IT security awareness and training program explains proper rules of behavior for the use of agency IT systems and information. The program communicates IT security policies and procedures that need to be followed. This must precede and lay the basis for any sanctions imposed due to noncompliance. Users first should be informed of the expectations. Accountability must be derived from a fully informed, well-trained, and aware workforce.

On the first day at a new employer, new employees usually go through an introduction to the organization. Usually it covers pay, vacation, parking, benefits, and so on. On that first day, new employees should receive an introduction to their responsibilities relating to information security. Does that happen where you work? Ten to 15 minutes on that day can set the tone for the length of their employment. Subjects to be covered on that first day should include the following:

- A review of the company's acceptable use policy. Every company has differing rules when it applies to using company networks and Internet connections.
- A review of the company's password policy.
- A clear explanation of every user's responsibilities for information security. While specific roles may add additional responsibilities to a user, there are a set of base responsibilities that should be covered.
- Explanation of the user's privacy. If e-mails are monitored, let the users know. If Internet access is monitored, let them know. Setting the tone early will avoid downstream problems.

Since the tone of security should come from the top, don't be afraid to stop down and deliver the message in person. The employee will know and remember your face, and understand that you felt it was important enough to deliver the message in person. I guarantee it will stick with the new employee for a long time. On our graph of easy to implement versus impact on risk, this small effort is a big winner.

The easiest way to start is with a centralized program. In this model, responsibility and budget for the entire organization's IT security awareness and training program are given to a single authority, typically the information security department. All directives, strategy development, planning, and scheduling are coordinated through this "security awareness and training" authority. Because the awareness and training strategy is developed centrally, the needs assessment—which helps determine the strategy—should also be conducted by the same group. This group also develops the training plan as well as the awareness and training material. The method of implementing the material throughout the organization is determined and accomplished centrally. Typically, in such an organization, both the CIO and CISO are organizationally located within the same group and should jointly format the overall message to address "technology risk" in general.

It probably goes without saying but communication is key. Training can't be developed from "on high" and pushed down. Organizational units have specific needs and business models: one size does not fit all. Communication between the central group and the organizational units must travel in both directions. Doing anything in a vacuum is a recipe for disaster. The central group should communicate the policy regarding IT security awareness and training, the strategy for conducting the program, and the material and method(s) of implementation to the organizational units. The organizational units provide information requested by the central group. For example, to meet its responsibilities, the central group may collect data on the number of attendees at awareness sessions, the number of people trained on a particular topic, and the number of people yet to attend awareness and training sessions. The organizational unit can also provide feedback on the effectiveness of awareness and training material and on the appropriateness of the method(s) used to implement the material. This allows the central authority to fine-tune, add, or delete material, or modify the implementation method(s).

Awareness Seminars

Ongoing awareness seminars are a valuable tool in the educational process. A standard presentation given on a regular schedule enables users to attend a yearly session at their convenience. It is recommended that an organization establish a requirement for at least annual attendance.

Preparing content that is relevant to the user is critical to the success of an educational program. In any organization, there are at least three main groupings of attendees that should be addressed. They are as follows:

Senior and Executive Management: Security awareness education that communicates bottom line cost advantages, business survivability, effects to shareholder value, attacks on confidential data, and offsetting resulting litigation.

Technical Staff and Line Management: In addition to the awareness education for all end users, technical staff and first line managers should have a focus on individual verification procedures, and features and attributes of software programs that can support increased security.

General Users: A high-level, nontechnical overview of what computer security is and why it is important. This overview should include elements of computer security, the threats to computer security, and countermeasures. All of the company policies and procedures should lend insight and support of the countermeasures.

Once the awareness and training strategy has been set, supporting material can be developed. Material should be developed with the following in mind:

- "What behavior do we want to reinforce?" (awareness)
- "What skill or skills do we want the audience to learn and apply?" (training)

In both cases, the focus should be on specific material that the participants should integrate into their jobs. Attendees will pay attention and incorporate what they see or hear in a session if they feel that the material was developed specifically for them. Any presentation that "feels" canned—impersonal and so general as to apply to any audience—will be filed away as just another of the annual "we're here because we have to be here" sessions. An awareness and training program can be effective; however, the material must be interesting and current.

At some point, the question will be asked, "Am I developing awareness *or* training material?" Generally, since the goal of awareness material is simply to focus attention on good security practices, the message that the awareness effort sends should be short and simple. The message can address one topic, or it can address a number of topics about which the audience should be aware.

The awareness audience must include all users in an organization. The message to be spread through an awareness program, or campaign, should make all individuals aware of their commonly shared IT security responsibilities. On the other hand, the message in a training class is directed at a specific audience. The message in training material should include everything related to security that attendees need to know in order to do their jobs. Training material is usually far more in-depth than material used in an awareness session or campaign.

The question to be answered when beginning to develop material for an organization-wide awareness program or campaign is, "What do we want all personnel to be aware of regarding IT security?" The awareness and training plan should contain a list of topics. E-mail advisories, online IT security daily news websites, and periodicals are good sources of ideas and material.

Awareness and training material can be developed in-house, adapted from other agencies' or professional organizations' work, or purchased from a contractor/vendor.

Changing peoples' attitudes and behavior in terms of IT security can be a challenging task. New security policies are often seen as conflicting with the way users have done their job for years. For example, departments and agencies that once operated with the full and open sharing of information are now being required to control access to, and dissemination of, that information. A technique that has been successfully used to acclimate users to these necessary changes is to begin an awareness module or session by discussing IT security issues in the context of personal life experiences (e.g., identify theft, inappropriate access to personal health or financial data, hacking incidents).

An organization may decide to mount a security awareness campaign to focus on a particular issue. For example, if users are becoming targets of social engineering attacks or a particular virus, an awareness campaign can be quickly implemented that uses various awareness techniques to "get the word out." Such a campaign differs from the normal implementation of an awareness program by the need for a timely dissemination of information on a particular topic or group of topics.

A significant number of topics can be mentioned and briefly discussed in any awareness session or campaign. Topics may include the following:

- **Password usage and management**—including creation, frequency of changes, and protection.
- **Protection from viruses, worms, Trojan Horses, and other malicious code**—scanning, virus protection, and updating virus definitions are critical to the survival of organizations today. The best technical systems can be overcome by a user's unintentional actions, such as opening an e-mail attachment from an unknown individual. Policies should cover the mandatory use of virus protection. Guidelines should cover the acceptable brands and configurations. Success factors include ensuring that the attendees know
  - How to identify a suspicious e-mail
  - What antivirus is acceptable per company standards
- **Policy**—Ensure that all users understand the potential penalties associated with noncompliance of information security policies. Because human interaction is involved and the surrounding circumstances are always different, the best that policy guidance can offer is that violations of policy may result in disciplinary action up to and including termination. Specify that Human Resources in conjunction with Information Security and departmental management will make the determination of the disciplinary action. To quote an old adage, "Let the punishment fit the crime."
- **E-mail/attachments**—E-mail and, to some extent, instant messaging have become a critical part of today's organizational environment. Try as we might to replace face-to-face communications with electronic messages, we have never found a way to effectively do business in a totally electronic environment. Because of this, each organization creates policies and acceptable use statements regarding the acceptable use of electronic messaging. Organizations may take a hard-line "business use only" policy. They may be required to monitor and archive e-mails. Whatever the controls, it is critical that each user understand what is acceptable by company standards. Success factors include ensuring the attendees know
  - The acceptable uses for e-mail
  - Restrictions on "business use only"

- If monitoring or archival is enabled
- Their rights to privacy

■ **Web usage**—allowed versus prohibited; monitoring of user activity. In addition to just quoting the policies, offer common sense advice: Given below is a list of a few more things that you should not venture into while browsing the Internet at work.
  - Pornographic sites
  - Funny videos
  - Chatting on instant messenger services
  - Reading e-books and jokes
  - Applying or looking for new job openings
  - Looking up good restaurants, movie lists, and so on
  - Downloading anything

  Better yet, advise them that there are some common sense things that you can do if you find yourself free of work for a while.

  Some people will always abuse their Internet privileges; it's really an issue of core values. I'll always remember my Dad's advice on getting ahead at work: "If you run out of work and there is nothing else to help with, grab a broom and start to sweep up." I'm not advocating that every CISO should have a broom in their office, but you get my drift. Tell them to
  - Read up some online study material, which will help you in your line of work
  - Look up sites that benefit you in your field of work

■ **Spam**—policies in place to reduce spam and what you can do to limit the influx of it.

■ **Social engineering**—In computer security, social engineering is a term that describes a *nontechnical* kind of intrusion. It relies on human interaction and often involves tricking other people to break normal security procedures. It can be called a "con game." A social engineer relies on the natural desire of people to be helpful. In fact, most organizations have some type of "service first" program that rewards helpfulness. They will appeal to the vanity of the target, impose some type of authority, or just do simple eavesdropping. It can be said that many very successful hackers were excellent social engineers possessing only marginal technical skills. If you can get a user to tell you their user id and password, there is no need to do a sophisticated attack on the system. The attendee should be given examples of how a social engineering example may work. Make sure the attendee knows their responsibilities to verify the identity of all individuals asking for information, and tips how to verify identity. Success factors include ensuring that the attendees know
  - The definition of social engineering
  - What methods may be used
  - How to verify the identity of individuals

TIP: If you have call center or help desk people who may be the targets of social engineering attacks, a good source of training may be no further than your local or federal law enforcement office. Find a contact and let them know that you have people who need basic training on how to identify deceptive behavior. Usually, they will be glad to come over and offer a "lunch and learn." If you want formal training, look at engaging an interview and interrogation speaker. They will have a great number of tips on recognizing deceit either in person or over the phone.

- **Logical access**—Each user must understand the policies regarding logical access to systems. These can range from acceptable use to understanding how to get approval to access systems. Cover all types of logical access including Internet activity, not just business applications. Success factors include ensuring that the students know
  - The procedure to request logical access to systems
  - The bounds of acceptable use

  Ask questions to ensure understanding. For instance, is a user allowed to browse the Internet looking for hobby information at lunch on their own time? The answer to these questions will vary by organization.

- **Password selection**—User id and password combinations are the most common form of authentication in use today. Because such a large degree of information system security relies on effective password selection, it is critical that end users are trained on how to choose an effective yet easy-to-remember password. A password such as *HayRide1* is easy to remember but is also easy to crack (discover) by standard password cracking utilities. A password such as *S,t,t@mws0d,s1020t* is hard to crack but is also hard to remember. Ironically, the first password *HayRide1* may be more secure because it is easier to remember and less likely to be written down than the second password *S,t,t@mws0d,s1020t*. Passwords that are hard to remember are often written down and placed in such "secret" places as under the keyboard, under the mouse pad, in the top desk drawer, or posted on the monitor. The logic of most security "experts" is that the password *HayRide1* is more secure and is therefore the logic used on security certification exams. This is because of the tendency of individuals to write down hard-to-remember passwords (making them easy to find and use in an unauthorized manner). My experience shows that most users will embrace a passphrase. It can be something from their life or family such as "My Grandson JJ is 3 years old." So the resulting passphrase is "MGJJi3yo." Pretty solid password, highly resistant to attack, and easy to remember.

Success factors include ensuring that the attendees know
  - How to construct a secure password
  - The restrictions on password sharing
  - Methods to protect their passwords
  - The required password change interval

There are some groups that need a specific focus. In my experience, system or network administrators are more apt to ignore the basic password rules. When reviewing logs at one of my employers, I noticed that there were a significant number of IDs that had not been changed in months, just reset. When I went down to the manager of the group and showed him the logs, he admitted that is was his "internal department policy" to allow his engineers to simply reset the same password instead of changing it. After all, they had enough to remember without the bother of a password that changes every 90 days. We had a short but sweet discussion and expired all the administrator passwords that night. OK, I never said I was popular, but you have to protect the company.

Lesson learned? When doing ongoing awareness for administrators and network engineers, ensure they know that policies are for everyone.

- **Incident response**—contact whom? "What do I do?"
- **Handheld device security issues**—address both physical and wireless security issues. Mobile devices are a boon to business functions and a bane to information security purists. Although they enable portability of data, they are easily stolen, and the data can be compromised. Awareness training should include material on methods to physically secure these devices, protecting them from loss or theft.

    Success factors include ensuring the students know
    - How to secure a device while traveling
    - How to password protect sensitive documents and information
    - Their personal responsibility for the equipment
- **Use of encryption and the transmission of sensitive/confidential information over the Internet**—address agency policy, procedures, and technical contact for assistance.
- **Laptop security while on travel**—address both physical and information security issues. Include items such as the following:
    - Allow yourself enough time. Airline travel is a hassle that only gets worse when you don't allow enough time to get on your plane. Mistakes can be avoided if you slow down your pace.
    - Do not check your laptop with your other luggage.
    - Do not send your laptop through the airport X-ray conveyor belt UNTIL it's your turn to walk through the metal detector. That way, you'll be able to pick it up promptly when it comes out the other end and prevent anyone else from walking away with it. X-ray equipment will NOT harm the laptop.
    - When using the laptop, keep it with you and in sight at all times, including when on breaks while attending a conference.
    - Do not leave laptops in places with little protection, like a car or hotel room. Use a hotel safe to lock your laptop or use a strong cable to attach it to a secure object in the room.

- Do not keep the username and password with the computer.
- Do not subject your laptop to extreme climates or lock the laptop in your car's trunk for long periods of time.
- Limit confidential information transmission, such as any credit purchases and reservations or anything with a Social Security number. Unfamiliar networks are always potentially dangerous. If you need to, use a one-time password and then change it as soon as you can, once you're out of the public eye.

■ **Personally owned systems and software at work**—state whether allowed or not (e.g., copyrights).

■ **Software license restriction issues**—address when copies are allowed and not allowed. This is an issue with the potential to cause serious harm to an employee's career and/or the company. Ensure the attendee knows who to contact with questions, and that they understand basic unacceptable behavior including the following:

- Downloading and sharing MP3 files of music, videos, and games without permission of the copyright owner.
- Using corporate logos without permission.
- Scanning a photograph that has been published and using it without permission and/or attribution.
- Downloading licensed software from nonauthorized sites without the permission of the copyright or license holder.
- Making a movie file or a large segment of a movie available on a website without permission of the copyright owner.
- Using images found on the Internet without proper attribution and/or permission. Some images that are licensed under a Creative Commons License can be used by simply attributing the source. Others that do not specify a license may only be used after permission is granted from the creator.

■ **Supported/allowed software on organization systems**—part of configuration management.

■ **Access control issues**—address least privilege and separation of duties.

■ **Visitor control and physical access to spaces**—discuss applicable physical security policy and procedures, for example, challenge strangers, report unusual activity. Physical access is just as important to information security as logical controls. The best logical controls are ineffective without good physical security. Ensure that attendees understand their responsibility for physical security. Subjects should include visitor access to the facility, special restrictions for sensitive areas such as data centers, requirements to wear badges, and temporary employee access. Success factors include that the attendee

- Understands the organization's visitor policy
- Would ask a person without a badge for additional information
- Understands how to properly treat vendors

- **Desktop security**—discuss use of screensavers, restricting visitors' view of information on screen (preventing/limiting "shoulder surfing"), battery backup devices, allowed access to systems. Also discuss whether the company or department has a "Clean Desk" policy and what that means to the employee. Items to include are as follows:
  - A personal computer is anything but personal.
  - Practice good physical security.
  - Use up-to-date antivirus software.
  - Use a locked screensaver.
  - Disable file sharing unless set up by company IT.
  - Remove all spyware from your machine and how to get help.
- **Protect information subject to confidentiality concerns**—in systems, archived, on backup media, in hardcopy form, and until destroyed.
- **E-mail etiquette**—While not truly a security issue, a reminder of these principles can save embarrassment and reduce conflict for new employees.
  - Be concise. Longer messages are difficult to read, and most people will not read them carefully, so be sure to bold or underline important action items.
  - Avoid sarcasm. It can come across as rude or abrupt because the recipient can't gauge your body language.
  - Include a descriptive, concise subject line. Many people are inundated with e-mails, so give them a clue as to your content so that they can prioritize.
  - Don't send an e-mail when emotional or angry. Sit on it for 24 hours.
  - Use emoticons...sparsely. Sometimes, it helps communicate the tone of your message when you add an emoticon. However, only do so as necessary for it can end up being annoying to readers if you have too many.
  - Think twice before hitting "reply all." Ask yourself, "Do all these other people really need to hear my reply?" If not, reply only to the original writer.
  - Respond within 24 hours. If you require more time, let the sender know you're reviewing the e-mail and when you'll get back to that person.
  - NEVER USE ALL CAPS or all lowercase.
  - Start with a greeting (hi, hello, good morning, etc.) and end with a closing (Thanks; I appreciate your time; until then; best wishes, etc.).
  - Never try to resolve a conflict via e-mail. Back and forth e-mailing is almost guaranteed to make the situation worse. Pick up the phone, walk down the hall, or set up a time to talk.
- **Additional sources**—There are a variety of sources of material on security awareness that can be incorporated into an awareness program. The material can address a specific issue or, in some cases, can describe how to begin to develop an entire awareness program, session, or campaign. Sources of timely material may include the following:
  - E-mail advisories issued by industry-hosted news groups, academic institutions, or the organization's IT security office

- Professional organizations and vendors
- Online IT security daily news websites
- Periodicals
- Conferences, seminars, and courses

Awareness material can be developed using one theme at a time or created by combining a number of themes or messages into a presentation. For example, a poster or a slogan on an awareness tool should contain one theme, while an instructor-led session or web-based presentation can contain numerous themes. Regardless of the approach taken, the amount of information should not overwhelm the audience. Brief mention of requirements (policies), the problems that the requirements were designed to remedy, and actions to take are the major topics to be covered in a typical awareness presentation.

Keeping your audience in mind, there are specific areas that need to be covered when planning your awareness seminars. These areas are covered in the following sections.

Security Policy

It seems that policies appear to be written by people who actually wanted to be lawyers. On one of my job moves to a new company, I took the time to review the security policies. I was shocked to see the length of the documents.

For instance, the company password policy was pretty basic: 90-day expiration, 8 characters minimum, uppercase and lowercase with a special character, and no reusing the last 10 passwords. For some reason, the resulting policy was 12 pages long. So, what is the purpose of policies? I believe it is to guide the user to take appropriate actions. If a user needs to sort through a dozen pages to identify what is an acceptable password, they will get frustrated and never look again. You lose, the company loses, and the security posture loses.

Lesson learned? Creating targeted, usable policies are your job. Focus on the audience, ALWAYS.

Lesson learned? Create a high-level overview of all the policies to be included in the employee handbook. No legalese, just a clear, concise statement of employee facing policies.

Take the time to review the organization's high-level policies.

During awareness training, avoid a simple reading of the document, which is sure to put your audience to sleep. Use real-life examples, bringing the message to a personal level. Ensure that every attendee understands his or her personal responsibilities to safeguard the information assets of the organization. Success factors include ensuring that the employee

- Knows where to find the policies
- Knows where to seek clarification on policies
- Understands his or her responsibilities for compliance

Roles and Responsibilities

While it is important to understand the policies that require companies to develop and implement awareness and training, it is crucial that organizations understand who has responsibility for IT security awareness and training. This section identifies and describes those within an organization that have responsibility for IT security awareness and training. Some organizations have a mature IT security program, while other organizations may be struggling to achieve basic staffing, funding, and support. The form that an awareness and training program takes can vary greatly from company to company. This is due, in part, to the maturity of that program. One way to help ensure that a program matures is to develop and document IT security awareness and training responsibilities for those key positions upon which the success of the program depends.

Company Board and Executives

Executives must ensure that high priority is given to effective security awareness and training for the workforce. This includes implementation of a viable IT security program with a strong awareness and training component. Executives should

- Designate a CIO or another person responsible for the overall awareness program
- Assign responsibility for IT security to a person in the organization
- Ensure that an organization-wide IT security program is implemented, is well supported by resources and budget, and is effective
- Ensure that the organization has enough sufficiently trained personnel to protect its IT resources

Chief Information Officer

Chief Information Officers (CIOs) are tasked to administer training and oversee personnel with significant responsibilities for information security. CIOs should work with the organization's IT security program manager to

- Establish overall strategy for the IT security awareness and training program
- Ensure that the executives, senior managers, system and data owners, and others understand the concepts and strategy of the security awareness and training program, and are informed of the progress of the program's implementation

Differences in organizational culture are indicated by the placement of the IT security program, funding support, and access to and support by management.

IT security awareness and training responsibilities can be documented in company policy, position descriptions, and, where applicable, performance or individual development plans. The CIO must ensure that the agency's IT security awareness and training program is funded. They must also ensure that personnel with significant security responsibilities receive awareness training and ensure that all users are sufficiently trained in their security responsibilities. Since compliance audits require proof, the CIO must ensure that effective tracking and reporting mechanisms are in place.

Information Technology Security Program Manager

The IT security program manager has tactical-level responsibility for the awareness and training program. In this role, the program manager is responsible to ensure that awareness and training material developed is appropriate and timely for the intended audiences. Effective awareness and training material must be effectively deployed to reach the intended audience, and since continuous improvement is critical, users and managers have an effective way to provide feedback on the awareness and training material and its presentation. As part of this program, it is important to ensure that awareness and training material is reviewed periodically and updated when necessary.

Managers

Managers have responsibility for complying with IT security awareness and training requirements established for their users. Managers must work with the CIO and IT security program manager to meet shared responsibilities. For users in roles with significant security responsibilities, the manager should consider developing individual development plans as necessary.

Since professional certification is a standard measure of knowledge, management must promote the professional development and certification of the IT security program staff, full-time or part-time security officers, and others with significant security responsibilities. Managers must also ensure that all users (including contractors) of their systems are appropriately trained in how to fulfill their security responsibilities before allowing them access, understanding any specific rules for each system they use. The company will benefit through reduced errors and omissions by users because of a lack of awareness and/or training.

Users

Users are the largest audience in any organization and are the single most important group of people who can help reduce unintentional errors and IT vulnerabilities. Users may include employees, contractors (foreign or domestic), other agency personnel, visitors, guests, and other collaborators or associates requiring access. Users must understand and comply with agency security policies and procedures and be appropriately trained in the rules of behavior for the systems and applications to which they have access.

It is not a one-way street for users however. Users must work with management to meet training needs. It is also the user's responsibility to keep software/applications updated with security patches and to be aware of actions they can take to better protect their organization's information. These actions include, but are not limited to, proper password usage, data backup, proper antivirus protection, reporting any suspected incidents or violations of security policy, and following rules established to avoid social engineering attacks and rules to deter the spread of spam or viruses and worms.

Owners of information have the responsibility to determine the value and importance of that information resource and to authorize access and assign custody. Custodians of information have the obligation to include information protection concepts in the design, development, or selection of systems that store and process the information. Custodians of computer information resources are primarily application development areas within the Information Technology Department.

Although the specific roles may differ, everyone is responsible for understanding the security design of an organization, and their roles in that design. The roles are not universally applied. For example, a person may be a user of one type of information, and an owner of another type. Ensure that the training is applicable to all the needs of the attendees.

Eventually, an individual's responsibility may include the reporting of a security incident. Individuals must be trained how to report security incidents. Incidents will be more likely to be reported earlier if people understand the importance of information security to the organization. It has been shown that many incidents go unreported because people do not know how to do it, or are afraid that they will be viewed as a whistleblower. Ensure that people know that their anonymity will be protected. Management should commend individuals that report problems.

If the organization is successful, the attendees will understand their roles, understand the responsibilities related to a role, and know how to report violations.

Formal Training

Success factors include ensuring that the attendees understand

- The company stance regarding mandatory compliance with policies
- Potential disciplinary actions and penalties for noncompliance

Brown Bag Lunches

Most people are busy and pressed for time at the workplace.

Taking time out for a security awareness session is not always a high priority. Establishing a "brown bag" lunch session gives users an opportunity to hear a security message while enjoying lunch. Be creative, supply the beverages, or better yet, supply the dessert.

Note: You can also draw users in with creative speakers. One winner is a "Meet your Fed" day, where an FBI agent is invited to give a presentation on identity theft. A session topic such as this will most likely be standing room only, and will receive rave reviews.

The technical staff is a critical part of any organization and must not be forgotten in the security awareness-training plan. Although the standard message of strong passwords may be lost on a senior system administrator, a session on advanced server security may be necessary. Refresher courses on network security, LAN and WAN security, workstation security, firewall, and other security equipment should be held on a regular basis. Utilize personnel available from selected vendors as a source of instructors. They are usually free and provide pertinent content to the attendees.

Another area of formal training that should not be overlooked is the area of Security Certifications. The Certified Information Systems Security Professional (CISSP) and the Security Plus certifications are two that should be pursued by information security professionals. Holding formal and informal training in-house to prepare for the tests is an excellent method of increasing the technical security knowledge of an organization.

Organizational Newsletters

If you have a good security story to tell, tell it! A monthly security newsletter with relevant tips and tricks is a valuable method of conveying the security method. Incorporate timely topics such as identity theft, making it hit home for the general user. If you cannot issue your own security newsletter, talk to the publishers of the company newsletter and institute a "security corner" column. Talk to a cross section of users and find out what hot buttons they may have, or check with management or internal audit for current topics of interest.

Awareness Campaigns

Nothing builds awareness like a well-planned campaign. This differs from standard awareness training in that it may incorporate posters, giveaways, contests, and awards. It is meant to build enthusiasm for the subject matter. Posters should be eye-catching. There are many sources for ready-made posters. Figure 11.1 shows a sample awareness poster based on a "Top 10 Tips" theme.

Figure 11.1   Awareness poster.

Contests should be easy to enter and complete. A good suggestion is an entry blank that has questions regarding information security practices or policy. Correctly answering the questions on the entry blank makes it eligible for a drawing. Use security-specific prizes such as home antivirus/firewall software, or a fireproof document container for home use. Have the security awareness event finish with a presentation featuring a well-known external security speaker. A review of information security publications will offer up a host of potential speakers.

Tests and Quizzes

When were you last in class? What was your last exam score? These are questions easily answered in academia today. This same thought process needs to be applied to organizational training. It is not uncommon for an external examiner or auditor to request proof that users have been trained. The two necessary pieces of information to track success are attendance and competency.

There are many methods that can be used in tracking security awareness training. In smaller organizations, a simple sign-in sheet that is archived can be used. In larger organizations, an alliance with the corporate training department may enable attendance to be tracked with the corporate training system. Use established, approved curriculum so that each class as well as subject can be tracked. Each industry may have a different standard for retention of training records. In the absence of a corporate standard, three years is recommended.

Many sources of information security quizzes exist. A quick search of the Internet will yield more than a few results. They range from paper forms for small businesses to online systems with test tracking for large organizations. As always, remember that a little inducement goes a long way; offer the user a reward for the successful completion of the quiz. You can always award an Information Security coffee mug.

Funding the Security Awareness and Training Program

Once an awareness and training strategy has been agreed upon and priorities have been established, funding requirements must be added to the plan. A determination must be made regarding the extent of funding support to be allocated based on the implementation model. The CIO must send a clear message regarding expectations for compliance in this area. Approaches used to determine funding sources must be addressed by departments based on existing or anticipated budget and other department priorities. The security awareness and training plan must be viewed as a set of minimum requirements to be met, and those requirements must be supportable from a budget or contractual perspective. Contractual training requirements should be specified in binding documentation. Approaches used to express the funding requirement may include the following:

- Percentage of overall training budget
- Allocation per user by role (e.g., training for key security personnel and system administrators will be more costly than general security training for those in the organization not performing security-specific functions)
- Percentage of overall IT budget
- Explicit dollar allocations by component based on overall implementation costs

Problems in implementation of the security awareness and training plan may occur when security awareness and training initiatives are deemed to be lower in priority than other departmental initiatives. It is the responsibility of the CIO to assess competing priorities and develop a strategy to address any shortfall in funding that may affect the department's ability to comply with existing security training requirements. This may mean adjusting the awareness and training strategy to be more in line with available budget, lobbying for additional funding, or directing a reallocation of current resources. It may also mean that the implementation plan may be phased in over some predefined time period as funding becomes available.

Summary

Security awareness training must bring the message home to the user. The subject matter must be presented in a manner that is relevant to their lifestyle and current position. Users must understand that information security is in place to protect their work. If a security event happens that was their fault, it may be their work that is lost as well as the work of others. Simply reporting that the company lost a large amount of money in dealing with a security breach does not bring the issue home. However, describing the hours of effort required repairing or reconstructing the systems brings the issue down to a more personal level and makes an impact that users will remember.

Focus on the things they are expected to do daily in their job. Ensure that what you are asking them to do is achievable and that you have given them the tools to be successful. For example, don't tell them they should shred all paper reports for disposal without ensuring that shredders are available in their work areas. The training is your formal opportunity to get in front of the only people who can truly affect the success or failure of your information security program. Without the end user's attention and cooperation, there can be no Information Security program at an organization.

While we focused on Awareness Training in this section, it is important to understand that there are multiple types of continuing education required to augment the security of your organization. The National Institute of Standards and Technology (NIST) states that a successful IT security program consists of (1) developing an IT security policy that reflects business needs tempered by known risks; (2) informing users of their IT security responsibilities, as documented in departmental security policy and procedures; and (3) establishing processes for monitoring and reviewing the program.

Security awareness and training should be focused on the organization's entire user population. Management should set the example for proper IT security behavior within an organization. An awareness program should begin with an effort that can be deployed and implemented in various ways and is aimed at all levels of the organization including senior and executive managers. The effectiveness of this effort will usually determine the effectiveness of the awareness and training program. This is also true for a successful IT security program.

Learning is a continuum; it starts with awareness, builds to training, and evolves into education. An effective IT security awareness and training program can succeed only if the material used in the program is firmly based on the company security policy. If policies are written clearly and concisely, then the awareness and training material—based on the policies—will be built on a firm foundation.

Security awareness efforts are designed to change behavior or reinforce good security practices. Awareness is defined in NIST Special Publication 800-16 as follows:

Awareness is not training. The purpose of awareness presentations is simply to focus attention on security. Awareness presentations are intended to allow individuals to recognize IT security concerns and respond accordingly.

In awareness activities, the learner is the recipient of information, whereas the learner in a training environment has a more active role. Awareness relies on reaching broad audiences with attractive packaging techniques. Training is more formal, having a goal of building knowledge and skills to facilitate the job performance.

An example of a topic for an awareness session (or awareness material to be distributed) is virus protection. The subject can simply and briefly be addressed by describing what a virus is, what can happen if a virus infects a user's system, what the user should do to protect the system, and what the user should do if a virus is discovered.

A bridge or transitional stage between awareness and training consists of what NIST Special Publication 800-16 calls *Security Basics and Literacy*. The basics and literacy material is a core set of terms, topics, and concepts. Once an organization has established a program that increases the general level of security awareness and vigilance, the basics and literacy material allow for the development or evolution of a more robust awareness program. It can also provide the foundation for the training program.

Training—The most significant difference between training and awareness is that training seeks to teach skills, which allow a person to perform a specific function, while awareness seeks to focus an individual's attention on an issue or set of issues. The skills acquired during training are built upon the awareness foundation, in particular, upon the security basics and literacy material. A training curriculum must not necessarily lead to a formal degree from an institution of higher learning; however, a training course may contain much of the same material found in a course that a college or university includes in a certificate or degree program.

An example of training is an IT security course for system administrators, which should address in detail the management controls, operational controls, and technical controls that should be implemented. Management controls include policy, IT security program management, risk management, and life-cycle security. Operational controls include personnel and user issues, contingency planning, incident handling, awareness and training, computer support and operations, and physical and environmental security issues. Technical controls include identification and authentication, logical access controls, audit trails, and cryptography.

Education—Education integrates all of the security skills and competencies of the various functional specialties into a common body of knowledge; adds a multi-disciplinary study of concepts, issues, and principles (technological and social); and strives to produce IT security specialists and professionals capable of vision and proactive response. Education gives the individual the ability to think about a new solution to a problem as opposed to reciting a canned solution to the problem they learned in a training class. Education helps the individual think strategically rather than tactically, which is the focus of training.

An example of education is a degree program at a college or university. Some people take a course or several courses to develop or enhance their skills in a particular discipline. This is training as opposed to education. Many colleges and universities offer certificate programs, wherein a student may take two, six, or eight classes, for example, in a related discipline, and is awarded a certificate upon completion. Often, these certificate programs are conducted as a joint effort between schools and software or hardware vendors. These programs are more characteristic of training than education. Those responsible for security training need to assess both types of programs and decide which one better addresses identified needs.

Professional Development—Professional development is intended to ensure that users, from beginner to the career security professional, possess a required level of knowledge and competence necessary for their specific roles. Professional development validates skills through certification. Such development and successful certification can be termed "professionalization." The preparatory work necessary, before testing for a certification, normally includes study of a prescribed body of knowledge or technical curriculum. Certifications may need to be supplemented by on-the-job experience.

Chapter 12

There Are Only Two Kinds of Organizations: Those That Know They've Been Compromised and Those That Don't Know Yet

The movement toward professionalization within the IT security field can be seen among IT security officers, IT security auditors, IT contractors, and system/network administrators, and is evolving. There are two types of certification: general and technical. The general certification focuses on establishing a foundation of knowledge on the many aspects of the IT security profession. The technical certification focuses primarily on the technical security issues related to specific platforms, operating systems, vendor products, and so on.

Some agencies and organizations focus on IT security professionals with certifications as part of their recruitment efforts. Other organizations offer pay raises and bonuses to retain users with certifications and encourage others in the IT security field to seek certification.

Over the years, I have seen many cases of attackers (both internal and external) operating on company networks with impunity for months before being discovered. Years ago, the initial reports were from government systems; lately, it has been major banks and retailers making the same confessions. Why can't we sense the bad guys? What is wrong with our approach to intrusion detection?

I had a personal experience, which led me to believe that there are only two kinds of companies, those that have been compromised and those that don't know it yet. While not a breach, I did get a call from a recording industry representative wondering why my company was running a music-sharing site on its network. In very clear terms, they told me I had to make sure it went away immediately and that they would be actively monitoring for further copyright issues. They were nice enough to give me the IP address, so we went right to work. We all envisioned an uber hacker who had compromised our defenses to set up an illicit music-sharing server share on our network. Instead, we found a network engineer's PC. He was shocked when we told him about the call, and swore he wasn't in the music-sharing business. So we looked at his laptop and found that in order to move files from home to work, he had set up an unauthenticated FTP server open to the Internet. He felt that no one would find it, and besides he was quite the tech god himself. He decided he would accept the risk for the company. Well, it was found, and the bad guy downloaded megs of music files, and shared the address with his friends. Malicious intent by the network engineer? No. Potentially damaging to the reputation of the company? Heck yes! If the Recording Industry Association of America (RIAA) had found that we did not do enough to stop this kind of copyright abuse from taking place, they could have sued the company in a very public way. They could have decided to make the company a very public example of what can happen to those who don't take adequate care. It doesn't take a major breach to hurt a company's reputation.

Sadly, compromises go on all the time. In many cases, it is your own employees. Fortunately, in most employee cases, it is a matter of them downloading licensed software the company has on its file shares and using it for their own personal use or obtaining personal data on other employees. Typically, it is not to cause damage to the company or for personal financial gain.

Do not underestimate the damage employees can cause. Just a single breach can cost a company hundreds of thousands of dollars not even counting the damage that may result to the company's reputation. So you need to protect against a single breach and not just mass penetrations.

Internal compromises are much more difficult to protect against. Employees already have access to a multitude of systems and networks. The IT staff in most cases pretty much has the keys to the entire kingdom. Certainly your database administrators have access to a considerable amount of data. Your employees also have a larger number of ways to get the data out of the building than your typical external hacker. Employees can dump data to CDs, DVDs, thumb drives, external drives, and even printers. They can physically remove storage media such as a hard drive from a PC and secret it out of the building.

A few years ago in Florida, a call center employee was convicted of stealing sensitive information. It seems that she had been contacted by a bad guy, who offered her money for every good credit card number she would give to him. So, she started taking information out with her when she went home and selling it to her contact. It may have started small, but it was reported that over five years she made about $300,000. It was only when the losses started ramping up that the company started an investigation, which led to her arrest. This was completely internal and perpetrated by a trusted employee.

Lesson learned? Compromises are not just the result of outside actors.

There are a number of data loss prevention (DLP) tools out there that can help stem the flow of information out of the building. DLP is a tool, not a panacea, as it requires configuration and tuning to meet business requirements. Configuring and monitoring these tools can be a challenge and even they cannot account for every contingency.

Do you know how many e-mails leave your environment every day? If they have attachments, do you know if sensitive information is contained within them? A company with whom I work receives about 20 million e-mails per month. About 80% of them are spam or junk and not delivered. That leaves about four million e-mails delivered. Assuming that 20% of them are answered, that results in 800,000 opportunities for an employee to send sensitive information in an e-mail. That is about 26,000 chances a day including weekends. Depending on the type of data loss experienced, an organization can suffer a variety of consequences, but in nearly all cases, it's both a financial and reputation cost.

Loss Types

We can divide data loss into two broad categories:

The first general category is referred to as **Leakage**. We see this when customer databases are hacked, usually falling into the news category of Identity Theft. We have seen hundreds of millions of identities and other sensitive data exposed from healthcare firms, financial firms, and retailers. We also see this when an insider intentionally or unintentionally sends sensitive information out in or attached to an e-mail.

Second is **Loss**. This is where the data are no longer available to the organization from which they were stolen. This results in a loss of availability. Another incident that falls into this category is the theft or loss of a laptop or thumb drive.

Consequences of Loss

As with other security incidents, data loss incidents can result in significant cost and reputational loss. Costs to the organization might be much more severe and could include liability costs or sanctions and fines that aren't always covered by corporate insurance policies. Additionally, the organization could face increased litigation or regulatory scrutiny for years to come.

How Can DLP Help?

Key drivers of privacy mandates include government or industry rules and intellectual property protection. The Health Insurance Portability and Accountability Act of 1996 requires that to ensure privacy and confidentiality, all patient healthcare information must be protected when electronically stored, maintained, or transmitted. The Gramm–Leach–Bliley Act of 1999 mandates privacy and protection of customer records maintained by financial institutions.

The Privacy Act of 1974 prohibits disclosure of information in personal records by any means of communication to any person or agency, except pursuant to certain statutory exceptions or to a written request by, or with the prior written consent of, the individual to whom the record pertains.

The Federal Information Security Management Act of 2002 provides a comprehensive framework for ensuring the effectiveness of information security controls on information resources that supported federal operations and assets.

The Payment Card Industry Data Security Standards helps organizations that process card payments prevent credit card fraud through increased controls around data and its exposure to compromise. Government and industry requirements are arguably the biggest drivers of DLP. In addition, many states have passed data privacy or breach notification laws that require organizations to notify consumers when their information might have been exposed.

Prevention Approach

DLP is an enterprise program targeted on stopping various sensitive data from leaving the organization. Today's DLP systems allow organizations to specify rules to detect sensitive information, which may be included in an e-mail or attachment. Many of the current offerings come with predefined rules for healthcare, financial services, and so on.

> At the time when DLP first came out, we were an early adopter. The DLP came preconfigured with standard templates for all the biggies: Social Security Number, Credit Card Number, and so on. We installed, thankfully, in the warn not block mode, and turned it on. It was as if we just launched a denial of service attack against our security mailbox. As it turns out, one of our business units had nine-digit part numbers. In the early days of DLP, the systems were not sophisticated enough to differentiate between the groupings of the numbers. Nine digits were nine digits.

Lesson learned? Tools must be configured to meet the needs of the business. Just as in this case, out-of-the-box controls seldom work well in any business.

Sensitive data can be stolen by many means. Just taking screenshots of sensitive data and e-mailing it as an attached image can foil most DLP tools. If you have functions with access to sensitive data like a help desk, you may want to restrict their ability to send to non-company e-mails from their desk. Most help desk providers that handle credit card information have strict policies for the work environment. However, sometimes where the help desk function is not a major department, the risk is ignored. The Payment Card Industry has specific requirements for handling credit card information. It applies to all functions that process or store card data. The following is a sample credit card information handling guideline/policy you can use as a basis for your own.

PCI DSS Credit Card Guidelines

> <COMPANY> accepts credit cards to provide a convenient way to handle business transactions. Credit cards must be processed in compliance with Payment Card Industry Data Security Standard (PCI DSS) requirements. The purpose of this document is to establish basic guidelines for accepting, processing, and storing or transmitting cardholder data to ensure PCI DSS compliance.

Guidelines

- Assignment of user privileges to Cardholder Data is to be based on individual job classification and function. The least amount of access necessary to perform job responsibilities is to be granted.
- Any job position that requires access to stored Cardholder Data will be considered security sensitive. Departments are to perform applicable background checks on potential employees who will have access to systems, networks, or cardholder data.
- Personnel involved in credit card processing, transmitting, or storing must attend card security training every year.
- Any person processing credit card information must agree not to disclose or acquire any information concerning a cardholder's credit card account without the cardholder's consent. Employees must sign and acknowledge that they have read and understood <COMPANY> and departmental payment card data security policies and procedures.
- Sensitive cardholder data (full account number, card type, expiration, PIN, and card-validation code [three-digit or four-digit value printed on the front or back of the card]) are NOT to be stored in any way.
- Credit card numbers should never be stored on a personal computer. E-mail, unsecured fax, or unsecure instant messaging systems are never to be used to transmit credit card numbers.
- All records that include cardholder data, including physical security of paper and electronic media (including computers, removable electronic media, receipts, reports, faxes, etc.) are to be in a secure environment. Secured environments include locked drawers and safes, with limited access to only individuals who are processing the credit card transaction. Departments must conduct an inventory of media as well as maintain inventory logs and audit trails of all paper and electronic media.
- Any cardholder information in paper format (recording, writing down or storing cardholder information) is to be kept at a minimum. Processing is performed as soon as possible and the credit card number is immediately blacked out to the last four digits. In addition, any Sensitive Cardholder Data should be masked.

- Stored credit card information and merchant receipts will be retained according to the respective <COMPANY> data retention policy (no longer than 18 months) so long as there is a business, legal, and/or regulatory purpose.
- Departments will notify information security regarding any technology changes affecting transaction processing.
- Network vulnerability scans shall be performed on machines that are involved in the processing of credit/debit cards on at least a quarterly basis and after any significant change in the network.

Credit Card Processing Procedures

With the help of Information Security, each department that processes, stores, or transmits cardholder data must complete an annual self-assessment questionnaire to ensure PCI DSS compliance. For specific requirements, please visit https://www.pcisecuritystandards.org/.

People usually get caught when they get greedy. The hacker that infiltrates your environment can remain undetected if they limit the amount of data they move across and out of your network. Small blips tend to go unnoticed. The thief walking out of your neighbor's house with diamonds stuffed in his pockets is less likely to draw attention than the one with the 65″ flat screen TV across their back. Even though your system administrators can grab a lot of information very quickly, don't discount the damage that can be caused by the average user. Their thefts may be smaller in nature but can go undetected for a much longer period of time, resulting in a much bigger cost to the company.

The employee who walks out with a DVD or thumb drive will go unnoticed. When they start carrying out whole PCs, then their crime spree will quickly come to an end. It is precisely these small thefts that actually embolden the perpetrators to escalate their activities. Back in the 1990s, New York City recognized this phenomenon and enacted their "Broken Windows" concept of crime fighting. The theory is that by cracking down on smaller offenses, there will be less likelihood that bigger offenses will occur. The success of this program in New York would seem to validate the theory. In the corporate environment, we need to similarly crack down on the smaller offenses. Besides the very fact that downloading licensed software is illegal and could jeopardize the company if caught by the vendor, by not enforcing copyright laws, it sends a message to the employees that certain socially unacceptable behaviors will be tolerated. Employees then continue to try and push the envelope until they get caught.

The best way to keep employees honest is to have a zero tolerance policy for anything not socially acceptable. I have to be careful using the term "socially acceptable." In today's society, a lot more appears to be socially acceptable than in the past. Probably, better that the company set the bar for what will be tolerated and well publicize this position. Then, the company has to strictly enforce this standard for it to carry any weight.

Employee screenings are becoming the norm across most industries. These are going beyond just a drug test. People's backgrounds and personalities are being far more heavily scrutinized these days. Besides background checks covering financial and legal history, employees are being subjected to psychological testing. We can certainly debate the ethics of all of this by corporations, but it certainly can identify potential problem employees. Unfortunately, the risk of false positives clearly exists. Good potential employees can be summarily excluded due to a bad credit check, not realizing they just went through a horrible divorce or had a major medical issue and they are now trying to rebuild their lives. Preventing people from getting a job only accelerates their slide into criminal activities. Guess which company might be high on their list?

Employee Loyalty Is a Factor

Remember when it was not uncommon for multiple generations of a family to work for the same company. Growing up in Wisconsin, there was a brewery that was one of those industries. Fathers and family members recommended other family members. Loyalty to the company was high. Company picnics, Christmas parties, all built the company family. Unfortunately, that has gone by the wayside in our new economy. When the beer business went down, the brewery was sold to a larger company, which was eventually sold to a larger brewery. Employees were laid off, buildings were closed, and while the brand still exists, it is not brewed in Wisconsin anymore. Do you think that employees losing their jobs after all those years were more or less likely to steal company information or equipment?

In a poor economy, employers have their pick of potential new employees. Sadly, employers also realize that they can dump a lot of existing employees and replace them with lower-paid staff either from the local economy or by using off-shore resources. This prevalent trend has caused employee loyalty to be a thing of the past. Employee loyalty is a critical factor in reducing internal threats. In a poor economy, expect greater instances of criminal activities. The Ponemon Institute, which conducts independent research on privacy, data protection, and information security policy, found in a survey conducted during the height of the economic downturn that of almost 1000 laid-off individuals, an astonishing 59% admitted keeping company data after leaving the business.

Corporations also tend to cut pay and benefits not only in poor economies but also whenever they want to boost earnings and the stock price. Unfortunately, these cuts are not across the board. While workers struggle to make ends meet, executives are rewarding themselves with huge bonuses, pay raises, and other perks. Resentment or worse by the employees is inevitable. What the executives fail to grasp is just how much damage a single employee can wreak. Poor managerial decisions related to employees may momentarily boost the stock but end up costing a career. A Verizon data loss report found that individuals with insider knowledge of organizations account for a significant percentage of all breaches. This same report also revealed that each internal incident compromised on average 100,000 individual pieces of sensitive information. This is at least 60,000 more pieces than the average external hack.

One approach that can be employed to guard against internal as well as external threats to some degree is by rewarding the reporting of any suspicious behavior that leads to identifying a bona fide risk to the company. People tend not to want to get involved, so by providing incentives, this will help change their attitude. Such programs need to be well crafted to avoid witch-hunts and personal vendettas. Anonymity also needs to be guaranteed. If monitoring is part of a person's normal job responsibilities, then naturally their specific monitoring activities need to be excluded from the reward program. Your employees are in the trenches each day, so they would naturally be in a better position to detect things that are out of the norm. If morale is very low in your company, do not expect great successes from such a program. You might find the employees actually rooting for the bad guys.

Key Point: Be sure and get Human Resource's buy-in for any suspicious reporting program. It may be a good idea for them to monitor the reports and distribute them for investigation. Whistleblower protection must be guaranteed or the program will die.

So besides using your employees for monitoring purposes, there are other options available to you. Cameras are a great deterrent to physical theft. There are two trains of thought on the use of cameras. One is to make them very visible so people know they are being watched. The drawback to this approach is once people know where all the cameras are located they can figure out ways to avoid their constant stare. Cameras in the bathrooms are forbidden. Carrying a stack of 50 papers into the bathroom and coming out with 48 will be totally undetectable. People also tend to dislike being monitored, so while a few cameras might be tolerated, employee resentment will grow exponentially as more cameras are added. Cameras should be sold to the employees as a safety feature and not a theft deterrent.

The other approach is to conceal the cameras. They will only act as a deterrent, though, if you acknowledge their presence without revealing their exact locations. You really should strive for deterrence and not apprehension. Catching the perpetrator after the fact may be too late, especially when related to cybercrimes. Plus, it is better to prevent good people from being tempted to pursue criminal activities. The one major drawback to cameras is that someone has to be monitoring them for real-time prevention. Otherwise, you need to review the tapes, which are rarely done unless a real or suspected incident has already occurred.

Let's not forget that employees aren't the only ones that have full access to corporate facilities and assets. While the cleaners have historically borne the brunt of accusations related to thievery, you also have physical security personnel, vendors, contractors, and a host of delivery services. It does not take much to attach a key-logging device on a computer and then retrieve it a few days later. While such devices might be more easily detected on a laptop, few people peer behind their desktop computers, which typically sit on the floor under their desk. There is a lot to be said for utilizing dumb terminals.

We all have our way of doing things. We tend to get into a pattern and stick to it unless something jars us from our routine. We may commute the same way to work every day until one day you notice a speed trap setup along your route. We get into routines at work as well. People might review logs a certain way, focusing on particular items that their experience has taught them as being important. We might use tools that we are comfortable using and never explore newer technologies. Third-party comprehensive audits are a necessity. You need an unbiased set of eyes looking at your environment. Like the ecosphere discussed earlier, third-party audits will shake up the environment and hopefully breathe new life into it or prevent someone from taking the life out of it.

Not all employees are bad, but even the good employees can place the company in jeopardy. Employees can cause a company breach in one of several ways. It can be intentional with malice, your typical insider threat. It can be intentional without malice, such as not following established policies or procedures in the mistaken belief some greater benefit will be achieved. Lastly, it can simply be unintentional. As we have discussed, it can include a visit to a malicious website or opening an infected e-mail attachment.

By only allowing access to data on a "need to know" basis, you greatly reduce your risks. This can be problematic with administrators typically having access to everything. Segregating responsibilities so your administrators only have access to certain pieces of the environment will help. Placing the sensitive data behind another layer of security such as password protecting files or using file level encryption will also work.

Key Point: Use tools designed to monitor administrative access (Super Users). These tools monitor the actions taken by those with sweeping rights and log those actions to a location NOT ACCESSIBLE to the system admins. You can use these tools for internal or external super users, as we all probably have systems that are administered for the company externally. The external auditors and regulators will want to see proof that you do this type of monitoring.

Of course, you have to know what data are sensitive and who has a legitimate need to see these data. Too often, the easy route is taken and everyone in a particular department or division is given access to certain data rather than really sitting down and evaluating the situation. Determining whether access should be granted based on an individual or a role is also a decision point that has to be made. In general, it is better to use role-based accesses since it is easier to justify the role as well as administer the access.

Whether the data are truly sensitive can be a challenge to determine sometimes. Data classification schemes help immensely but are difficult to implement and support. Separating sensitive data from other data makes managing and securing the sensitive data easier. By placing your secure data in specific locations, you can tightly control and monitor access. You need then only focus your DLP-type scanning to the other areas of your network and not waste resources and time scanning what you already know has sensitive information.

Auditing tools can greatly assist in determining who accessed what data and when. The drawback to this is the size of the log files that are created. You have to determine how long you wish to keep these data. Since some breaches go undetected for months at a time, you may want to keep your log files for quite some time.

The best way to handle the intentional without malice situations is by strictly enforcing the security policies and standards. Sometimes you have to make someone the example. It's a painful lesson, but without it, employees will continue to push the envelope.

The bad guys, just like everyone else, like to do things the easy way. Compromising employee end points is a much easier way to penetrate a corporation than by directly attacking the networks. Vulnerabilities in operating systems and applications that are left unpatched give the bad buys an opportunity to install their malware on the employee end point devices. It is not difficult for the bad guys to find the vulnerabilities. They increasingly are relying on exploit kits. Exploit kits are prepackaged software that can recognize vulnerabilities and install a malicious payload. It is commercial software available to hackers that can cost thousands of dollars. New to the cyber attack world are those who will attack others for you for a fee. The DarkWeb has many sites with price lists depending on what you want and how many computers you wish to attack. The really scary part? Now you don't have to have mad technical skills to be a hacker, you just need a Bitcoin account.

The myriad of file-sharing sites, software download sites, music-sharing sites, and so on are routinely exploited by the bad guys. While many of these sites are known and can be blacklisted, new ones continually pop up. Your employee can simply use their Internet search engine to search for the latest song by XYZ and they will come across dozens of sites offering them the ability to download it for free. Along with the free song comes embedded malware and the cybercriminals are now in your environment.

Once inside your environment, the bad guys can operate at their leisure. Time is on their side. Mandiant reports that the median time to detect an intrusion is well over a year. They can steal your data little by little or use your resources for other nefarious purposes. They may come and go and you may never even know they were there. Charles Baudelaire, a French poet, once said, "The greatest trick the devil ever pulled was convincing the world he doesn't exist." This is exactly what the hackers hope to achieve in your environment. It is only because of a third-party notification that most companies discover they have been compromised. An amazing 94% of victims according to Mandiant.

Cybercriminals come in several flavors. At the top of the food chain are the state-sponsored cybercriminals, which are no different than ordinary spies. They are at the top of the food chain because they are very well funded and equipped. Collecting intelligence and corporate secrets is their primary objective. Normally, direct economic gain or causing harm is not their immediate goal but not always. Sony was allegedly attacked by North Korea in retribution for a film they were producing that cast North Korea in a bad light. The infiltrators stole unreleased movies and distributed them across the Internet, causing considerable financial harm to Sony. State-sponsored cybercriminals may also cause isolated harm as they test their capabilities to be able to produce wide-scale damage at some future time.

Next down on the food chain are the cybercriminals supported by organized crime. In these cases, financial gain is the primary driver. While not as well funded and supported as state-sponsored cybercriminals, they are certainly a force to be reckoned with. Just like the bootleggers of the 1920s produced very powerful criminal elements, so does the Internet with its global reach and almost unlimited targets of opportunity. The financial incentive is very strong for these groups to continue to develop and expand their cybercrime resources.

Then you have organized groups with social agendas such as Anonymous. Their intents can vary widely from just trying to make a political statement to actually imposing financial harm. Usually, they are striving to promote human liberties, information ethics, and free speech, but their methods can be destructive and illegal. What started out as somewhat harmless prank calls and the sending of black faxes to waste fax toner to the Church of Scientology quickly escalated into full-blown Distributed Denial of Service attacks. The power of such groups cannot be underestimated. Anonymous took on the Los Zetas cartel, a Mexican drug cartel noted for its brutality, when the cartel kidnapped a fellow Anonymous member that they considered troublesome. Anonymous threatened to release details of those sympathetic to the cartel if their comrade wasn't released. He was eventually released. Whether you make toys or guns, there is bound to be some social group out there that has issues with your company's products, policies, or practices.

Further down the food chain are your lone wolves. These are people sitting in the relative comfort of their home or some Internet café or even within your own company using your resources to penetrate other organizations for personal gain. We have all heard the stories of employees running side businesses from their place of employment. The Internet has made this so much easier. These employees can also make your company an unsuspecting target through their actions. Lone wolves typically have more modest goals but can still cause considerable harm to a company financially or to its reputation. Lone wolves can be socially motivated, financially motivated, or revenge motivated such as a terminated employee or a highly dissatisfied customer. The end result is the same; the company is harmed in some way. In some ways, they are easier to catch due to less sophistication in their tools and methods. Though by the time you actually catch them, the damage may already have been done.

Lastly, you have the curiosity seekers. These are people meaning no damage at all. Some are just kids experimenting with their programming skills. Others may be honest White Hats looking for vulnerabilities that they can expose for recognition of their skills and as public service. You may have employees just trying to find out how their salary compares to others in the company. While no harm may be their goal, nonetheless harm can result.

The real challenge is distinguishing among the different types of hackers. Though, in the end, does it really matter? The potential for harm exists for every type, so you need to defend yourself regardless.

What Can You Do?

Have a plan: What will you do if you are attacked or breached? Do you have a written plan? Has it been tested? Has it been reviewed by an external expert? Does it include your business partners?

If you don't have one, I have included a sample template in the back of this book. Remember, you must make it work within your company. One size does not fit all.

Test your plan: Gather the people listed in the plan, shut the door and tell them the network has crashed and it may or may not be the result of a malicious attack. Make it painful. One person I know said the high point of his career was when the White House ran a simulation, he got to put a sticky note on the President's BlackBerry saying it was out of service.

Remember earlier when we discussed preparing for the moment when you can be excellent? This is part of the preparation work.

Prepare and train a core group of experts: I call these folks my "Cyber First Responders." Every emergency needs specialists capable of triaging the situation. These are those people in your organization. Look for content from the Certified

Ethical Hacker program, or other forensic certifications as training material. Recognize them, give them an incentive to excel.

Penetration Tests are mandatory! Have a world-class firm test your defenses and response programs. These firms have seen all types of attacks and the methods by which the bad guys exploited the company. Get the reports and FIX THE ISSUES! You would not believe how many pen test reports get filed away with no follow-up.

Don't be a statistic: It is up to you as the CISO to build the best program you can. The company will assume some risk and only give you so much funding. If you have done your job all around in talking to senior management and educating the company, you should have adequate resources.

I'd personally challenge you to come to work every day assuming you've been compromised, and spend time proving to your satisfaction that you haven't. If you tell me you can't, what is your program missing?

Chapter 13

In Information Security, Just Like in Life, Evolution Is Always Preferable to Extinction

Technology marches on—sometimes when you are immersed in controls, it is easy to forget. A good security person is always concerned with data walking out the door, right? Well, sometimes it seems that the technology vendors have made it their personal mission to drive security folks completely bonkers. Our only path is to follow the wisdom of the old prayer:

> Please grant me the serenity to accept the things I cannot change; courage to change the things I can; and wisdom to know the difference.

Many times, in our efforts to secure the business from all threats, we forget to speak the language of business. Business must change as its customer base does. They can't sell to Millennials with the same strategies that they used to sell to Baby Boomers. Millennials are tech savvy, want to use social media, want information at their fingertips, and use technology to stay in touch. If you only advertise in the

169

Sunday paper and avoid electronic marketing, your company will go the way of the dinosaur.

The function of information security is to allow the business to operate and grow securely. If Security is not in lock step with the business, how can we enable the business? If you are not in tune with the 3- to 5-year strategic plan for the business, how do you know what to focus on for your strategic plan?

Case in point:

BlackBerry created waves in the market by offering a device that could send and receive e-mail. This caused serious concern in the info security space as it was a whole new vector by which sensitive e-mails could be exposed. What if the exec lost his device? And while we are at it, remember that the first devices were brought in by executives who were not interested in having a login for their device.

There were those who sought to squash the devices and those who decided to offer limited services to a few key people. Soon after security tools came out, other manufacturers started to offer smartphones, and we know today the state of the industry.

How about you? What would you have done, or did do? Personally, I was aware enough to place the technology in my three-year security plan and let the company know that if this technology would proliferate, there would be costs and tools required.

It is never pleasant when common sense hits you in the face and shows you there is a lesson to be learned. I realized in that instant that as technology marches on, we must design and implement compensating controls to allow the safe use of new technology. We may be able to delay the introduction of new technology, but we will eventually have to cave in. Taking a curmudgeon approach also makes the security profession look inflexible and not tuned to the business. Staying an inflexible course is the fast lane to career extinction.

A few years ago at another company, we had a major culture shift when an industry-recognized company released a radically new piece of technology called the iPhone. Most businesses were completely BlackBerry and there was not much tolerance for anything new. Today, the iPhone is pretty much the de facto standard business mobile phone. BlackBerry, on the other hand, has basically gone the way of the dinosaur, primarily due to its slowness and reluctance in adapting to the times.

In security, we can never rest on our laurels. The lion devours the slowest in the pack. Though being the leader in the pack has its own set of perils. You could be galloping full speed toward the edge of a cliff. When it comes to security, the safest place might just be in the middle of the pack.

Simply from a morale perspective, you need to keep your systems up to date. People don't want to be working with outdated technology. It is not good for their professional development and it makes their jobs harder since newer technology has much needed new functions and features.

When I've needed to drive home the need to upgrade company systems, I've asked during a meeting for business leaders to pull out their cell phones. I then ask them how old their cellphone is or when was the last time they updated the software. Chances are it is highly unlikely any are more than two years old. Why should the company's future ride on outdated systems?

Flexibility is also a crucial characteristic of the successful CISO. The easiest target for the German U-boats (submarines) in World War II was the convoy ship that continued on a steady course. The security afforded by the convoy was negated if a ship would not zig now and then. Such maneuvers complicated the submarine commander's firing solution and could potentially put a greater distance between the two adversaries, thus placing the ship out of reach of the submarine's weapons.

The hackers are very much like a submarine. They are out there but we can't see them. However, they have us clearly in their sights. They are relatively small in number compared to their potential targets yet can impart considerable damage. US submarines in World War II comprised just 2% of the US Navy fleet, yet they accounted for the destruction of over 30% of the Japanese naval fleet and over 60% of the Japanese merchant fleet. They take their time. They search for the right targets. They probe for weaknesses in the lines of defense. When the time is right, they attack quickly and then as quickly disappear into the depths, leaving chaos and destruction behind. Modern submarines are maybe even more so like hackers in that they are less interested in wide-scale destruction and more interested in collecting intelligence without being detected. The longer a security breach goes undetected, the better the payoff for the perpetrators. Once the breach is detected, the value of the information gained drops off rapidly.

As a CISO, you need to recognize when things are not working and be willing to "zig." Even if things are working, changing things up a bit complicates the "firing solution" for the hacker. Changing how you do things internally can reveal weaknesses previously not recognized. As the saying goes, the first sign of insanity is when you do things the same way all the time yet expect different results. Using a different scanning tool now and then is a very effective way to find holes in your environment missed by your standard tool.

Security Strategic Planning

Do you have a strategic security plan tied to the business? Can you link your security projects and programs to a business initiative or need? If you can't, do you have problems getting yearly funding for the important security initiatives. Do you find yourself saying, "The Execs just don't get it?" Depending on how you answer the above questions, you may have a credibility gap with the executives of your company. In fact, the execs may be saying, "The Security guys just don't get it…we are in business to make money." The sad truth is that many good CISOs have lost their jobs because they were viewed as out of touch with the business or irrelevant. It is up to YOU to make sure that does not happen: it is bad for you and even worse for the company. While you will have to develop what works for you or your company, let's discuss a sample method you can use to get started.

The Planning Cycle

Any strategic planning process without a feedback loop is an exercise in futility. Since a long-term plan requires constant tweaking to map to the changing business direction, we must develop feedback mechanisms and revisit them constantly. Deming called it the "Plan, Do, Check, Act" loop, which will require a few more steps.

Foundation/Strategy

Just what is it that the business expects you to do? Have you ever asked? What do you think you are supposed to do? Have you ever documented it? If so, what are the gaps, and who is involved in negotiating the middle ground? Sounds simple, but you'd be surprised at the number of CISOs who have a mission statement copied out of a book with no thought of business linkage.

So, start with an assumption of your mission, where you feel you are now, and a road map to get to where you want to be in the next one, two, and three years (Figure 13.1). Document it with all assumptions that got you there, as well as any interviews that supported the plan.

Assessment and Measurement

So, you've made your assumptions; time to check and see if fact supports your plan. Select an external reputable vendor and perform a penetration test, both internal and external. My personal approach is two-phased. First, give the test team access to a network jack in an office: no credentials, no account, just a wire and their laptops. This phase will tell you what a skilled attacker could do if given access to the network. Typically, the testers will start just watching traffic and, with the right tools, capture a user id and break the password on some system. In many cases, it

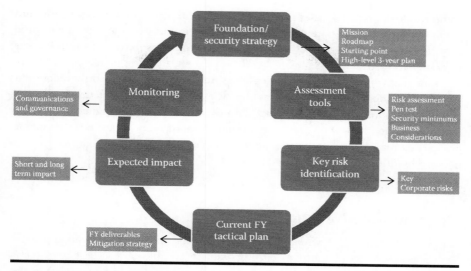

Figure 13.1   Security strategy.

is a system or device installed with the default account and password still in place. Once they get a foothold, it is just a matter of time until they escalate privileges until they get an administrator account. When that happens, the battle is over, you are owned. Let's be straight, there is no such thing as a pen test failure. You have taken the initiative to test and learn. When you understand how they got in, you can develop effective tools and processes to compensate for any weakness.

The second phase is to have the team do an outside-the-network scan and test. Similar to the first, you are looking for any weakness that could be exploited.

Key Tip: Be sure and define how far the testers can take action on any weakness found. Finding and identifying a vulnerability is a lot different from exploiting the vulnerability. Running an exploit may shut down or corrupt the target; if it is a production system, that is probably not a good thing. Typically, I do not allow exploiting a target on a test. If a finding is particularly troubling, I will schedule a secondary controlled test.

Key Risk Identification

Take all the findings from the penetration tests, along with any open audit findings and known issues, and define the key or primary risks that these issues present. For instance, if the testers found they could exploit systems because of missing patches and software updates, the key finding might be, "The lack of a formalized and monitored patching process places company assets at risk of compromise, which could result in financial losses or adverse publicity to the company." No geek babble, just a solid precise statement of what the risk is and why the company should care. There are a lot of Internet resources available on the subject of identifying key risks such as ISACA.org.

Now that you've defined a few risks, be sure to list them in a central repository. I refer to the document or system as the "Risk Tracker." It can be as simple as a spreadsheet as long as it lists the risk, definition, impact (high, medium, low), due date, and owner. Follow up and issue quarterly reports on progress to the executive group. Be organized and professional above all: disorganization will never get you good recognition or respect.

Develop the Strategic Plan

Let's look at Figure 13.2, which describes the inputs and outputs of a good plan.

The preparation of the plan encompasses three phases. The first is to compile the process inputs. These are mine; you should define the ones that make sense to you. These are the issues that you must take into account when defining which projects and programs you should drive as being the most impactful to the business.

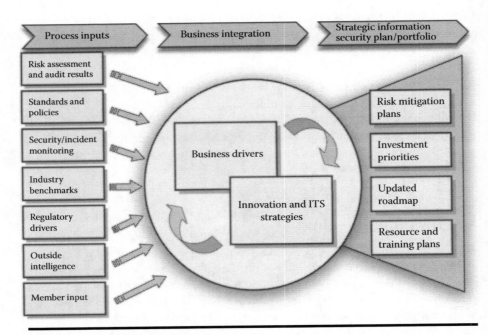

Figure 13.2   Security plan.

Process Inputs

Items to include when planning the projects and programs.

- Items from the Risk Tracker, Open Audit Items, any other risks identified. Be sure and include action items to address any critical or high-risk items. You must be able to show the Audit Committee of the Board of Directors that you are making progress in reducing risk for the company.
- Issues related to compliance with existing or new policies and procedures. They are not always yours so look around. It may be a new HR or Legal policy that you must support and for which you must supply reporting.
- Security Incident/Monitoring issues must be accounted for in your plan. What are you seeing? Is it different (type, intensity, source) from last year? What steps will you take to remediate? Be sure and include actionable items. If you remember the Target company breach, the papers reported that the security staff ignored multiple alerts that something was going wrong. What will you do to ensure that does not happen at your company?
- Benchmarks are critical. How many of you have been asked if the security at your company is comparable to a competitor or partner? How will you know if you have not asked? Find a few sources and have a meeting or call to discuss. Make sure you share information with the company as well as getting data. Typical things to ask:
  - How big is your staff?
  - What are your key metrics that you report to management?
  - What keeps you up at night?
  - Do you have a formal set of policies? Have you implemented any new ones and why?
  - As a percentage of company revenues or IT budget, how big is your budget?
  - What are your key projects for next year?
  - What new technologies are you looking at for this year?
- Regulatory Drivers are a major part of many security programs. Have you kept track of the new and emerging regulations? If so, what impact will they have on your projects? Are any technologies or processes required to support? Do you expect any new regulations over the span of the strategic plan? What are they and what was the source of the information? The successful CISO gets out ahead of the changes. You have a chance to show that you are a leader and a strategist, not just an isolated security function.
- Outside Intelligence is a critical piece of proactively identifying future threats and trends that will affect your company. If you do not subscribe to a world-class threat feed, get it in your budget and do so as soon as possible. You and your staff will never get the inside information and actionable intelligence that a threat feed will supply. I'm not just talking about the CVE vulnerability

feed. A good threat feed will supply plain English information as well as the motivation for a threat. Is it financially motivated, or political or trade secret theft driven? What country is the source? Do you have operations there?

■ Member or Customer Input is critical as customers are the ultimate consumer of your company's products and services. How would they like to interact with your company? What is the sales department saying about customer feedback? Are there authentication problems? What are their concerns about breaches and identity theft? All of these are drivers for your security programs, and they are a chance to tie your initiatives to a specific member or customer desire.

Business Integration: Tying your projects to Business need. A world-class CISO will be able to articulate how all the security initiatives support the needs of the Business and the IT projects and programs underway. Many new CISOs miss this piece thinking that the company should "get" security on its own. Look at it from their perspective. Why would they give you money to do something that does not support the ultimate company goal of making money?

As you can see from Figure 13.3, it does not have to be incredibly complex or sophisticated to get started. A simple table that shows the intersection of security goals to business goals is a great start. Everywhere there is a checkmark, be prepared to discuss why and what your group will do to address/support the interaction.

Information security and compliance program goals	Grow the company	Increase customer satisfaction	Deploy Salesforce.com CRM	Reduce operating costs by 5%	Establish sales presence in Europe
Prevent hacker- and threat-related downtime due to attack or compromise	✓	✓	✓	✓	✓
Improve performance and security of the ecosystem	✓	✓	✓	✓	✓
Provide a unified offering of threat alerting to all locations	✓	✓	✓	✓	✓
Protect the environment from attack while legacy apps are decommissioned	✓	✓		✓	✓
Security issues prevented, analyzed in advance	✓	✓		✓	✓
Achieve all regulatory and recertification goals	✓	✓	✓	✓	✓

Figure 13.3 Compliance program goals.

My best advice: start simple and small. Make sure it adds value and can be understood in a stand-alone document for a nontechnical Board member. Remember, we should never do security just for security's sake. It must address a business need; the better job you do in explaining it, the easier it will be for you to get support and funding.

Deliverables: Telling the company what you will do, when, and why. The odds are that the company doesn't keep you around because you are so good-looking or smart. Trust me, the company wants to know what it is getting from the money it is giving you. Remember, the executives must make decisions about where to get the best return on the limited capital they have to invest back in the company. You must be able to articulate the value of your activities to the overall company success. Never ever use a hammer to try and get money. Saying that a new regulation "demands" that a project be funded is a self-defeating strategy. Instead, work with legal to define the risk (financial, reputational) that noncompliance would bring. Also make sure that the right people in your firm weigh in on the issue as there are many facets to any regulatory or legal question. Make absolutely sure the execs hear a common line.

Risk Mitigation Plans must be clearly identified along with a cost–benefit analysis of mitigating the risk. Be prepared to answer the question, "What if we do nothing this year?"

Investment Priorities must be clearly identified so that the company can plan the financials for the year. If a project will not start until the third quarter, state it, and explain the rationale for the program being lower on the list than others. An easy way of illustrating it is to use a simple scoring method. My favorite is to rate each project against two factors; the first is the potential impact to the company if the issue the project addresses is exploited, and the second is the maturity of the EXISTING controls to address the issue. Figure 13.4 is a quick example.

Project	Description	Impact if not addressed 10 (high), 1 (low)	Effectiveness of existing controls 10 (low), 1 (high)
Intrusion detection expansion	Add sensors to internal segments to address internal threats	8	5
Digital leakage protection	Implement system to monitor for IP leaving company network	10	1
Security awareness training	Implement mandatory awareness training for all employees	4	5
Two factor VPN access	Security to address the new partner VPN system	7	2

Figure 13.4   Investment priorities.

When scored, it is a simple matter to make a powerful graphic that is easily understood by executive management. Let's take a look at Figure 13.5.

The placement of the bubbles on the chart clearly conveys the criticality of the project to even a casual observer. Remember, the plan you are preparing is to convey the high-level strategic plan and to prompt discussion, not explain each point in gory detail.

The Road Map is the next critical piece of information you must convey. This can be a simple Gantt chart that shows when each initiative will start and finish. Be sure the dates are achievable and realistic. There are few things worse than having to explain missed dates, even if the reasons are acceptable. Also, be careful what you name a project. My worst naming mistake ever was to name a project I expected to finish in October—Project October. Needless to say, it came in six months late, and at every update meeting, it was painfully obvious the project was late. I learned to survive a whole bunch of ribbing and being the butt of all sorts of jokes.

The Training Plan is yet another critical deliverable. Develop and document an all-encompassing plan that covers Training to support the initiatives, User Awareness Training, and Staff Development Training. Unless the company can use and execute on security tools and principles, they are useless. Never forget about the ongoing training necessary to secure an organization. It will pay back in both the short and long term. As I've said before, use "lunch and learn" sessions based on user interest. Please use outside speakers to provide interest and different opinions and viewpoints. Some of my best-attended sessions are when I use a local FBI or Secret Service agent to talk about cybercrime or identity theft. They are free, highly skilled, and eager to get the message out.

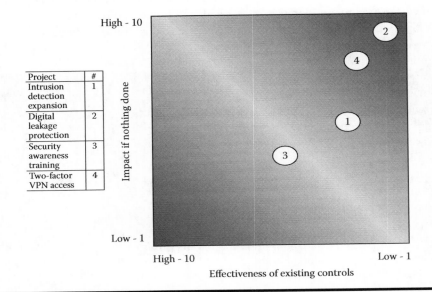

Figure 13.5   Impact versus effectiveness.

Money, Money, Money…

All this drives your funding planning. Develop a three-year projection, broken into quarterly buckets that includes the following:

Capital Expenditures

Your next year plan should be accurate. Given the process you just went through, there should be no surprises for the next 12 months. Months 13–24 should be fairly solid, but realize that you will have the next year strategic planning cycle to hone the numbers. Months 25–36 will be strictly projection. Why go through this process? It lets the company know that you plan and have a process to address new and emerging risks. It also allows you to project expenditures to the finance folks, and they will appreciate the advance heads-up.

Operational Expenses

Same thing with the three-year cycle, but focus on two main exceptions: First: Will additional headcount be required to support the business? The earlier the planning starts, the higher your probability of success. Second, remember that any Capital Expenditures will probably bring additional year-over-year maintenance cost increases. A good projection is to take 20% of the anticipated CapEx, and project it for an OpEx increase. Again, work with your finance group to detail the specifics. Once you show them you care about the budget and you are proactive, you will make a powerful ally.

As a CISO, one of the things you must do well is budget planning. It's not incredibly difficult, but missing a major project or budget line item can cause you a significant yearend miss in your budget. You are expected to be a manager as well as a technical resource and security guru. Many people in the company will judge your effectiveness by how you fare in the financial management area. Regardless of where your budget rolls up to, you must make sure the organization allocates funding and resources to protect critical assets in a rapidly changing technology and threat environment.

The most common scenario today is where the CISO reports to the CIO because security operations and budgets are part of the IT department, and a major portion of the security budget is technology driven. As the CISO role matures in an organization, they will directly control more of the budget, whereas in an immature organization, the CIO will control the budget. My advice: Stand up and take responsibility; trust is earned and you must earn trust through successful financial management.

The CIO control of the security budget does have some conflict of interest issues, in that funds can be redirected away from a security project to other IT programs. Keep records, do good project management, and communicate frequently with the

CIO and program owner. You can't always control what happens to the budget, but you can control how you respond. Learn your lessons and apply it to the next budget cycle. God knows I have quite a few scars from financial floggings over the years.

Change is constant, and budget planning is no different. Things will change over the course of the year, which will push and reorder priorities. Be flexible, but don't take your eye off the ball. Build a strong relationship with the finance department and find a person who can mentor you on how the organization plans and executes budgets.

As a help, here is some advice for you as you get started:

1. **Know the state of your current systems:** As discussed earlier in this book, know where your existing systems are in their life cycle. How many do you have? Where are they in the support life cycle? Will support no longer be offered or will it be offered at a significantly increased price? This planning will go a long way in helping you avoid the surprise of a critical security tool no longer being eligible to product support or updates, and you have no money to replace it.

2. **Know the status of your staff, both employees and contractors:** Do you have people who may leave or retire? If so, are you planning for agency finder's fees or relocation packages? These can be huge expenses that can kill a budget.

3. **Benchmark:** Find peers in the area or in like industries and compare your budget as a percentage of IT overall budget, or as a percentage of company revenues. This will give an indication of whether or not your company is adequately funding the security program. The more comparisons, the better. Be sure and take geographic issues into account. Don't compare Minot and New York wages without adjusting the cost of living and other supplier issues.

4. **Work with Finance on new projects and programs to get "creative" with funding:** Just as the accountants are not cyber geeks, the odds are you are not a financial wizard. The rules governing what is capital and what is operational expense changes frequently. How expenditures are classed can make the difference in getting a project funded or not. You will have to build a business case for any major project. Involve the finance folks early and often, so when the proposal gets to them, there are no surprises.

5. **Measure the effectiveness of your security program:** A successful CISO will measure the effectiveness of his or her organization's security program. There are a variety of frameworks to help managers achieve this goal. The National Institute of Standards and Technology Cybersecurity Framework and Assessment tool is a great way to establish your position on the maturity continuum and monitor your progress to higher levels. The Federal Financial Institutions Examinations Council also has an assessment tool that is very effective. Complete the analysis of your current systems and establish continuous improvement plans. Establish a goal of where you want to be on the maturity curve every year.

Chapter 14

A Security Culture Is In Place When Talk Is Replaced with Action

Introduction

Just like countries, regions, and communities, companies also have their own inherent culture. There are a number of ways to define culture. For our purposes, culture is a shared way of thinking, behaving, or working that exists in an organization to achieve a common goal. Once a culture is established, though, it is very hard to change it without an influx of a large number of new people and ideas or a catastrophic event. For the most part, company culture is a reflection of management ideas and principles embodied in your employees. Employees are the public face of a company since it is through employees that others interact on a daily basis.

To build a culture of security, it is important to have a core group of professionals who are living examples of the culture. As you build your staff, take care to evaluate the character of applicants as well as their technical skills. In my career, I have been lucky to find a few world-class people who exactly fit the bill. Every good CISO should hire people capable of leading the organization when the time comes. Pay attention to finding someone who can effect cultural change by leading through example. As for me, I have multiple people with the capability to lead. David (listed in the "Thanks to" section in

181

the Introduction) has been with me at multiple companies for 15 years. Lori and Rich worked with me at prior employers. Brad was here when I arrived, but has great leadership and technical skills. It's your job as CISO to apply those leadership talents and assets where they will have the greatest impact.

With today's ever-increasing cyber threats, developing a security-based culture is more important than ever. A security-based culture achieves two key outcomes. First, it improves an organization's security posture by integrating security practices with business functions. Second, it shows that security is more than just an activity relegated to what is usually a small and undervalued IT department.

While the culture typically emanates from the top of a company, it can take years for a new leader's ethos to permeate throughout the company without some sort of affirmative actions. International Business Machines Corporation (IBM) was noted for years for its white shirt, black suit, and tie attire. This all changed when Louis V. Gerstner Jr., the freethinking chairman of IBM, let it be known that employees could dress more casually. Yet, even after his pronouncement, it took years for it to be fully embraced by the employees. The so-called C level can certainly steer the organization to a security-based culture, but it must be fostered, developed, and espoused by the entire company for it to be effective. We cannot underestimate the influence employees have on a culture. Everyone in an organization has a collective effect on the overall culture. While the executives may define the culture, it is created from the bottom up. Unionized organizations are a good example of the tremendous influence that can be exerted from the bottom up. If your organization is unionized, they can be a tremendous asset in promoting a security-based culture. Everyone must be equal partners when it comes to developing a security-based culture. It is certainly in everyone's best interest to do so.

It has been well established that the human being is the weakest link when it comes to security. A security-based culture must start with the individual. A security-based culture means employees at all levels must be actively involved in promoting and enforcing security. Nearly everyone in a company will have access to some assortment of the organization's computers, systems, networks, and company data. Those at the top of an organization are prime targets because of their potential access to highly sensitive information. On the other end of the spectrum, the frontline employee is a similar target for attackers since they can provide a conduit to gain access into the network. Once in the network, the attackers are quite adept at elevating their privileges so they can freely move around to gain access to sensitive data. Thus, from the top to the bottom of an organization are opportunities for attackers to achieve their goals. Your employees must serve as the first line of defense in the protection of company assets.

The following will focus on some key areas that can have a major impact on influencing a security-based culture. These various components of a security-based culture, if addressed properly, can elevate the overall security posture of an organization.

Training

Training non-security personnel can go a long way in breaking down barriers between security and the rest of the organization. Security training, while needed, and in many cases mandated by external requirements, tends to be viewed more as punishment than as a true learning experience. Just one of those things you have to do to get the checkmark in the box. Avoid at all costs the "death by PowerPoint" type training or some generic computer-based training that is just a repeat of what was seen and done in prior years. What people are most interested in seeing and hearing are things that are directly relevant to them. If you want to get their attention, start talking about the foreign hackers that were detected and blocked by your systems and staff. Talk about the person that was fired for taking sensitive data home on a thumb drive. Naturally, you wouldn't mention anyone by specific name unless it was already printed in the newspapers, and if that is the case, you probably have much bigger problems right now. Show actual video of tailgating occurring at your site. Bring in someone from the FBI to talk about threats to your very company. Find a retired hacker to talk to your employees about how easy it was for them to breach systems.

Security training is best approached collectively. Remember, security is not just a problem for the security department but for the organization as a whole. Involve your executives, management, and employees from all across the company into the same room. Even include your key vendors and business partners, especially for outsourced functions whenever possible. Such opportunities allow everyone to share their experiences, thereby enlightening the collective group on the types of threats they have each personally experienced. Such open and frequent discourse will not only tend to unify the company in regard to security but also identify where there are strengths and weaknesses in overall security awareness.

Training is your best opportunity to promote a security-based culture. You really should throw out the annual user security awareness training. Such training becomes a compulsory necessity rather than a valuable opportunity to inform and educate. By having frequent interactive training, you will be able to better prepare your employees for the current threats. Use these sessions to draw attention to the tactics, techniques, and procedures being used by hostile actors to gain unauthorized access into your environment. Rather than blindly patch a recently discovered vulnerability, educate the employees on exactly what the vulnerability is, how it got into the environment, and the danger it poses. Such frequent interactions not only make your employees more knowledgeable regarding security but also make them a more viable component of your defensive strategy.

Get the business and rest of IT directly involved in the security presentations and training. Make them part of the show and ultimately part of the solution. Every company has some very creative people. Security folks tend not to be right brain thinkers. Creativity is needed to get the message across, which is why you need to engage people outside of security to effectively promote a security culture. Part of Walt Disney's success can be attributed to his willingness to embrace others' ideas. He said, "I use the whole plant for ideas. If the janitor has a good idea, I'd use it." Live presentations are far better than anything canned. Being able to interact with others helps drive the message home. Effective training should educate the educators as much as the students.

It is hard to imagine a corporate culture where people don't enjoy having a little fun. Incorporating security into enjoyable activities will go a long way to making security a notable part of the corporate culture. Have people identify security lapses in a recent TV show or movie. Critique the infamous Red Wedding episode from *Game of Thrones* or the episode where Jon Snow was murdered. Security is more than bits and bytes; physical security is equally important. There are a number of TV show episodes where one could have a lively debate on the efficacy of their data security. How often does a document on a copier or printer end up in the wrong hands?

Put on security-related contests and competitions. Create trendy calendars with a security theme. Have celebrations based on meeting security milestones such as running a phishing exercise and beating the previous threshold. Take full advantage of National Cyber Security Awareness Month, which occurs in October, to promote security awareness and a security-based culture. Use training as a means to educate not only the users but also your staff to the pain points the business and rest of IT are feeling and use this opportunity to try and develop ways to make life easier for all parties involved.

An effective way to conduct training is to construct it similar to how one obtains a college degree. Provide electives and mandatory "courses." Have different types of "degrees" a person can achieve based on the courses they take. Structure the training so people can actually obtain industry-recognized security certifications. In this way, people can focus on areas of interest and obtain the type of training they need for their individual jobs and commensurate with their capabilities. People learn better the things they embrace and choose for themselves over things they are forced to consume.

Effective training is your best means of creating a security-based culture. It gives the workforce the knowledge and tools they need to be a valuable component in the organization's overall security structure. It all boils down to resource management. Use everything you have in a constructive matter to achieve a desired goal. Ignore the contributions your employees can make to security at your own peril. Training should actually be removed from your lexicon and replaced with employee security awareness. Such security awareness should become an ongoing integral aspect of your security-based culture.

Basics

What tends to happen is security professionals get too wrapped up in the technical aspects of security. While knowing something about SQL injection and cross-site scripting is important, unless the employees understand basic security concepts, this techno jargon will only confuse and alienate them. This will be very detrimental in the process of creating a security-based culture. Introducing the more technical aspects of security to the employees will keep the conversations fresh and interesting, but only after they have fully embraced basic security concepts. These concepts and the technology associated with them need to be conveyed to the employees in quick and easy-to-understand terms. Security is not their primary job, so there won't be a lot of effort on their part to grasp the concepts if it turns out to be difficult to learn on their part.

It is important to convey to the employees not only basic concepts presently embraced by your company but others typically utilized throughout industry as well. As an example, consider two factor authorizations. Some companies use this technology while others do not. Educating the employees on the benefits of a technology or process not currently utilized will make it easier in the future to introduce such a technology or process. Prior training and awareness reduces the fear associated with change.

Passwords are one of your greatest security risks since they are the keys to the kingdom. Most users are rather careless about how they manage their passwords. Password management is a very basic but extremely important concept to include in employee awareness. Don't place too much emphasis on how to make effective passwords if your applications force you to regardless. Rather, offer secure ways employees can manage their multitude of passwords. Providing options to writing them down such as approved password managers goes a long way in reducing this risk. Implementing single sign-on systems is a double-edged sword. While it reduces the risk of people writing down their passwords, it also means a hacker only needs to crack one password to gain access to multiple systems. Single sign-on systems provide a good argument for two-factor authentication.

The importance of keeping devices and laptops updated has to be stressed. While most companies have automated this process, employees should be taught to verify their devices are indeed being routinely updated. Occasionally, a device will slip through the cracks and not be updated. It only takes one vulnerable device to open the door to a hacker. Remember this truism, as a CISO, you have to be correct 100% of the time; the hacker only needs to be correct once. If your users can directly download applications to their devices (not really a good idea), then these will most likely not be part of the corporate automated updates. The user will have to update these independently. Users need to be educated on this and take responsibility for doing this regularly.

Automated update processes are only good if they are achieving the desired results. Security patches need to be implemented as soon as possible. In many cases, such patches cannot wait till the normal patch cycle. Patching once a quarter is not conducive to promoting a security-based culture. The more often you patch, the better. Patching needs to be all-inclusive. You cannot exclude certain systems from the patching for fear it would break the system. If the system is that fragile, then every effort should be expended to replace the system. Patching should also not be limited to just operating system security patches. Application security patches need to have the same level of urgency and attention. Many third-party applications pose a greater security risk than the operating system itself.

Something I don't see a lot of anymore is laptops and desktops that are secured via cable locks. Securing these devices with cable locks sends a clear message that this is a company that takes security seriously. If theft is a problem in your company, then this should be a no-brainer. Carrying out a laptop is rather easy in most organizations and the data on most laptops can be quite sensitive and used to your company's detriment in the wrong hands. A password-protected laptop provides little defense once the device leaves the building and is in the hands of a dedicated hacker.

Need to know is the foundation by which access is granted to systems and data in the military. The same sort of rigor should apply in your organization if not already mandated by various auditing agencies. No one in your organization should ever need access to everything all the time. A consistent and well-documented access policy needs to be in place. Accesses that are granted likewise need to be well documented and continuously monitored. The more granularities in the accesses granted, the better. Accesses should be restricted by/from location, time of day, environments (Development, Test, Production, etc.), operating system, application, and so on. Those that develop the software should never have access to it once it is in production, commonly referred to as separation of duties. Similarly, those with access to a system should not have the ability to modify the logs associated with that system. A comprehensive system of checks and balances should be in place to reinforce the notion of a security-based culture.

A very basic concept yet one that receives marginal attention in many organizations is asset management. If you don't know what you have, how can you possibly protect it? Everything in your environment should be tagged, documented, tracked, and monitored. What you should have is a literal chain of custody. This does not just involve hardware but software as well. Applications and databases get loaded on servers that people quickly forget who or what they are for, and there they sit for ages since everyone is afraid to delete them for fear someone just might be using them or need the data contained therein.

The above basics have been shown to thwart many of the most common attacks. They are effective measures to employ to prevent data breaches. They are cost-effective and simple to employ and will be easily embraced by your employees. They are fundamental to a security-based culture and can help reduce the workload on your scarce security and IT resources. Leave the fancy security measures to your trained security staff.

If your executive leadership sets the example by choosing to follow these basic secure behaviors, it sets the right tone for a security-based culture. If they fail to follow them, employees will not have any clear incentive to comply. Security will be an afterthought rather than a prime directive. Your executives must embody organizational security.

Technology

A security-based culture is more than just people and process. It also involves technology. Yet, a security-based culture does not necessarily mean you have to increase your budgets or apply greater effort. Rather, it means changing how you do things and thinking differently. A great deal of technology is required if one wants to position an enterprise for the best chance of resiliency in an ever-changing threat landscape. If you were to inventory the technology you currently have, you might find that a lot of it is underutilized, improperly utilized, or shelf ware. People and processes, if properly applied, can help reduce the amount of technology you need to deploy and manage and better utilize the technology you currently have in place.

The breadth and depth of technology employed and how people view it play a role in defining the security culture of an organization. Even the specific manufacturer of a group of technologies can define the security-based culture. Very often, we hear people refer to their location as a McAfee or Symantec or Cisco shop. Technology coupled with such things such as training, user awareness, policy guidelines, and information sharing on threats both internally and externally is what will define the security-based culture of an organization.

Fear of change and the comfort associated with the status quo are huge impediments to moving an organization to a new culture. History has shown that companies that fail to change with the times tend to fail. When it comes to security, failure to adapt is a definite path toward a breach. While those Windows 2000 servers may be working fine and your staff is fully adept at managing them, sometimes you just got to let go. Just like I gave up my leisure suits, I also have let go of old technology no matter how much I liked the technology. When it comes to security, the axiom "If it ain't broke, don't fix it" doesn't really apply.

Unless the security technology is simple to use and understand it is best not to push it down on the employees. It will either not be used or used improperly.

If people resist adoption, it will certainly detract from crafting a security-based culture. Likewise, never take something away from the employees in the name of security that you don't have an alternative for. For example, if employees are using a non-secure method of file sharing, provide them a secure alternative. Employees are resourceful, so chances are if you take something away from them, they will find an alternative on their own that may be worse than the original option from a security perspective. Think of all the technology that has been put in place to prevent a user from copying the contents of a file, yet in the end they could just take a picture of their computer screen with their cell phone.

Any technology and security in general must be viewed as an approachable process and an ongoing commitment of the organization in order to be successful. Technology needs to be standardized as much as possible within an organization. Enforced standards and change management processes are essential to limit the spread of conflicting technologies within an organization. What is referred to as Shadow IT occurs when parts of the organization decide to go their own way regarding a particular piece of technology. Once this happens, you lose control of the technology and the ability to manage any vulnerability it might present. A good example is the plethora of cloud-based file storage and collaboration sites that are readily accessible to users within an organization.

Data Security

Security needs to be promoted as being there to protect the employees and not just the company. Protecting the company is simply an added benefit. The organizational culture needs to be one that values and respects confidentiality and privacy. While hackers pose a serious threat to businesses because they steal corporate-sensitive information, they can also compromise employees' personal and medical health information. Personal data are just as valuable as corporate data on the dark web. Both an organization's and an employee's reputation can be damaged through a security breach.

Security requirements need to be included in the recruitment of employees to ensure they will contribute positively to the security-based culture. Any new arrival to the organization such as new hires, contractors, and vendors must be made familiar with the values, traditions, and requirements of your company's security-based culture. Data security along with data privacy must be emphasized.

Security needs to be part of everyone's performance reviews from top to bottom to facilitate inculcating a culture that embraces security. Rewarding people for executing good security practices goes a long way in moving to a security-based culture. Promotions should be partially contingent on a person's contributions they have made to support a security-based culture. The dilemma we face is balancing security while trying to instill a culture of trust. Without trust, you create a potentially hostile environment and one where work is certainly impeded. A true security-based culture will promote greater internal as well as external trust.

When I was growing up, I remember that we seldom if ever locked the house when running errands around town, and we never locked the car in a parking lot. Sadly, that was another time. Maybe we were naive, or we lived in a safe, small community, but ultimately we trusted our neighbors, even those we didn't really know. We had a culture of trust and security. We watched out for each other and unconsciously kept an eye open for threats to that community culture.

Company culture is certainly influenced by external factors. World events are driving a greater appreciation by everyone for increased security. While there once was a time when people left their houses and cars unlocked, those days are sadly gone. But just as we won't leave a window open in our homes these days, how careful are we at closing a port on the firewall that is not being used? While most of us would not let a stranger in our home, how many of us are equally careful with whom we let on our network or into our data center? This is an area that has clearly tightened over the years but can still be improved upon. How carefully do we monitor our guest wireless network? While we are careful about examining our internal network for exfiltration, your guest wireless network could be an easy exit point for someone on the inside.

Laptops being what they are, portable, pose a whole new set of challenges to a CISO trying to protect the corporation's assets. Data, like Elvis, has left the building. People tend not to apply the same care and attention to things they do not own as they do to their personal property. While a laptop is a valuable asset, it is far less valuable than the data it holds and the potential it carries in the wrong hands to allow less desirables into your network. In a security-based culture, employees value company assets as if they were their own. Educating users on ways to protect these portable assets is important.

And let's not forget the multitude of other portable devices out there such as cell phones, tablets, and external drives. All of these can contain a considerable amount of sensitive corporate data. Mobile device management is a hugely important role for the security department. These devices require a greater level of care on the part of the users since they are more easily lost or stolen. Attaching some form of liability should an asset go astray would certainly increase an employee's attentiveness to their devices when outside the company walls. This is certainly one advantage of Bring Your Own Device (BYOD)–type policies. It was amazing to see how many corporate cell phones were lost or damaged beyond repair right after a new model version was released. Strangely, this problem never seemed to occur in a BYOD environment.

The amount of data even a small company deals with on a daily basis is astounding. Not only does data flow into a company but a great deal is generated internally. Most data have a finite useful life span, but in many organizations, the data seem to live on forever. The original intent and purpose of the data tends to get lost in time and there is a general reluctance to delete the data for fear someone just might still need it. Maintaining and protecting these data is a huge expense as well as a potential liability. In a security-based culture, employees realize that all documents must be appropriately labeled and have defined retention periods. Automated deletion processes are a CISO's best friend. Everyday documents, both physical and electronic based, should be destroyed as a matter of course. All documents need to be protected in some manner from the moment they are created until the time they are destroyed. While individual documents may not pose any security concerns, the aggregation of apparently benign documents can bring to light highly sensitive information.

Productivity

Security tends to be viewed as an impediment to productivity. My staff has been referred to in the past as "Checkers" that do little other than identify vulnerabilities and add workload to the rest of IT to address their findings. This is a dangerous attitude to allow flourishing since it creates a culture of "us versus them" rather than a cooperative environment. One can argue that if proper security policies and procedures were followed, then there would be no need for the "checkers." Such reasoning fails to recognize that not everyone is an expert at security and only reinforces the "us versus them" culture. Security should never be viewed as a hindrance to achieving corporate objectives.

Should that be the case, then security is an insignificant component of the overall culture of the corporation. Security needs to be seen as an enabler. A person who is not part of the security department may view security as someone else's responsibility. Such a person sees security as having very little to do with anything that person does or fails to do. It is important to view a security culture as the sum of the environment; that of pure security-related positions and that of non–security-related positions. Understanding the differences between security and non-security personnel is vital to a balanced and appropriate security-based culture. While most employees will take some degree of ownership of security, it is likely that there will be divergent views among the workforce.

Unfortunately, security is not an idea or concern of high import to most leaders unless you are a CISO or happen to work for a security-related business. On a positive note, though, this attitude is changing. What is in the forefront of most leaders' minds is making the numbers. The culture then is one of productivity, efficiency, and a general work ethic. Security is rarely viewed as having a positive contribution to any one of these. Leadership typically doesn't think about security until the organization is violated in some manner. As we know, blame then tends to roll downhill, with the CISO bearing the brunt of it.

Changing the mindset of the leaders to recognize the importance of security is a difficult task for a CISO. Unless the CISO has access to the company's Board of Directors, their efforts are further impeded. The Board exerts a considerable influence over the direction and culture of a company. The CISO needs a seat at the table with the Board, or at the very least, a direct conduit to one or more Board members to provide an unfiltered overview of the company's security posture.

The CISO's relative position in the company will clearly determine how important security is viewed within the company. Ideally, the CISO should be at the same level as the CIO to ensure security has the same standing as operational matters. Since security is directly related to the level of funding available, it is important that security be high enough in the food chain to not have to fight for whatever scraps remain. Products and services tend to garner the most attention and the most funding. The best products and services can become worthless overnight without a solid security infrastructure in place.

Security is like an insurance policy. You know you need it but it is difficult to see any return on investment. How much you spend on security is similar to what you spend on an insurance policy; it is a matter of how much risk you are willing to accept. Quantifying that risk though is a major challenge. The costs to a company for a security breach are pretty well defined across the industry, but the likelihood that a breach will occur is a lot harder to put a number on. There is a good argument to be said, though, that it is not really a question of if you will be breached but rather when. A strong security culture will certainly help push the timing out a bit.

If you have teenage drivers, then you certainly recognize you are at a higher risk and the insurance companies do as well to your detriment. Leaders, though, may not necessarily recognize the level of risk their company or even industry segment is exposed to. The fact you have not been breached develops a false sense of security, reinforcing the notion that attention and resources can be devoted to areas outside of security. This false sense of security is reinforced by the reality many companies do not discover they have been breached until months after the fact. A certain level of fear is not a bad thing to inculcate in your company culture. A security-based culture is a lot like car seat belts. At one time, seat belts were an anathema to drivers. Having never been in an accident, most drivers saw no need for them. Now, it is rare for anyone not to buckle up in the car, though that nagging seat belt warning bell might have a little to do with it.

Financial institutions are the first to come to people's minds as being at high risk. Yet, while people tend to focus on security breaches being driven by monetary motives, even a nonprofit can be at considerable risk from those trying to make a political statement or simply gaining access to personally identifiable information to be used for other nefarious purposes. The smaller, less likely targets may actually be more susceptible to a breach because of their misplaced naïveté. The Ferrari behind the gate and in the locked garage may be a lucrative target but the VW parked on the curb is far easier pickings. You might also find the VW useful to knock down the gate protecting that Ferrari.

An easy gauge to determine how much you are at risk is by looking at insurance premiums. Ask any homeowner in Florida about their homeowner's policy and you will quickly realize how much more at risk a homeowner in Florida is than say someone in Utah. Besides alligators, snakes, and hurricanes, Floridians now need to contend with climate change and the associated rising ocean levels. Homeowners in southern Georgia may be sitting on future prime oceanfront properties. Wherever there is perceived risk, you can be sure it will be reflected in your insurance premium.

Various insurance companies offer coverage for cyber-related incidents. The size of the premiums compared to say fire insurance can provide an indication of just how much risk your company is at. This is a tool a CISO can use to put things into perspective with senior leadership. Insurance companies like to reduce their risk exposure so they can also be used to help drive changes in your environment that can be translated into return on investment via reduced insurance premiums. Just like insurance companies offer the parent of a teenager who has taken a safe driver course lower premiums, they may do the same for your company when you show evidence of strengthening your security posture. CISOs normally don't get involved in the insurance riders for your company, but this is an excellent opportunity to show the value a good security-based culture provides.

The creation of Information Sharing and Analysis Centers (ISACs) and Information Sharing and Analysis Organizations (ISAOs) are an excellent means of sharing data related to cybersecurity risks and incidents within a business sector. CISOs should actively participate in these organizations and engage their leadership team as well. Peer influence can have a great effect on helping to change the culture as it relates to security. These organizations provide real-world data that are sector specific and more meaningful to the participants. Data related to a cyberbreach at a financial institution would have far more relevance and interest to a credit union than say a telecommunications provider. Such free exchange of information can have a positive effect on productivity as resources are more efficiently deployed to address sector-specific problems.

Communication

Communication is an integral part of a security-based culture. Without effective communications, it will be impossible for employees to become active participants in the organization's security efforts. Communication takes many forms. It can be verbal, visual, written, or a combination thereof. It can be top-down such as policy guidelines that are directed from executive leadership, or it can be bottom-up such as frontline employees reporting potential security situations. It can be driven externally from vendors, threat monitoring organizations, and ISAOs advising of new threats affecting the sector. Or it can be driven internally, such as security personnel informing the organization of identified vulnerabilities.

One must keep security awareness in the forefront of employees' minds across all levels of a company's workforce. This can only be accomplished through frequent socialization of security-related information. This will reinforce the notion that security is a shared undertaking. It will also highlight the fact that each employee has a vested interest in ensuring all sensitive information and system accesses are safeguarded and well maintained for the protection of the company.

And while everyone also has shared accountability and responsibility when it comes to security, this should not be conveyed in a draconian fashion. Policies and procedures cannot account for every contingency. People need to have some flexibility in how they conduct business operations. Employees should not, just for the sake of compliance, impede the business or fear undue punishment for using some degree of discretion in dealing with security-related matters. The best advice to communicate is that, when in doubt regarding security, just ask and always error on the side of caution. Open communications related to security is an opportunity to strengthen an organization's commitment to protecting information and system accesses that support the goals of the business and enhance the security-based culture. An example of the deleterious effects of strict compliance to policies and procedures was demonstrated some time back by airline pilots who were in a contract dispute. By following the rules and regulations to the letter, they basically crippled the air traffic control system, resulting in considerable delays and cancelled flights.

Some companies like to send out bulletins or put security posters on the walls. Posters are fine if they can grab the reader's attention. Pictures are more effective than printed words. Real-world examples and relating how security could personally affect each employee has a great impact. Everything in moderation though. Too much communication and people will simply begin to tune out the message. Think about all the advertisements at presidential election time. Now, try to recall some of those advertisements and the message they were attempting to convey. With a few notable exceptions, it is unlikely you remember the majority of them. It is the notable exceptions though that you should reflect on. What was it about those exceptions that grabbed your attention and the message stayed with you? These are the kinds of messages you need to craft and deliver to your company if they are to have any long-term impact. If you can capture the user's attention, then you increase the probability that the information will actually sink in and be retained. What I have seen very successfully used is the creation of little jingles or mnemonics related to security. Memes can be effective with the newer generation once you figure out what they are.

I would highly recommend you avoid the e-mail blast. Everyone gets too many e-mails as it is, and these will just be added to the ever-growing list of unread e-mails. Security intranets are a good place for people to find forms and policies but don't rely on it as an effective communication tool. Unless you have a really interesting site with lots of real-time feeds to keep the content fresh, you are not going to find a lot of people saying, "I need to go visit the security intranet site today." If you have a closed circuit TV feed in your company, ensure that it has a security component to it. Like a moth to a flame, TVs do attract people's attention. Make sure, though, that you refresh the content. People don't like reruns.

Use your corporate experts in tailoring your communication channels and crafting your communiqués. Marketing folks are quite good at this sort of stuff. That is why they are called marketing. If you are really lucky, you might have a separate communications group. They are even better at this than marketing, that's why they are called communications. Security is rarely viewed as a great communicator. Security is seen more as the cloak-and-dagger type hiding in the shadows watching your every move. Consider many of us work in confined spaces behind locked doors with no windows and lots of monitoring equipment; there might be an element of truth there.

Security needs to work hand in hand with the rest of IT and the business. Being an integral part of new initiatives as early as possible in the process will mitigate the consequences of subsequent security checks. Security needs to promote a culture of openness and assistance. Individuals need to feel they can come to security without fear of retribution. When groups avoid interacting with security, you have a culture problem. Walt Disney recognized the importance of communication. In his words, "Direct and easy communications—freedom of speech in all forms and its broadest sense—has become vital to the very survival of a civilized humanity." This is equally true for a corporation.

Communication means opening up the kimono a bit. Security issues and incidents tend to be kept behind closed doors. Unfortunately, you will never build a security-based culture if no one is aware of the very real threats that exist in their company. Imagine considering moving into one of two communities. One openly publicizes their crime statistics and the other does not. If you were unaware that the one does not publicize its crime statistics, you would probably feel more secure living there since it has no crime, but this would be a false sense of security. Knowing the true crime statistics gives you the ability to make a more informed decision. Another example would be deciding between buying two used cars, one has a detailed report highlighting the life of the car including accidents it was involved in while the other does not. Which would you be more comfortable owning and driving? Giving your employees security-related information allows them to be more informed and more sensitive to their cyber surroundings and eliminates an otherwise false sense of security. If you publish the fact there were X number of phishing attempts against your company in the last week, then employees might be more reticent about opening up that attachment for a free vacation.

E-mail

E-mail is a necessary component of business. Unfortunately, it is also a hacker's easiest way to infiltrate a company. Having a well-trained workforce as part of a security-based culture can go a long way in mitigating this vulnerability. An alert and savvy employee is your best line of defense against this sort of threat. Everyone in a company needs to understand the risks of clicking on an attachment or a malware embedded link in an e-mail. The expenses incurred in time and labor as the result of someone being deceived into opening a malicious link or attachment are substantial.

One way to bring home how easy it is to be breached via e-mail is through a phishing exercise. Conduct such an exercise before your security training and then show the results. Talk about the executive who clicked on the link not once but seven times or the person who e-mailed their login credentials in response to the phishing exercise. Educate the users that social engineering and spear phishing e-mails are used to target one particular class of worker and may not target others within a company. They can be highly personalized and extremely convincing. It is still crucial that everyone in the company be mindful of what these types of exploits entail. In a security-based culture, users are no longer complacent when it comes to e-mails. They should know how to recognize and check suspicious e-mails and know what actions to take should one be received.

E-mail also carries the risk of disseminating company-sensitive data. Employees need to be made aware of what is not acceptable to include in an e-mail, especially those destined for outside the corporate domain. A data loss prevention (DLP) system can help but it can't catch everything without affecting productivity due to excessive false positives. As an example, an invoice number might appear to a DLP system to be a social security number or credit card number and get quarantined. Time and effort then must be expended to validate its contents. Even personal e-mails to family and friends can innocently include information on corporate initiatives that are not ready for public consumption. Such information in the wrong hands could seriously affect a company's market strategy.

Many a person's career has been ruined due to an ill-advised e-mail. Think twice before hitting that send button. If it is company e-mail, then it should pertain to company business. Don't use the corporate e-mail system for personal e-mail. This can be difficult since many companies restrict access to personal e-mail accounts but nowadays almost every cell phone supports e-mail so you are not completely cut off. E-mail systems should have defined retention periods with auto deletion. E-mail is a huge financial liability when it comes to any legal discovery. The more you have, the greater the costs. E-mail also tends to become a document management system. Auto deletion mitigates this problem.

Morale

Corporate culture has a direct effect on employee morale, which can have a significant impact on the security posture of a company. We all know that the biggest threat to security is from an insider. Low morale increases that threat. Even if employees don't take any overt actions to subvert your security, they are less likely to proactively address indications of a potential threat. There are many ways to gauge the morale of a company such as turnover, absenteeism, work ethic, and the extent of social gatherings. There are many behaviors that can disrupt groups and impact morale. Whether someone is liked or not does not matter. Your attention needs to be focused on addressing bad behaviors. Some of the behaviors to watch out for are sexism, abusive behavior, gossip, and creating conflict between individuals or groups.

Whether low morale is endemic or isolated, it needs to be addressed. It only takes one bad actor to cause a breach or bring down the morale of others. While company culture can affect morale, likewise morale, both positive and negative, can have a huge impact on the culture of a company. While you can't please everyone, a positive culture will minimize the influence of the disaffected. If the attitudes of the few cannot be improved, then you will be doing yourself and them a favor by severing the relationship. Just the act of showing a genuine concern for their issues and feelings can go a long way in improving the morale of an employee. You simply cannot afford to ignore the matter and hope it will go away on its own. It won't and it will most likely get worse. Never let security violations just pass without any sort of action on your part. When security abuses are ignored, they then become habitual and adopted by others eroding the social fabric of a security-based culture. Chronic security violators have the same detrimental effect as an outside infiltrator. It is important and necessary to set clear boundaries.

The importance of a security culture has been officially recognized in what is known as the Security Culture Framework. This is a free and open framework to build and maintain a security culture in any organization. It is certainly a useful resource to help guide a security-focused culture change in your organization. The starting point in the Security Culture Framework is establishing metrics to measure progress in instituting a security culture. You need to ascertain your current posture and identify where you want to end up. You can't change what you don't monitor. Measure only what you feel you can realistically change. Metrics are frequently abused, resulting in collecting a lot of useless data.

To effect any change, you have to involve senior management, for without their support, there will be no change. Getting their support will be a challenge since, as previously mentioned, security is not normally one of their priorities. Support has to go beyond just lip service. People see right through that. If the leaders aren't committed, the employees surely will not be either. Human Resources should be a major player in your efforts to create a security-based culture. They are typically well versed in human nature, change management, and corporate culture. Don't expect results overnight. Corporate culture has a lot of momentum. It will take a lot of time and effort to change directions. To achieve long-term results, you will need to carefully craft a plan to build the security culture you want and follow the plan over the course of several years, carefully monitoring the metrics you have put in place.

Jurgen Habermas (1929), a German philosopher, defined a modern society as one that is able to examine and criticize itself. Such self-examination is needed to enhance the security culture of a company. Employees must be able to have a free and open dialogue about security. An employee should never be reticent about expressing concerns they have regarding security for fear of retribution. To accommodate those that fear "big brother," put up a security suggestion box and you might be surprised at the submissions you receive. Pleasantly surprised that is. People tend to be more open under the cover of anonymity. Habermas succinctly stated, "One never really knows who one's enemy is." The suggestion box may help you in this and other areas.

Noam Chomsky (1928) is an American political philosopher that has questioned whether our political rulers are actually more ethical than those of foreign governments. Chomsky espoused that citizens should examine the facts and not accept government pronouncements at face value. The same can be said for employees in regard to their corporate leaders, especially when it comes to security. Corporate leaders tend to downplay the security threat that exists. Chomsky said, "Either you repeat the same conventional doctrines everybody is saying, or else you say something true, and it will sound like it's from Neptune." Being receptive to differing opinions builds a culture of trust and openness. A good security culture is one where you don't need the suggestion box anymore because people are willing to express themselves. As the amounts of suggestions you receive begin to dwindle, this is a good sign you are transforming the culture in a positive way. As a CISO, you do need to stand up for your convictions. If the CEO, President, or Board is downplaying security, you have to alter their thinking. Remember, the corporate culture springs from the top. You need them to set the tone for a security-based culture.

Metrics and Measures

Metrics should help you monitor the level of security awareness in your organization. Metrics can help you determine what tools and procedures you need to document and enhance your security-based culture. The strategy you take to improve security should be driven by the metrics you have collected. Metrics are a vital tool in motivating management as well as employees to take the necessary actions as related to security. Again, remember, if it is not being monitored, it is not going to change. The ultimate goal is to create a security-based culture that reflects positive personal behaviors such as professionalism, integrity, personal accountability, adherence to procedures, teamwork, forthright and timely communication, and attentiveness. These are all traits that should be welcomed and embraced in any corporation.

To be effective, metrics need to have an established baseline, so make sure you collect a representative sample before measuring progress. Collecting too little data initially to establish your baseline can result in trying to measure progress against a baseline that is constructed from outliers. This would not be a true representation of the current state of the environment. Once you establish your norm, then it is easy to measure progress and to identify deviations that may require decisive action.

As part of any training exercises that are conducted, you should include periodic tests designed to evaluate user security awareness and the effectiveness of the training. These should not be implemented so as to evaluate the individuals themselves. Participation can be anonymous, but it must include a representative sample of those partaking in the training in order to properly gauge the effectiveness of the training and to direct future training to areas needing increased focus.

For an effective security culture, a little paranoia isn't necessarily a bad thing to help in averting an insider threat. Recognize, though, that too much paranoia can be counterproductive. Again, do things in moderation. Security cameras protect not only company assets but also employees and are far more accepted these days than in the past. Everyone should operate on the assumption that all Internet and phone communications are potentially being monitored. Restricting access to key areas, even if just normal workspaces, enhances security. People leave computers on all the time without invoking a screen lock and set papers on their desks that could contain sensitive information. Segmenting your office spaces is just as important as segmenting your network, especially in light of increasing bodily threats to employees. No one should have free flow access throughout your entire company. The front desk guard should not be your last line of physical defense. Security and safety should reinforce each other in achieving the common objective of protecting the people and the organization.

Hard data are better than rhetoric any day of the week. Hyperbole may get people's attention but solid facts get you respect and the funding you need. Emphasizing and engaging in risk analyses supported by solid metrics will contribute to a positive security-based culture. By employing defensible and rigorous risk analyses, you and the rest of the management team will be able to make informed and sound decisions about security. This, in turn, will increase the security posture of the company, contributing to the overall security-based culture and, as an added benefit, will increase the credibility of the security organization.

Workplace

An unattended computer is a perfect opportunity for you to make a lasting point. Use the occasion to send yourself a rather critical e-mail from this machine. Then, call the person into your office to have them explain themselves. Show them the e-mail. It is doubtful they will ever leave their PC unattended again and no harm was done in the process. The grapevine will quickly spread the word not to leave one's PC in an unprotected state. Your reputation might also be enhanced among the workforce when it is relayed as to how magnanimous you were in handling the situation considering the content of the e-mail.

Clean desk policies are not a bad idea, though you have to be willing to walk the talk. If you've seen my desk, this would be a challenge. With every phone having a camera, it is so easy to get a quick copy of anything these days. The potential to acquire sensitive information increases after normal working hours. Regular staff has left the facilities and is supplanted by various contract resources such as maintenance personnel or cleaning staff. It is always entertaining to see the highly secure sensitive paper disposal receptacles throughout a building yet the material that ultimately ends up in these receptacles lies openly on many desks. Another way to make a point is to pick up some of these papers and post them on a bulletin board in your office highlighting the sensitive information, a wall of shame. You will need to ensure, though, that you have an office that can be secured and that has no windows, or you are just as guilty of not protecting sensitive information.

Speaking of windows, this is an area that is not given much thought except in department of defense circles. Go outside your building some time with a good set of binoculars and see how many computer screens you can actually read. A lot of sensitive data can be gathered by just sitting out in the parking lot. Taking a picture of what you can see from outside the building could really drive home the message of how easy it is to gather information from a company. Repositioning computer monitors so as to not face the windows or providing filters that obscure them from any angle but dead on will reflect a security-based culture. Don't rely on users to lower the shades when they happen to be working on sensitive information.

Rather than scatter the secure sensitive paper disposal receptacles around the office, put a personal shredder in every office that handles sensitive material. I hate to say it, but people are inherently lazy. Chances are a lot of sensitive material ends up in the regular trash. Making it easy to shred documents will help ensure sensitive data is properly disposed of. Make it a policy to shred all paper products, not just sensitive documents. Sometimes, people don't realize what is and is not sensitive. Shredding everything eliminates that concern. It also reinforces the concept of a security-based culture.

Cell phone cameras are problematic. We have all been in meetings where every square inch of a whiteboard is filled with the collective knowledge of the assembled group. Rather than risk the loss of this mind dump, the cell phone cameras come out and the knowledge is saved for posterity on a dozen phones you have little control over. Replacing whiteboards with electronic equivalents would help mitigate this situation. Restricting who can take the pictures and with what devices might reduce some of your exposure. With everyone these days having a PC, collaborative idea generation-type software may be a viable solution.

Your security-based culture has to extend beyond the walls of your organization. It is a scary world out there. Your employees may very well be already targeted to gain access to your company's secrets. Social engineering is highly effective at acquiring the information needed to get through the barriers you have so painstakingly put in place. The cloak-and-dagger approach of seducing the target at a neighborhood bar while still in use and certainly effective is being supplanted by taking advantage of the wealth of information readily available through social media. It is amazing the information employees freely post in social media. Such information not only threatens your company but can pose real grave danger to them. A cursory scan of various social media outlets where you can see your employee posts may identify some serious security exposures. Education and training are your best defenses against this threat.

Organizations that support BYOD must ensure that comprehensive policies are in place to protect not only the company but the employee as well. Such policies need to guide employees on the safe usage of these devices both inside and outside the corporate walls. In essence, anything accessed outside the corporate walls should not be trusted by the employee or the corporation. Additional safeguards will need to be put in place through technology and process. BYOD has many benefits for the company and the employee, but it requires additional work on the part of management and the security department to ensure its safe execution. For example, anything you would expect on a corporate device such as antivirus protection will equally need to be found and verified on any BYOD apparatus.

User education on BYOD and a higher degree of monitoring are definitely in order. Employees must understand the importance in maintaining the same robust security standards at home as they do at work. A security breach at home has potential work implications as well. Acceptable online behaviors need to be communicated to include the types of information that should not be shared on social media. This will help employees reduce security risks at both their homes and their places of work. A security-based culture has to extend from the workplace to the home.

Conclusion

A security-based culture will make you more effective. Nothing can guarantee safety, but a security-based culture will improve the odds. Just like you need to be streetwise when walking a city street, you also need to be cyberwise when strolling through the Internet. Your employees make decisions every day that can potentially negatively affect the security of your business, usually without even realizing it. When employees are grounded in a culture of security, there is far less potential for improper actions. A primary motivation for a security-based culture is that it can help with the alignment of security with the business as a whole. Having a security-based culture is a means to an end. It allows you to achieve and maintain other corporate objectives, such as meeting various outside security audits and regulations.

An effective security-based culture depends on a number of factors. These would include but are not limited to training, awareness, proper planning, operations, and maintenance. The thoughts and actions of the people who plan, operate, and maintain your systems are an integral component of a security-based culture. No matter how technically competent your resources may be, you will remain vulnerable if the very important role the human plays in regard to security is not taken into consideration. At a very minimum, employees must understand that a credible threat exists and recognize how important security is to your corporation. A robust security-based culture needs to be an essential component of every security plan for it to be fully effective. Any security culture must be periodically reassessed to ensure that it continues to meet the needs and goals of both the corporation and its employees. It is beneficial to institutionalize such reassessments within the organization.

You will know your organization has achieved a security-based culture when everyone from top to bottom understands that very real and credible threats from both within and outside the company exist, and when the whole workforce, not just those directly involved in security, recognizes that security is important and understands the company is constantly vulnerable. Lastly, you will know when your organization has achieved a security-based culture when those outside your company easily recognize the importance your company and its employees place on security.

You will achieve many benefits with an effective security-based culture. You will find that your employees are more observant, they question anomalies more frequently, they execute their work assiduously, and they exhibit high ethical standards along with both personal and collective accountability. A security-based culture will not solve all of your problems, but it can effectively contribute to an energetic and robust security regime encompassing the entire workforce. It will certainly assist your corporation in keeping pace with a threat environment that is constantly changing.

As you can see, a security-based culture depends not on any one person or group but on the collective contributions of everyone in an organization and even outside an organization. As long as the executives provide a consistent positive security message and you keep the employees engaged in frequent interactive security awareness education, you will soon have a security-based culture in which everyone has a stake in its success. This also frees up the organizational security group to be more proactive rather than reactive when it comes to security. Your security personnel can only do so much by themselves, for they are not the only ones interacting with corporate networks and the data it contains.

No matter how much effort you put into security or how many valuable resources you expend in strengthening your security posture, your endeavors will not have the overall desired effect if there is no strong and consistent security message delivered from the top. While I have mentioned this several times, it cannot be overemphasized that your senior leadership has to be an enthusiastic advocate and fully supportive of your security goals and objectives and the concept of a security-based culture.

Chapter 15

NEVER Trust and ALWAYS Verify

It was a typical project: development ran long and testing revealed problems that required additional development work. It seemed that everything was fluid in the project except the delivery date. True to form, two days before the cast in stone "go live date," I got the code for security validation. Now, in my time, I'd seen some crap code, but upon verification, this code was a textbook example of every security coding mistake possible. No thought was given to proper input validation and output filtering, which led to numerous problems including cross-site scripting, SQL injection, command injection, and buffer overflows. Total problem count? About six hundred!

If you're a veteran CISO, you know what is coming next. I submitted the report, and within the hour, I had a crowd in front of my desk. Some looking angry, some with sweat on their forehead, and some with the company concerned frown. The spokesman started, "Look here's the deal, we respect your security concerns, but this is a high visibility project and we have some very important customers lined up to test starting Monday morning. How about if we allow the application to move forward but lock down to the internal network only. Anyone testing would have to come in via VPN." I thought about it, and trying to support the business, I agreed, ONLY if they committed to fixing all the issues before exposing it to all customers. They agreed; we all parted friends. Fast forward to 2 a.m. the next morning when I got a call from our Security Operations Center saying that as part of their scans, they found a new in-house application exposed to the public Internet. Sure enough, they had installed it open to the Internet. Intentionally? Maybe not, but that wasn't the immediate issue. I took steps to have it taken off the Internet immediately, and quickly became the most unpopular person in the company.

So, what did I do wrong? Should I have given permission to move the application to pilot? I think that my decision was appropriate given the visibility and the limitation of it being an "internal only" deployment. Should I have assigned my staff to ensure it was not exposed to the Internet after deployment? Absolutely yes. I should not have trusted that the team would do as it promised given the risks.

The original phrase "Trust but verify" was made famous by Ronald Reagan in December 1987 after the signing of a treaty with Mikhail Gorbachev. The Russian leader quipped, "You repeat that at every meeting," to which Reagan replied, "I like it." The origin of the phrase is actually from a Russian proverb, *doveryai no proveryai* (trust but verify). However, "trust but verify" is an oxymoron when you consider that the word "but" usually changes the meaning of the whole statement. I remember the painful high school dating discussions that started with "I really like you, but…" We've also all had the performance reviews that started with "You are really good at your job, but…."

I'm not talking about "blind trust." In management training classes, I've been told that blind trust is not a sane strategy to employ across all decisions in a low trust world. For instance, if you ask the clients that trusted Bernie Madoff, they would probably say that they would have achieved a better result if they had verified what he was actually doing with their money. In our security world, CISOs are tasked with protecting the company. Understanding that people have different motivations, ethics, and values, it is not possible to put absolute trust in others, and if we do, I'd argue that you are not performing the job for which you were hired. A "trusted" insider can do more damage than any external hacker. Let's look at a couple of real-world incidents and then discuss what could be done to detect and limit the damage of their actions.

Timothy Lloyd was fired from a company named Omega Engineering. It was a company that produced equipment for the US Navy and NASA. Tim's supervisors thought he was a true pain in the butt. He was like every bad IT jerk put together. His peers often accused him of throwing up roadblocks and taking credit for others' work. They were happy he was finally gone. What they didn't know was that even after he was gone, he had left a small program that continued to work.

When he first started, he was an IT superstar. But, as the company grew and more people were hired, he began to feel like his talents were no longer appreciated, and he felt his assignments were of less importance than before. Rather than stepping up, he decided to get even unless things got better. In early 1996, months before his firing, he began testing a little program that would be triggered at a specific date, running a simple line of code that would delete a certain sector of the main server. It was an incredibly simple piece of code that goes as follows:

1. 7/30/96

    The date is the triggering point in the code string, executing the rest of the commands as long as it is after July 30, 1996.

2. F:

    This line of the code gives access to the server.

3. F:\LOGIN\LOGIN 12345

    This automatically piggybacks User 12345, which has supervisory rights and no password security, with which-ever user first logs in on the file server.

4. CD\PUBLIC

    This line gives access to the public directory, a com-mon storage area on the file server.

5. FIX.EXE/Y F:*.*

    FIX.EXE is a DOS-based executable that served as the deletion command but showed the word "fixing" on the screen instead of "deleting." This is a slightly modified ver-sion of Microsoft DOS' Deltree.exe.

    /Y answers "yes" to the implied question of "Do you want to delete these files?" F:*.* refers to all files and fold-ers on the entire server volume.

6. PURGE F:\/ALL

    This line calls for all of the deleted information to be immediately purged.

Simple, deadly, and using only system commands to cause massive damage to the company. At the same time, he started moving the most important documents in the company's file system in a single folder, and then got access to the only backup tapes for those files.

Finally, on July 10, 1996, the hammer dropped. He was finally fired from Omega, but going out the door he knew that the plan was already in place to get his revenge. Twenty days after his firing, on July 30, employees at an Omega manufacturing plant in New Jersey logged in to a computer terminal and absolutely nothing was there. Thousands of design files and machine production programs were wiped out. The company estimated the cost to the company at 10 million dollars and putting all their contracts in jeopardy.

A few days later, a production worker at an Omega factory fired up the file server just as he did every morning. This time, the server crashed. But it didn't just crash. When the server went down, it took nearly every program down along with it, destroying any means of finding or recovering them. They called in a company to do data recovery, but the programs were nowhere to be found.

It was only a matter of days before three different people called in to do data recovery all reported that the programs were nowhere to be found.

What about the backup tape? It was nowhere to be found. How could something like that even happen? Didn't they have backups or something for such important files? Well, Lloyd had taken them home in the weeks before his firing and deleted them. He was eventually sentenced to three years in prison and ordered to pay a $2 million restitution.

Here's another insider case:

A former network engineer for oil and gas company EnerVest has been sentenced to four years in federal prison after pleading guilty in January to sabotaging the company's systems badly enough to disrupt its business operations for a month. He was also ordered to pay US $428,000 in restitution and a $100,000 fine, according to an announcement from the US Attorney.

In June 2012, the engineer found out he was going to be fired from the company. He decided to reformat company servers, disabled cooling equipment for the computer systems, and disabled a data-replication process.

According to court records, it left the company unable to "fully communicate or conduct business operations" for about 30 days. The company also had to spend hundreds of thousands of dollars on data-recovery efforts, and a big part of the information could not be retrieved. He was sentenced to prison for his actions.

So, since trust doesn't always work, what are some of the lessons learned that we can take away from this?

- Make sure no one person is controlling the system front to back.
- Every logon must have a password that meets policy (System Admins may have the right to bypass length and complexity rules).
- As few people as possible should have supervisory rights.
- Mission-critical systems should be backed up every day at a minimum based on risk.
- Limit access to backed up data.
- Back up desktops and laptops, as well as servers.
- Change passwords per policy, change shared administrative passwords whenever a person with that access leaves.
- Keep servers in a secured area.
- Stay up to date on software patches.
- Use intrusion detection software that alerts you when you are being hit and make sure your response time is faster than a fast penetration.
- Code should not be put up unless at least two pairs of eyes have checked it over.
- Information security personnel should be aware of any employee who is showing signs of being troubled or disgruntled, particularly if that employee holds an information-critical position.
- Beef up security during certain events, such as mergers or downsizings, that could upset workers and cause them to lash out at the company.
- If an employee, particularly an IS employee, is becoming a problem, start locking down—monitor the network, set up software that will alert you if she is in a different part of the network than usual, or if she's working at a different time than usual. Also, scan e-mails to see what's going out of the company, double check backup tapes, and have someone else do the backups if that person is the one in question.

Trust Your Vendors: Home Depot

Probably the one breach that sticks in our mind of late is Home Depot. This is a classic example of why it is so important to manage any third-party relationships, particularly those with access rights to core company systems. Home Depot admitted that 53 million e-mail addresses were stolen along with the previously disclosed 56 million credit and debit card details. They also disclosed that the information was lifted from their network because a third-party vendor's credentials were stolen or compromised.

Investigators found that the criminals used a third-party vendor's user name and password to enter the Home Depot's network. While the credentials did not have the rights to access the company's point-of-sale devices, the hackers laid in wait on the network until they acquired elevated rights. These rights allowed them to deploy custom-built malware on self-service checkout systems in the United States and Canada.

That accounts for the credit and debit cards, but what about the 53 million e-mail addresses that were also taken during the breach? Remember that for those who make money by phishing scams, a set of viable e-mail addresses, probably susceptible to home improvement scams, would be worth real money. A comment from an investigator read as follows: "Insider threats are not only the No. 1 cause of breaches, but also lead to the biggest damage; this is because once on the network, an outside attacker looks like any other employee and can take their time siphoning off data without being seen."

Home Depot isn't alone. Target was also a victim of a supply chain partner's lapse in security. Their data breach was started through a compromised HVAC vendor's credentials whose security controls were admittedly lax.

Just like any other criminal, they look for the easiest entry into a target. If a large company with large resources can make major investments in security, the criminals will actively look for a backdoor or easy way in. One easy assumption is that if you know the supply chain for a company like Target or Home Depot, you have a list of potential targets. Supply chains are a good target because they often have liberal access to company resources.

Companies need to get tougher regarding third-party controls and be willing to pay a little more for better security. If you beat them into submission on product/service price, you can't expect them to support a million-dollar security system to protect your business. Compounding the issue of control is that your partner may have downstream suppliers doing work for them that ultimately supports you. When you look at the whole issue, there are just too many gaps or holes in the supply chain today. There is little doubt that the real-time nature of business today makes it nearly impossible to monitor everything.

Here's a real life story to drive the point home.

Medical transcription is one of those areas that is important and critical, but can easily be outsourced to a firm that specializes in the business. A regional medical center in California decided to use a US-based outsourcer for medical transcription services. Shortly after the process was established, the medical center received an extortion demand from a medical transcriptionist in Pakistan: Pay a ransom or your patients' medical records will be posted on the Internet. Strange, the medical center didn't think they signed up for a service that would allow its sensitive medical data to be shipped overseas but they were wrong.

The medical center contacted the outsourcer and resolved the issue. With proper awareness and oversight, they wouldn't have been in that situation. They were put in a position of violating a number of state, federal, and international privacy laws because of an outsourced vendor. The lesson? Companies may be able to outsource the processing of sensitive data, but they cannot abdicate their responsibility to protect the data. They will be held liable and accountable for the information entrusted to them by their patients, customers, and users. Outsourcing functions requiring access to sensitive information puts your company at risk of serious privacy violations and security breaches.

As I was walking through the main lobby of the office, I noticed one of the Human Resources people flagging me down. When she got to me, she said, "Just wanted to give you a heads up: We have a new project to move our in-house HR system to the cloud. Are you interested?" Interested? Heck yes! "Where are you in the process?" I asked. "We have selected the vendor and are planning to sign the contract this week." I can sense all you veteran security folks nodding your heads. We've all been here.

Employers will continue to use the cloud to outsource business functions such as Human Resources. In fact, a recent survey by the Society of Human Resources Management said that 58% of its members reported having sent one or more functions to cloud-based providers. The result: US businesses are becoming more vulnerable to security attacks and breaches. From a risk and security perspective, there is nothing wrong with outsourcing as long as programs are in place to mitigate the risk. However, we should seek to achieve the benefits of outsourcing and the use of a Cloud infrastructure while minimizing the risks of privacy violations and security breaches.

Nervous about Trusting the Cloud?

Not sure where your data are stored? As I've said many times in this book, you can outsource storage and processing, but you can't abdicate your responsibility to protect and secure the information entrusted to you. Here are five questions to suggest your clients ask potential vendors before allowing employees to use these cloud-based tools.

Does Your System Encrypt Our Data while They Are Stored on Your Cloud?

This might surprise you, but very few providers encrypt customer data at rest, as part of its base offering. You absolutely can't take anything for granted, even an established, well-regarded company may offer encryption only as an option. There are also many flavors and strengths of encryption. What is acceptable? Is a specific strength required by regulatory constraints? **You must also consider who holds the keys to your encrypted data.** By default, most providers will maintain the keys for the customer. You need to decide if that is appropriate and understand where these administrators may be located. Are you comfortable having an administrator in Taiwan having the keys to access your data?

Does the Provider Have a Disaster Recovery Plan for Your Data?

Code Spaces, a code-hosting company, was put out of business by an attacker who deleted the company's data and backups. Officials posted an explanation and an apology on the company's website. "Code Spaces will not be able to operate beyond this point, the cost of resolving this issue to date and the expected cost of refunding customers who have been left without the service they paid for will put Code Spaces in an irreversible position both financially and in terms of ongoing credibility. As such, at this point in time, we have no alternative but to cease trading and concentrate on supporting our affected customers in exporting any remaining data they have left with us."

It started with a DDoS attack that was accompanied by an intrusion into Code Spaces' system. Extortion demands were left along with an e-mail address they could use to contact the attackers. Code Spaces said it changed its passwords, but the skilled attacker had created backup logins. When the attacker saw that the company was not going to pay, they began deleting code repositories and backups from the system. Code Spaces said, "In summary, most of our data, backups, machine configurations, and offsite backups were either partially or completely deleted." Within a day, the company had gone from a progressive, profitable company to finding themselves out of business. They advertised that they had a full DR program, but in essence, the data and backups were held on the same system. It wasn't just a disaster for the company, but also for all the companies that had stored their data on the systems that was now lost forever.

Lesson learned? Before you entrust your data to any cloud service, you need to know whether that vendor has a disaster recovery plan in place to recover data lost due to theft, natural disaster, or human error. Many do not; don't take chances with your information assets. If possible, you need to understand the details of their DR plan to ensure that the backup data are secure.

Don't Confuse Compliance with Security

There's one problem that always surfaces, regardless of which regulatory "flavor" (e.g., PCI, HIPAA, etc.) you discuss. Different people in your organization will have differing views about the difference between compliance and security. Some people think they're the same. Some get so wound up in dotting all the "i's" mandated by compliance they can't help but think that after months of compliance work, the organization must be secure.

The big example we can all point to is Target, who was certified as PCI compliant two months before the breach. Despite being compliant, the company was breached for 70+ million credit and debit card numbers.

As we often say, compliance does not equal security—Compliance is a "batch" process while Security is "real time." I've heard compliance called a snapshot of how your security program meets a specific set of security requirements at a given moment in time. In fact, PCI Compliance is defined as adherence to a set of specific security standards that were developed to protect card information during and after a financial transaction. PCI compliance is required by all card brands.

You need both. To truly protect sensitive data, both security and compliance are critical. Without a smart, thorough, and active security program, coupled with a solid compliance plan, you're at significant risk of being breached. To protect your environment from threats and attacks, you must build and manage a proactive security program that goes far beyond compliance requirements.

Has the Potential Vendor Earned Certifications for Security and Compliance That Can Provide Assurance of Their Capabilities?

Does the potential vendor have external certifications that matter to you? If you process and store credit and debit card numbers, is the vendor PCI compliant? If you are a health care firm, is the vendor HIPAA certified? If you are required to be certified, you must look for independent, third-party verification that the vendor has processes for managing and protecting your data to those standards.

Remember, this is compliance with standards, not a guarantee that your data are secure. Yet another good standard for certification is the best practices of the ISO-27002:2013 standards for information security management.

What Physical Security Measures Are in Place at the Supplier's Data Centers?

The best technical and process security controls are of little use if the physical security at the vendor's data center stinks. Many times, your supplier will sublet space from a larger data center provider.

Is your data physically segregated from other customers or is it co-mingled? Is the supplier's equipment caged or locked to stop unauthorized physical access?

I actually had a case in a previous company where a server was stolen from a data center by people dressed as maintenance people. We reviewed the surveillance tapes and saw that the criminals entered through an unalarmed window that was actually connected to the roof of an adjacent building. By the way, the tapes also showed the guard at the main station asleep while the incident happened.

Where Are My Data Being Stored?

When you put your data into the hands of a provider, make sure you know whether or not they have data centers in many different places, countries, or even continents. Just because their address is in the United States, don't assume their data centers are in the United States. Ask, verify, and you should even plan a visit.

It's not just the security of the data, there are laws that govern where data can be stored or processed. Governments continue to implement common laws to cover data—for example, in the EU, the Data Protection Directive requires data to either be stored in the European Economic Area or in a territory that has equivalent legal privacy laws. Several other countries require information about its citizens to be stored in that country. Many companies have found to their pain that ignorance of the law is no excuse and have suffered multiple sanctions and penalties. From circumstances like this, if you still want to outsource data storage or processing, your only option is to look at developing a Vendor Oversight Program. Basic or Advanced? It's all based on your assessment of risk. The following is a good place to start:

Vendor Oversight Program Basics

These six steps are key for starting a vendor risk management program:

1. **Corporate Governance:** The place to start is with strong internal governance systems and policies. Establishing a corporate-wide policy supported and enforced by executive management is a mandatory foundation for the program. Tone from the top and educating the staff is required before you can get all the parts of the company to participate.

2. **Vendor Contracts and Review:** Contracts define the vendor relationship. Getting the necessary terms and conditions agreed upon by both parties is critical. Use standard security language and provisions wherever possible. Ensure that the "right to audit" is a mandatory part of the language. Ensure they have adequate insurance and indemnification clauses to cover you should a breach of their systems cause your company harm.

3. **Risk Assessments before, during, and after the Contract:** There are three components of a vendor risk assessment: Relationship, Business Profile, and Control Risk. To get a complete view of risk, it is important to collect all pertinent information. You will get most of that input from the business unit, finance, and legal. Pick a standard methodology and stick to it. This will ensure consistent results across the program.

4. **You May Need an Onsite Audit:** Depending on the business model, the only way to fully understand the risk may be to do an on-site audit. You will need to develop a standard audit plan that focuses the due diligence effort on critical areas. Develop a standard list of "red flags" that may indicate possible problems within the vendor's environment.

5. **Ongoing Reporting:** Follow up all audits with standard, well-written reports for the review of all areas within the company. All identified risks must have a management response from the organization and those responses should be reviewed by the business unit, legal, and security teams.

6. **Ongoing Risk Monitoring:** Your initial audit was only a "snapshot" in time. Unless you regularly review your vendors, you will not be aware of any significant changes at the vendor and as such assume additional risk for your company. Key areas to monitor include the company's financial status, security controls, and regulatory status. A change in any of these areas could significantly increase the risk the vendor poses to your ongoing operations and financial stability.

Internal Trust

If your goal is to develop the strongest possible computer security for your company, "trust no one" is the strongest policy. Absolutely any piece of software or hardware could deliver a Trojan Horse or other malicious features, but ultimately you have to trust someone. Just learn to pick carefully. Here's a flashback from the '90s:

Chuck was the product manager for a brand new industrial controller line. The greatest thing about this product was that you could edit the control program on a PC and then transfer it to the factory controller. Those of you who were process engineers remember the joys of punching in a program on a controller on a 110-degree factory floor. This product was a godsend for hot sweaty engineers everywhere.

Since it was a new product, Chuck had the newest, cutting-edge two–disk drive PC on his desk, and he was responsible to copy and label the control disks for the product. If you remember those days, with no hard drive, you booted from a floppy disk and then did your work. Unfortunately for our friend Chuck, he had been given a boot disk with a virus on it.

Chuck worked hard, created 100 disks for the initial controller shipment, taped up the boxes and shipped them. About two weeks later, the company started to get complaints from customers that they had found a virus on their disks and were not happy. They had tracked the virus down to the disks shipped with the product. As much as it might seem otherwise, this is not a virus story, it is a trust story. For the customers who had been burned by the bad disks, would they be likely to trust the supplier again? Given a choice of a new or alternate vendor, would the trust issue come into the decision? Absolutely!

True, it's an old example, but operating in a mode of low or zero trust is becoming more common. We live in a plug-and-play world, even with security and production devices. Unless you decide to write all your own code and build all your own hardware, you will have to trust someone. Luckily, most computer and software companies are relatively trustworthy, even if they aren't as transparent as we'd like them to be.

OK, let's talk about trust. I'd argue that trust is multifaceted. If we go back to the three foundational elements of security, People, Process, and Technology, we can see that there are factors that can elevate our levels of trust.

Even in Table 15.1, there are many judgment calls and potential risk assumptions necessary to decide if an element should be treated with trust. If we added one more column that talked about the value of the assets being accessed, it would change again (Table 15.2). After all, we make those decisions every day. The person who cleans our house has a key to get in when we aren't home; however, they don't have the combination to the safe. If I was giving access to my safe without me being there, I'd probably do an in-depth background check before giving them the combination.

If the value of the asset is low, like public information, then almost everyone is trusted. If the information is critical, then even trusted technology might not be "trusted enough" to have access to the information such as Merger and Acquisition plans.

That is pretty much how we operate today. The business makes all kinds of critical decisions regarding legitimate access. If we compound the issue further by introducing malicious traffic and actors, network issues, and the increasing speed of business, the attempt to secure information using yesterday's methods and technologies becomes an insurmountable problem.

Table 15.1   Trust

Element	Training in Place	Mature Yes/No	Resultant Trust
People	Yes—roles based	Yes	High
People	No—informal	No	Low
Process	Yes	Yes	High
Process	No—not documented	No	Low
Technology	Yes—run books	Yes	High
Technology	No	No	Low

Table 15.2   Trust with Value

Element	Training in Place	Mature Yes/No	Value of Assets	Trust
People	Yes—roles based	Yes	High	High
People	No—informal	No	Low	High
Process	Yes	Yes	High	High
Process	No—not documented	No	High	Low
Technology	Yes—run books	Yes	Critical	Low
Technology	No	No	Low	Low

As part of my first 90 days at a new company, I met with the infrastructure manager to talk about the physical and logical structure of the network. He drew the obligatory bubbles and lines on the whiteboard and assured me the network was physically segmented into Production and Non-Production areas. That coupled with firewalls and network controls ensured that only authorized people and traffic could access sensitive data.

A few days later, I talked to the Database Administrators, Developers, and Production Support Analysts. As I dug deeper, I found out that while the segmentation concept was good, the actual implementation had gone horribly wrong. Shortly after the network layout, multiple test and production applications were mixed on the segments. The Database servers were on both segments. To keep the access and connectivity locked down, several firewalls were installed with hundreds of complex rules written over the years. As I dug deeper, I found that it was not uncommon for production systems to be affected when installing new systems due to the complexity of the rules. It was a major disaster waiting to happen.

Note the lack of a common IT vision and language. Did the network group have a segmented physical network? Absolutely yes. Did IT have a network where the data and applications were segmented? Absolutely not. Did the complexity of the systems throw a wrench in most upgrade and patching activities? Absolutely. With the overlapping rules, segments, and access control lists, can you trust that the network will only let the appropriate people access the critical data? Absolutely not.

The cybersecurity universe evolves continuously as threats and business needs morph. Just as castles added inner and outer walls in response to new methods of breaching perimeters, we must also evolve our approach for cybersecurity. I'm not advocating that we start from scratch. This new approach should combine "defense-in-depth" with the new ideas of "zero trust" and "adaptive perimeters." We need to constantly evaluate and change our protection strategies. Business changes, threats change, people change, vendors change, and **TRUST CHANGES.**

This is all about trust. To go back to the beginning of the chapter: Trust but Verify. That is your job, do it well, and the company will be much better off from a risk perspective. To close out, let's review some of the great "Trust Me" lines of all time:

■ Trust takes years to build, yet seconds to shatter.
■ Trust me, I do this all the time.

- Trust me, what could possibly go wrong?
- Trust me, I'm in sales, this is the best possible deal.
- Trust me, I'm an IT expert.
- Would I lie to you?
- Trust me, I'm a simple e-mail: no viruses here!

SUMMARY

A valuable asset for any successful CISO is a set of templates and reference material. Never ever reinvent the wheel when you don't have to. I've included a core set of templates and references to get you started.

If you've been around for a while, I'm sure you have a set of your own. My hope is that these will add value. If you are new to the field, use these as a starting point for your own library. They are as follows:

Appendix A: The Written Information Security Plan
Appendix B: Talking to the Board
Appendix C: Establishing an Incident Response Program
Appendix D: Sample High-Level Risk Assessment Methodology

The written information security plan is a mandatory part of any security program. This template and description is a great starting point for you to develop you own. Talking to the board is a skill that you will need to develop. Hopefully, this section will provide you tips and tools to successfully navigate this part of your career. Documenting and establishing an incident response program is a critical process for you to go through as you build your own group. When the wheels come off and an emergency hits, a well-developed response plan is worth its weight in gold. Finally, I've added a simple risk assessment tool. It is not sophisticated or comprehensive, but it will get you started.

Use these tools and build your own set!

Chapter 16

My Best Advice
for New CISOs

You, my friend, have picked a strange career. It can be a thankless job while at the same time being personally rewarding. So, where are you headed as a CISO? Are you destined to repeat the mistakes of the past, or are you going to continue to be a trailblazer in a still emerging field? Much of the choice will be yours. I've tried to share some of my practical lessons and observations; you will have your own. I urge you to record them and pass them along to others.

Over the years, some of our less visionary brethren have created an environment where Security is viewed as an obstacle and not an enabler. We are seen as the purveyors of "No." But, you can't blame your lack of success on them, or the past. It is up to you to "sell" security to the business. When I say sell, that is exactly what I mean. Maybe I had a head start as my Dad was an incredible salesman and I watched him work deals from beginning to end. *Maybe your next seminar should be sales or negotiating.*

Success is hard to measure. You go for weeks and weeks with no security incidents. Are you doing a good job, just lucky, or have you already been breached and just don't know it? As one of my best managers says, "We have to be right a million times a day, the bad guys only once." Unfortunately, failure is easy to measure. Usually, you will read about it in the papers.

You can never be too secure in your environment or your position. Stay hungry and have a voracious appetite to learn about your business, not just Info Security. Also, realize that you will never have the budget you need; spend wisely. The reason that I talk budget and learning about the business in the same breath is that to be successful, you must incorporate a security component to every new business initiative to help subsidize and account for the true costs of security. Also, knowing the business will help you get a seat at the strategic table where mergers and acquisitions are discussed. This is how you get out ahead of the business where security is concerned.

Communicate frequently to elevate awareness of the existence of the security group and its importance to the company. Do this internally and externally. Develop a presence in the community. I'm often asked if Info Security people should actually talk at seminars as it may prompt hackers to attack who would take the session as a challenge. Since this is a "G Rated" book, let's just say that I think that is crap in today's world. What is the greatest thing that the hackers do? Communicate! They actually hope that we don't share information about how they hack.

Get to know your peers in the industry and develop professional relationships. Share information. McAfee (*Underground Economies*, McAfee, SIAC, March 2011) has reported that "Only three in ten organizations report all data breaches/losses suffered, while one in ten organizations will only report breaches/losses that they are legally obliged to, and no more. Six in ten organizations currently 'pick and choose' the breaches/losses they report, depending on how they feel about them."

Keep yourself educated. Take advantage of the knowledge of your security vendors both in person and what they provide on the Internet and in various reports. Just a few samples of excellent material available to you are *Symantec's Internet Security Threat Report*, *Verizon's Data Breach Investigations*, *McAfee Threats Report*, *Sophos's Security Threat Report*, and *Trusteer blog entries*.

Be creative. Antivirus/antimalware software is no longer enough. The bad guys use a concept known as polymorphism. The result is that malware files mutate with every changing appearances that signature-based malware detection software cannot keep up with. Certificates are no guarantee of legitimacy. Cybercriminals have been known to use stolen or forged certificates. These then give malicious files the appearance of being legitimate applications or updates. The malware files will be successfully downloaded, evading your malware protection applications.

Focus on the people, not the technology. Never assume technology can replace the human element. Always ask probing questions, never assume you are safe. The questions should include the following:

■ What are the most significant security threats?
■ What do we know about them? What don't we know?
■ What is just around the corner that we should be preparing for now?

These are the kinds of questions we must ask ourselves every day. It's part of our intelligence-driven, threat-focused approach to defending our company from a wide array of threats. Tomorrow, we must combine investigations and intelligence operations to be more predictive and preventative—more aware of emerging threats and better able to stop them before they turn into breaches.

Talking to the Board

I wouldn't be doing a good job unless I said a few words about addressing the Board. This can make or break a security program. There are some great resources out there. For instance:

The National Association of Corporate Directors, in conjunction with the American International Group and the Internet Security Alliance, published a report outlining the five principles that all corporate boards should consider "as they seek to enhance their oversight of cyber risks." This is expounded upon in Appendix B: Talking to the Board.

The Board is the Supreme Court of a company. The final decisions on the direction of the company are made here. Keeping them apprised of the current state of the company's cybersecurity posture and the threats to the company are critical to ensuring security gets the proper attention it deserves. This is especially important if you have a CEO or CIO that did not view security as a priority.

People do not get appointed to Boards because of their good looks. They are politically astute and very business savvy. They are good at separating the wheat from the chaff. Never assume you know more than they do on a particular subject. Boards are composed of a number of people with varying backgrounds. Invariably, someone on a Board will have some degree of expertise on security. You still need to make sure whatever you present to them is in terms that they as a whole can understand and relate to business goals. The Board is no place to show how technically smart you are.

Getting granted access to the Board is a lot like getting backstage passes to a hit performing group. Such access is highly coveted and sparingly given. In some cases, you may find you are considered not high enough on the totem pole to warrant such an honor, usually by those competing for the access themselves. These same individuals may also harbor a concern that you might embarrass them if granted access. The advantage you have over them is you have the knowledge the Board needs and they do not. Chances are, these same individuals will highly filter any information you develop for the Board presentations. Sending in a proxy for the CISO is done at great risk should the Board have any questions. If you do get the chance to meet with the Board, you certainly want to vet your presentation with your superiors and get their buy-in ahead of the meeting. You don't want to surprise them. In the end, they are your bosses. Don't ever think the Board will protect you. The Board has a closer relationship with your superiors than they do with you, for now. It will take time to build their trust and respect. Now, when the Board asks you questions, you certainly should answer truthfully but also respectfully.

With the increased emphasis on security, just bide your time. Eventually, your day will come when you will be granted the vaulted access. Security is becoming all too important for the Boards to ignore or discuss with intermediaries. Get yourself recognized in industry circles through attendance at conferences, giving presentations and writing articles for prominent magazines related to cybersecurity. Board members will eventually hear about you through their circles and want to meet you in person. Certainly, promote yourself internally through companywide communications and face-to-face meetings. Of course, a major data breach might also grant you a onetime visit with the Board.

Finally: Despite the title of this book, there is no Silver Bullet for security. Believe me when I say that I wish I could leave you one. The best I can do is pass along some of my thoughts and lessons learned.

Best of luck as you develop your own path. I look forward to reading and hearing about your thoughts on this book, security in general, and lessons you have learned over time. I am never too old to continue learning from my peers. Plus, I enjoy a good "war" story now and then.

Appendix A: The Written Information Security Plan

The Written Information Security Plan or WISP

The following section contains information regarding the importance of developing and maintaining a Written Information Security Plan (WISP) for your organization. Aside from being required by many states in their data breach and privacy laws, it is an excellent framework for you as the CISO to think through and document your program. It also provides a method for you to clearly convey the program to your executives and Board of Directors.

You need a WISP in place for your business. Without one, you are putting your company at risk for legal action and punitive fines should you have a breach. The law in virtually all states now dictates that you must take steps to safeguard personal information and contains provisions for how you must report breaches and in what time.

As we've discussed before in this book, it is likely that a breach will happen to your company. Don't bury your head in the sand and assume it will never happen to you. The need to have a WISP is made clear in one of the most stringent of the regulatory laws, the Massachusetts Data Security Regulations, 201 CMR 17.00. If you want a model to build your WISP upon, this is a great start. It's generally accepted that if you meet the Massachusetts standards, you will be good in all jurisdictions.

The Commonwealth of Massachusetts states:

> Every person that owns or licenses personal information about a resident of the Commonwealth shall develop, implement, and maintain a comprehensive information security program that is written in one or more readily accessible parts and contains administrative, technical, and physical safeguards.

225

Remember that this does not just apply to you if your business operates in Massachusetts; it is a law that protects the residents of the Commonwealth. It applies to you if you have even one customer that lives there.

Writing a Comprehensive WISP

There are lots of things to think about when you create a WISP. How do you protect data, both in transit and at rest? What about encryption? What about access controls and how you regularly review access to ensure that only authorized people see sensitive information? Do you allow personal devices? How about personal laptops? Do you allow company e-mail of personal phones? If this sounds like it may be tough to collect all the data, it is unless you create a committee to build and review the WISP. Include IT, Audit, Legal, HR, and so on. The diversity of the views will make the WISP stronger and more comprehensive.

Remember our earlier discussions about third-party connections and their part in data breaches? Ensure that your WISP includes third-party provisions and make sure they comply with your WISP. Write it into your standard service agreements and vendor contracts.

Education and Awareness

Writing the WISP isn't going to improve your security in and of itself. Unless you educate the users on their responsibilities to adhere to the WISP and their personal role in protecting sensitive information, you have wasted your time. Ensure the education is formalized and the employees have to sign off that they read and or reviewed the plan. Awareness is key; ignorance will never be accepted as an excuse by your customers or by the law. When conducting training, don't forget about the third parties and contractors.

A regular review of the plan is critical. I would recommend that you use an oversight committee, preferably your existing (I hope) information security oversight committee. Review it in light of the business and regulatory need. Pass it by the internal audit department and the legal department. Look at new products and services the business and IT will offer. Unless it reflects the business and the needs of the business, it is an exercise in futility.

Your role must be fully defined as well as the others in the WISP. Define all roles to a person, not a committee. As always, committing a deliverable to a committee is the kiss of death; make sure a person is on the hook for all critical activities.

You will find that drafting the WISP will be a complex task with the input of many people and functions required. I've listed some key considerations below to help you through the process.

Know your data. Do you have existing data classifications? How is access segmented? Unless you know what is to be protected, you cannot develop a plan. If you are in Financial Services, then you are probably concerned about financial information, possibly PCI, and definitely PII. If you are in a service or manufacturing sector, it may be Intellectual Property or Trade Secrets. Don't forget about financials and plans to acquire new companies or businesses. Understand where it is stored, and what protections are available to the data or paper documents.

Now that you have identified the types of data at a high level and where it is stored, map the information protection controls to the data and sources. This should tell you if the data are encrypted, stored on site, or in the cloud; who administers the data; and who administers the systems and networks that support the data stores. You must realistically describe the protections in place today.

Communicate and Educate

As I said before, a document of policy on a shelf is a waste of company resources. Particularly with a WISP, ensure you communicate the plans as well as any updates to all stakeholders, employees, and users. A good plan must not adversely affect the business; be sure that the business and product leaders review and have an opportunity to provide ongoing feedback to the plan.

New to many regulations is the requirement to extend controls to third parties. You can no longer assume that the third parties handling and processing your data are doing a good job when protecting your information. You must evaluate the vendors and agreements that govern the relationships. You must also ensure that those providers have a WISP and that you have reviewed it and identified any gaps that could put your data at risk.

Even before the WISP, your organization should already have a plan for responding to a data breach. The plan should identify a specific incident response team led by a member of senior leadership with decision-making authority and access to a company's Board of Directors, and also include employees with relevant skills (technology and otherwise) who are assigned clear responsibilities in advance. Don't forget to include Public Relations and Legal as they will be key in communicating and dealing with potential negative publicity. If you have a call center or other customer-facing teams, make sure they have a script of what to say and how to escalate issues. Ensure that the plan is tested at least yearly, and don't forget to mix it up. Throw in a scenario not covered in the current plan. Remember the old military adage: "No battle plan ever survives first contact with the enemy." Your attackers will never follow your script.

Review and Update Security Plan

Since operations and technology are subject to significant and repeated change, a WISP should be viewed as a living document. Review the plan at least quarterly, but at the very least conduct an assessment annually and in the face of a material change in the business. Ensure that you maintain a change log on the document including the mandatory levels of management review and approval.

Drafting a WISP may appear to be a huge program, and let's be honest, it can be. Develop a team; it is better if created with multiple viewpoints. Use the steps outlined above, and the basic template that follows below. Get started. Remember, the WISP is a great planning and documentation tool. It is useless if you put it on the shelf and never look at it again. Socialize it. Circulate it. Regularly review and update the plan.

The section below contains a sample WISP you can use to get started. My comments are italicized so you can separate them from the WISP text.

<YOUR COMPANY> Information Security Plan

Prepared and Maintained by the Information Security Group

Introduction

This first section is where you will scope your plan. Don't try to "boil the ocean" with your document. If you notice, this document discusses the company plan to secure sensitive information, not all information.

This Information Security Plan ("Plan") describes <YOUR COMPANY>'s safeguards to safeguard protected information. Protected Information for the purpose of this plan statement includes customer information (defined below) required to be protected under various legislative and regulatory instruments. Protected information includes both paper and electronic records.

In addition to an aggressive information security infrastructure, <YOUR COMPANY> also performs the following third-party assessments to ensure a strong security practice:

Network penetration tests
Application security code reviews
Application vulnerability assessment
Quarterly full vulnerability scans
External audit review
Continuous network event monitoring
IT Controls performance benchmark
IT Process risk assessment

The Information Security and Compliance office performs several critical roles, including managing the risks and protection of <YOUR COMPANY> information assets; the development and implementation of global security policies, standards, guidelines, and procedures; and managing security incidents to minimize impact to the business.

> In the following section, define the scope of the security group in the light of protecting sensitive information. Remember, you may be asked to prove that the scope is correct and that you actually do everything you say. Be factual and careful with words like "all, never, etc."

The information protection responsibilities of the Information Security Group include network security architecture, application and network access authorization, risk assessments, monitoring, and employee security awareness and training. The group maintains our corporate relationships with local, state, and federal law enforcement, as well as other related government agencies. The team members have been recognized as industry professionals, earning multiple top certifications in a variety of information protection disciplines. As part of their risk management responsibilities, in conjunction with additional departments of the company, the team conducts incident response planning and immediate investigation of suspected security breaches and assists with disciplinary and legal matters associated with any data compromises.

What Is Personally Identifiable Information (PII)?

> The Office of Management and Budget (OMB) defines personally identifiable information as:
> Information which can be used to distinguish or trace an individual's identity, such as their name, social security number, biometric records, etc. alone, or when combined with other personal or identifying information which is linked or linkable to a specific individual, such as date and place of birth, mother's maiden name, etc.

Customer information is the information that <YOUR COMPANY> has obtained from a customer in the process of offering a product or service, or such information provided to the Company by another company or third party. Examples of customer personal information include addresses, phone numbers, bank account numbers, credit and debit card account numbers, income and credit histories, and Social Security numbers, in both paper and electronic format.

These safeguards are provided to

- Ensure the security and confidentiality of protected information
- Protect against anticipated threats or hazards to the security or integrity of such information
- Protect against unauthorized access to or use of protected information that could result in substantial harm or inconvenience to any customer

This Information Security Plan also provides for mechanisms that identify and assess the risks that may threaten protected information maintained by <YOUR COMPANY> by the

- Development of written policies and procedures to manage and control these risks
- Implementation and review of the plan
- Adjusting the plan to reflect changes in technology, the sensitivity of protected information, and internal or external threats to information security

Identification and Assessment of Risk to Customer Information

<YOUR COMPANY> recognizes that it has both internal and external risks. These risks include but are not limited to the following:

- Unauthorized access of protected information by someone other than the owner of the protected information
- Compromised system security as a result of system access by an unauthorized person
- Interception of data during transmission
- Loss of data integrity
- Physical loss of data in a disaster
- Errors introduced into the system
- Corruption of data or systems
- Unauthorized access of protected information by employees
- Unauthorized requests for protected information
- Unauthorized access through hardcopy files or reports
- Unauthorized transfer of protected information of a third party

<YOUR COMPANY> recognizes that this may not be a complete list of the risks associated with the protection of protected information. Since technology

growth is not static, new risks are created regularly. Accordingly, the Information Security groups will actively participate and monitor advisory groups for identification of new risks.

<YOUR COMPANY> believes that current information technology safeguards are reasonable and, in light of current risk assessments, are sufficient to provide security and confidentiality to protected information described above maintained by the central Company units. Additionally, these safeguards protect against currently anticipated threats or hazards to the integrity of such information.

Security Plan Roles and Plan Administration

The **Chief Information Security Officer** of <YOUR COMPANY> is the administrator of this Plan. The <Working Title> is identified as the CISO for purposes of this plan. The CISO is responsible for assessing the risks associated with customer data and implementing procedures to minimize those risks to <YOUR COMPANY>. Internal Audit personnel in partnership with the CISO will also conduct reviews of areas that have access to protected information and assess the internal control structure put in place by the administration and will provide verification that <YOUR COMPANY> departments comply with the requirements of this policy.

Note: The following section is critical: Executive Management MUST formally identify the person who is functioning as the CISO. Without this, there is no oversight by executive management and the Board that many state laws require.

The Executive Team has appointed the CISO as the entity responsible for overseeing the development, implementation, and maintenance of the <YOUR COMPANY> information security program, and making senior management accountable for its actions.

> All regulators from the SEC on down are now demanding that the Board of a company be involved in the monitoring of and decisions around cybersecurity. Consequently, it is important that the CISO delivers a report to the board at least annually. The review of the report must be memorialized in the minutes of the meeting, along with any request for additional information or follow-up actions.

At least annually, <YOUR COMPANY> shall deliver a written report to the board that describes the overall status of the information security program. At a minimum, the report shall address the results of the technology risk assessment process, risk management and control decisions, service provider arrangements, results of security monitoring and testing, security breaches or violations and management's responses, and recommendations for changes to the information security program. The annual approval should consider the results of management assessments and reviews, internal and external audit activity related to information security, third-party reviews of the information security program and information security measures, and other internal or external reviews designed to assess the adequacy of information security controls.

The CISO shall ensure that Senior Management

- Clearly support all aspects of the information security program
- Implement the information security program as approved by the Board of Directors
- Establish appropriate policies, procedures, and controls
- Participate in assessing the effect of security issues on the company and its business lines and processes
- Delineate clear lines of responsibility and accountability for information security risk management decisions
- Define risk measurement definitions and criteria
- Establish acceptable levels of information security risks
- Oversee risk mitigation activities
- Design and implement a Safeguards Program

Employee Management and Training

References of new employees working in areas that regularly work with protected information are checked. During employee orientation, each new employee in these departments will receive proper training on the importance of confidentiality of customer records, customer financial information, and other types of protected information. Each new employee is also trained in the proper use of computer information and passwords.

Training also includes controls and procedures to prevent employees from providing confidential information to an unauthorized individual, including "pretext calling" and how to properly dispose of documents that contain protected information. "Pretext calling" occurs when an individual improperly obtains personal information of company customers so as to be able to commit identity theft. It is accomplished by contacting the Company, posing as a customer or someone authorized to have the customer's information, and through the use of trickery and deceit, convincing an employee of the Company to release customer identifiable information.

Each department responsible for maintaining protected information is instructed to take steps to protect the information from destruction, loss, or damage due to environmental hazards, such as fire and water damage or technical failures. Further, each department responsible for maintaining protected information should ensure, annually, the coordination and review of additional privacy training appropriate to the department. These training efforts should help minimize risk and safeguard protected information.

Information Systems

Access to protected information via <YOUR COMPANY>'s computer information system is limited to those employees who have a business reason to know such information. Each employee is assigned a user id and selects a password that meets <YOUR COMPANY>'s complexity requirements. Databases containing personal information, including, but not limited to, accounts, balances, and transactional information, are available only to <YOUR COMPANY> associates in appropriate departments and positions.

Systems requiring passwords must conform to the <YOUR COMPANY> Policy on User ID and Passwords. Systems that allow remote log-ins over the <YOUR COMPANY> VPN network must have passwords on all accounts.

<YOUR COMPANY> will take reasonable and appropriate steps consistent with current technological developments to ensure that all protected information is secure and to safeguard the integrity of records in storage and transmission. The Chief Information Officer is responsible for all servers and ensuring that they meet necessary security requirements as defined by information technology policies. These requirements include maintaining the operating system and applications, including application of appropriate patches and updates in a timely fashion.

In addition, an intrusion detection system has been implemented to detect and stop certain external threats, along with incident response procedures defined by <YOUR COMPANY> for occasions where intrusions do occur.

All protected information will be maintained on servers that are behind <YOUR COMPANY>'s firewalls. The Company has a number of policies and procedures in place to provide security to <YOUR COMPANY>'s information systems. These policies are available in the Company's Policy and Procedures Manual. The Company presently maintains a secure network for protecting the protected information of its customers and employees.

General Security Measures

<YOUR COMPANY> has identified and implemented several security measures to enhance our ability to monitor and prevent intrusions and situations that may compromise account information. Additional security measures are as follows:

- Antivirus <NAME> are utilized to monitor system files for planned or unplanned modifications and correlating general security events.
- Mail Gateways to monitor e-mail communications for sensitive information.

- Antivirus is utilized to automate the detection of malware on workstations and servers.
- Automated control and monitoring systems <NAME> to manage security controls and vulnerabilities.
- Digital Leakage Protection to identify sensitive data and quarantine, encrypt, or alert on inappropriate use.
- Configuration and patch management software.
- Web proxy filters.
- Outbound traffic monitoring alerts for APT and BotNet traffic leaving <YOUR COMPANY>.

<YOUR COMPANY> has enhanced its risk management processes as well as its tool portfolio to evolve with the increasing threat landscape. Enhancements to core processes and controls will continue to improve the security posture to manage risks to the company's information assets.

Data Center Redundancy

<YOUR COMPANY> utilizes a Redundant Data Center strategy. <YOUR COMPANY> has two geographically separated data centers each with its own redundant power infrastructure, generators, and bandwidth. This allows them to provide high availability business applications and backend storage.

System and User Account Administration and Management

<YOUR COMPANY> has an Access Administration team dedicated to assigning, modifying, and revoking access, which controls all aspects of user and administrative accounts on the network. User access is managed through Windows Active Directory and other LDAP-capable applications. Internal applications utilize custom authentication applications for access control management. Controls are in place to ensure user access meets password requirements and expiration periods. Access reviews are performed periodically for Active Directory and critical applications.

All data transmissions between <YOUR COMPANY> and our business partners use a combination of TLS or VPN encryption. In the event a data transmission is needed via CD or portable media, the data are encrypted and the media is shipped with tracking information. E-mail is protected via a Message Gateway that facilities e-mail encryption to authorized parties.

Remote access to the <YOUR COMPANY> network requires multifactor authentication using secure tokens. Without the tokens and a unique password, remote access to the network is prohibited. As a final line of defense, the internal network is protected from unauthorized devices by requiring each device to contain an authorized 802.X certificate.

Encryption

Database Encryption

Sensitive data stored at rest in a database are encrypted at the column level.

For internally developed applications, sensitive information is replaced with a token unique to that data element. The token is a unique identifier within <YOUR COMPANY> databases.

Third-party applications that do not have encryption built into the application and cannot support the use of the <YOUR COMPANY> custom security API may be encrypted using other approved encryption packages.

File Storage Encryption

<YOUR COMPANY> goes to great lengths to secure its customers' information. The primary storage environment for <YOUR COMPANY> file storage is a robust solution. Encryption appliances use AES (Advanced Encryption Standard) 256-bit algorithm to encrypt all data stored on the NAS (Network Attached Storage).

Encryption keys are managed by the appliances and are not accessible by system administrators. Keys are rotated regularly to ensure data security and meet the highest standards across the regulatory compliance landscape.

Monitoring and Audits

<YOUR COMPANY> has implemented a System to deliver constant security event monitoring and alerts related to anomalous activity at the firewalls and Intrusion Detection Systems (IDS). In addition, a variety of vendors and tools are used to conduct systematic network and application-level information security risk reviews. Monitoring solutions are used to ensure data integrity.

<YOUR COMPANY> also conducts monthly discovery for new devices in the network, as well as vulnerability scans and regular penetration tests to further increase visibility into the company's security posture. The scope of the assessment program includes the evaluation of the security posture of <YOUR COMPANY>'s environment supporting critical systems and applications. Retesting is conducted after remediation of findings is completed.

In summary, <YOUR COMPANY> conducts the following third-party assessments:

- Annual internal and external network and application penetration tests
- Application security code reviews
- Quarterly ASV vulnerability scans
- Industry (such as SSAE 16) assessment and certification
- Externally supported IT General Computing Controls (IT GCC) Audit
- Continuous perimeter security event monitoring (MSS)

And the following self-assessments:

- Monthly vulnerability and discovery scans
- Ad hoc risk assessments of processes and procedures
- Ad hoc event log monitoring

Internal Audits

<YOUR COMPANY> has an internal auditing group responsible for conducting audits on physical and electronic security, application and system controls, general computer controls, sensitive data access, and department policies and standards.

The methodology consists of reviews of existing documentation, one-on-one and group interviews of personnel in the effected departments, and access to any information needed for successful completion of the audits. After the evaluation, follow-up meetings are held with IT Management to review any concerns or questions identified during the audit, and an action plan to correct or modify the systems in question is created. Internal Audit will then follow the completion of the corrective action and retest as needed to ensure compliance.

Advanced Persistent Threat (APT)

APT Prevention

<YOUR COMPANY> has installed APT appliances that help protect internal resources against the increasingly dynamic nature of today's advanced attacks. Most defenses leave significant security holes in the majority of corporate networks and traditional tools are designed for the known patterns of attack not the attacks specifically devised to evade detection. Attacks now blend tactics like delivering malicious URLs and infected attachments through highly personalized and effective spear phishing e-mails. Then, malware infiltrates data and spreads laterally through file shares. By combining new technology with best-in-class external resources, <YOUR COMPANY> has positioned itself to defend against today's advanced targeted attacks.

Database Activity Monitoring (DAM)

<YOUR COMPANY> has incorporated a Data Access Management (DAM) technology for monitoring and analyzing database activity performed continuously and in real time. DAM provides privileged user and application access monitoring that is independent of native database logging and audit functions. It can function as a compensating control for privileged user separation-of-duties issues by monitoring administrator activity. The technology also improves database security by detecting unusual database read and update activity from the application layer. Database

event aggregation, correlation, and reporting provide a database audit capability without the need to enable native database audit functions (which become resource-intensive as the level of auditing is increased).

Some other advanced DAM functions include the following:

- The ability to monitor intra-database attacks and back doors in real time (such as stored procedures, triggers, views, etc.)
- Is agnostic to IT infrastructures
- Blocking and prevention, without being in-line to the transactions
- Active discovery of at-risk data
- Improved visibility into application traffic
- Data Loss Prevention capabilities that address security concerns, as well as the data identification and protection requirements of the Payment Card Industry (PCI) and other data-centric regulatory frameworks
- Database user rights attestation reporting, required by a broad range of regulations

Business Continuity and Disaster Recovery

Business Continuity

A Business Continuity Plan is documented to guide the organization in the event of a business interruption or natural disaster (Figure A.1). The business continuity plan is reviewed and updated annually. Information technology components of the business continuity plan are tested throughout the year according to a predefined schedule.

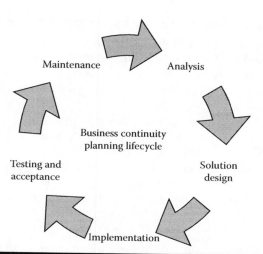

Figure A.1 Business continuity.

Disaster Recovery

A Disaster Recovery Plan documents the steps to be taken by the Data Center Infrastructure team to recover the hardware and all accompanying components. In the base case, this plan is reviewed and exercised annually to ensure that all changed environments are updated and, when necessary, replaced.

Physical Security

<YOUR COMPANY> has addressed the physical security of protected information by limiting access to only those employees who have a business reason to know such information. For example, personal customer information, accounts, balances, and transactional information are available only to <YOUR COMPANY> employees with an appropriate business need for such information.

Paper documents that contain protected information are shredded at time of disposal.

Management of System Failures

<YOUR COMPANY> is developing written plans and procedures to detect any actual or attempted attacks on <YOUR COMPANY> systems and has defined procedures for responding to an actual or attempted unauthorized access to protected information.

Selection of Appropriate Service Providers

Every organization should establish and maintain effective vendor and third-party management programs because of the increasing reliance on external and cloud providers. You must understand the details of arrangements with outside parties and ensure adequate controls and oversight for the engagement of the relationships and ongoing monitoring.

To ensure functions are conducted appropriately, organizations should have comprehensive contract provisions and adequate due diligence processes. They should also monitor service providers for compliance with contracts and service-level agreements. Contractual provisions should define the terms of acceptable access and potential liabilities in the event of fraud or processing errors.

Because of the specialized expertise needed to design, implement, and service new technologies, vendors may be needed to provide resources that <YOUR COMPANY> determines not to provide on its own. In the process of choosing a service provider that will maintain or regularly access protected information, the evaluation process shall include the ability of the service provider to safeguard confidential financial, PCI, and PII data. Contracts with service providers may include the following provisions:

- An explicit acknowledgment that the contract allows the contract partner access to confidential information
- A specific definition or description of the confidential information being provided
- A stipulation that the confidential information will be held in strict confidence and accessed only for the explicit business purpose of the contract
- An assurance from the contract partner that the partner will protect the confidential information it receives according to commercially acceptable standards and no less rigorously than it protects its own confidential information
- A provision providing for the return or destruction of all confidential information received by the contract provider upon completion or termination of the contract
- An agreement that any violation of the contract's confidentiality conditions may constitute a material breach of the contract and entitles <YOUR COMPANY> to terminate the contract without penalty
- A provision ensuring that the contract's confidentiality requirements shall survive any termination of the agreement

Continuing Evaluation and Adjustment

This Information Security Plan will be subject to periodic review and adjustment. The most frequent of these reviews will occur within <YOUR COMPANY>. The constantly changing technology and evolving risks mandate increased vigilance. Continued administration of the development, implementation, and maintenance of the program will be the responsibility of the designated Chief Information Security Officer who will assign specific responsibility for implementation and administration as appropriate. It may be necessary to adjust the plan to reflect changes in technology, the sensitivity of customer/customer data, and internal or external threats to information security.

Questions regarding this policy should be sent to the Chief Information Security Officer.

Appendix B: Talking to the Board

I've run into more "talking to the Board" experts than any other kind in my career. Granted, there is some political capital in getting granted access to the top management group of an organization and somewhere along the way people forget that the Board just wants information. So put away your tuxedo and tap shoes, and focus on creating and delivering a meaningful message.

Case in point: When Boards first started asking for a cybersecurity update as part of the risk overview of the company, the expected happened: I was scheduled to write a slide deck so the EVP of operations could update the Board on security. There were about 40 rewrites with a lot of talk about "optics," how the Board would view our efforts, and the message he wanted to deliver. Got a solid deck (finally) and our EVP hopped a jet to deliver his message.

Unfortunately for him, there were at least two Board members that had a good cyber background. As soon as he started, the Directors threw away the deck and told him what they wanted to talk about, unfortunately not what he had prepared for. He came back bloody and bruised, and like a good seasoned manager, he blamed the people who prepared the message. He hadn't done the background work to research the Board members. He forgot to talk in business terms, and he hadn't researched the subject of cyber beyond the deck he was given.

After one more bloodied EVP took a hit from the Board, they finally decided to send someone truly expendable: me. I took the time to read the minutes from the two previous meetings. I read the bios of all the Board Members and tried to figure out, based on their background, what questions might be coming.

Finally, I made sure that all the technical and operational programs had clear linkages to business goals and objectives. I also felt confident in my ability to answer any technical question they might throw at me. I knew I had to earn their trust.

It might have gone better, but based on the recent history, it was a stellar success. It was the first of many meetings, and as we built trust, the meetings were more productive. Moral of the story? When talking to the Board, just being a security guru doesn't guarantee success. They will not be impressed by the letters after your name, because many of them have letters like CEO. Do your homework, it will pay off.

If asked what has changed most in my job over the years aside from the threats, it would be an easy answer. It is talking to the Boards and Execs. When I started my career, we used to talk about the "ostrich defense" used by Execs and Boards. It said that if management had delegated the responsibility for an activity to a lower level of management, and they were not aware of any malfeasance or failure to perform, it wasn't their fault because they "didn't know." In other words, they buried their heads in the sand to avoid responsibility.

The courts took care of that defense over the years. They made sure that management clearly understood they were ultimately held liable for overseeing all things performed in the business under their watch. A series of laws and regulations have been enacted to regulate and enforce the direction and provide penalties for companies and individuals who do not comply.

Given all that, I wouldn't be doing a good job unless I said a few words about addressing the Board. Your skills and success in this area can make or break a security program. There are some great resources out there. For instance:

The National Association of Corporate Directors, in conjunction with the American International Group and the Internet Security Alliance, published a report outlining the five principles that all corporate Boards should consider "as they seek to enhance their oversight of cyber risks." I'd suggest you find and read the report. They list five principles, which fundamentally say

1. Directors need to understand that information security is not just an IT issue.
2. Directors need to be aware of the legal and regulatory impact to the company related to information security.
3. Boards should have regular access to competent information security expertise.
4. Directors should set solid expectations to the senior management of the company regarding their responsibility to implement and support information security experts.
5. Board-management discussions should include risk discussions about what to accept and what to mitigate.

There is now an understanding that Boards will have knowledge of the company's information security programs supported by open access to the cybersecurity expertise of the company. The external auditors and regulatory examiners now routinely ask for Board minutes that detail the discussions about cyber risk management. This is why it is now given regular and adequate time on the Board meeting agenda.

Boards now regularly meet with the chief information security officer (CISO) of the organization. Even though the Board is getting reports from Enterprise Risk Management and external independent sources, the Board is now taking the time to meet with the CISO at least annually. The purpose of the meeting is to get the state of cybersecurity from the organization's information security program expert. They want to know (be prepared to discuss the following topics when you address the Board)

- What the key cybersecurity issues are from the CISO's perspective. Important: Tie in the business view here. They do not want to hear how many viruses you stopped last month.
- Given the key issues you identified, what are your security strategies and current projects to address the issues?
- Identify any key roadblocks or competing strategies that may affect your ability to deliver (key roadblocks, e.g., budget, political agendas, arrogance).
- Be prepared to discuss current data breaches within the organization's industry and how your program compensates for the vulnerabilities that led to other breaches.
- The CISO is generally the "heart and soul" of an information security program in most organizations. The Board will value your input. Give it professionally and listen. Become a trusted advisor of the Board.

Talking to the Board of Directors

Why is it important that the Board understand the current state of cybersecurity in the company? Let's start with the value proposition as driven by the world in which we live.

Given the following circumstances:

- Significant cyber-attacks are occurring more frequently—There is no doubt here: not only more frequently, but also exponentially increasing in technological sophistication. This makes every company more susceptible to breach or significant damage to the financial health of an organization.
- No company or organization is immune. We can't name a sector that has not been affected. Even our most secure and sophisticated military systems have been compromised. This is because of the three vectors that can be leveraged

in an attack (remember our recurring theme through this book): people, process, and technology. Technological sophistication is not a guarantee against compromise.

■ The effects of a breach can significantly affect the profitability of a company long term, resulting in risks to investors. It's not just the immediate impact of the news of the breach, or the fines, or the publicity. Long term, clients and customers will react to a loss of trust in an organization, and may, as we say, vote with their feet to go somewhere they feel safer or more comfortable.

Therefore, we can reasonably assume that

■ Public companies must report significant breaches. The SEC feels that investors must know about cyber risks that could affect their investment and past breaches are a significant indicator. Remember hearing that "past performance predicts future results?" It may not always be true, but in the area of cyber, it is difficult and is a slow process for an organization to change its security culture.
■ The Board should include formal actions to monitor, assess, and govern cybersecurity based on the company's risk profile. If the Board is ultimately responsible for the oversight of cyber risk, then it must have formal processes and procedures on how to accomplish this responsibility. However, it is YOUR responsibility as the CISO to help them define that process and ensure they are fully informed. It won't be easy, and you may feel the culture doesn't support your efforts, but that is no excuse. Stand up and keep trying!

But, we understand there are barriers:

■ There is uncertainty regarding what is expected or required. Just as I experienced uncertainty or a lack of rules in my early career, the same exists today in the area of formal Board oversight of cyber risk.
■ SEC guidance and cybersecurity legislation is constantly changing. I've been told that laws and regulations are written in Washington, but defined in the courts. This is no different. The actual implementation of this direction will be defined through hard work, litigation, and industry leadership. This is an area that every CISO should continuously monitor. Use peer groups, industry organizations, news feeds, or any other source you can find. The only certainty here is that more change is coming for the next few years. Be aware and brief your leadership on new trends and actions.
■ Audit Committees traditionally focus on financial risk, so significant cybersecurity expertise may not be available to the Board. Let's face it, this is new to them too. They have organized for years to deal with "traditional" areas of market and financial risk. Yes, the audit committee did review internal audit findings, but they were not in-depth cyber reviews as we see today. Boards will recruit cyber expertise, but it will take time.

Given that, what are firms doing today? In an era of uncertainty, Boards are reluctant to add a full directorship focused on cyber. While I believe that it will eventually be commonplace, here is what I've seen today:

- Engage external advisor to the Board. Boards find an experienced consultant to provide the cyber expertise and advice to the Board. This is not a bad way to start for many Boards as they seek the right long-term solution.
- Add Director with formal cybersecurity and risk expertise. Adding a permanent director is a big step for a company and must be taken in deliberate steps. The challenge is finding a truly experienced cybersecurity expert whose experience matches the mission of the company. There is no existing certification for "Board Security Expert," and as such there are many people claiming expertise they simply do not have. Care must be taken to avoid a bad decision. The most prudent approach depends on Board expertise and composition, business strategies, and risk profile.
- While not recommended, an organization may choose to ignore the issue until mandated by SEC or a Regulator. This is a risk decision that must be carefully weighed. Failure to provide oversight could be construed as negligence if the organization has a problem or gets sued.
- Reliance on CISO for guidance and expertise. This is happening today. However, be aware that there will always be a question of independence and objectivity. The Board will also rely on external advice as it is required to do. It is not a reflection on you, it is required separation of duties and due diligence by the Board.
- The Board may rely on an External Audit Firm. However, care must be taken to ensure that the advisor provided by the firm has adequate operational experience that matches the business.

Liability—Best Left to Legal Staff

There has been much discussion regarding the liability of Board Directors and Executives in the event of a breach. I will pass on a few points in this section, but this is an area where the expertise of your legal group is needed. Here are a few points of note that have occurred in the fast few years.

In the case of Home Depot, a class action suit was filed by investors claiming "inadequate oversight" by executive management and the Board. This is similar to a lawsuit filed by shareholders following the Target data breach. Experts expect this trend to continue as derivative actions become more common.

The experts recommend that companies **proactively manage cybersecurity risks** by implementing and adequately documenting procedures to prevent and prepare for data breaches. Please note the requirement to adequately document procedures. It is also critical to keep logs and log files that prove the procedures were actually followed. Ask yourself, "Could I prove in a court of law that I actually follow my procedures?" You will need proof; your word will not be good enough in all cases.

While state corporation law is careful not to permit shareholders to second-guess every well-informed business decision adopted by the Board of Directors, inadequate oversight over corporate risk can serve as a basis for individual member liability. It must be determined that **the directors consciously failed to implement any reporting or information system or controls, or the directors, having implemented such system or controls, consciously failed to oversee its operations and thus failed to be informed of risks.** The seminal Delaware case defining the scope of the Board's duty of oversight is in re Caremark International Derivative Litigation, 698 A.2d 959 (Del. Ch. 1996). Go out and take a look, ask your General Counsel for the specifics. Every CISO should know the high-level facts of the decision.

The corporate jewels: what are you trying to protect? Sometimes the answer is easy. If you process credit cards, then it is a PCI data. If you are a healthcare provider, then it is healthcare information. If you are in the "other" category, it may not be so easy to positively identify, but in order to know what to protect, you must identify and locate your critical information. The critical information may include the following:

- Business plans, including merger or acquisition strategies, bids, and so on
- Contracts with customers, suppliers, distributors, and joint ventures
- Employee log-in credentials
- Information about company facilities, including plant and equipment designs, maps, and future plans
- Product designs
- Information about key business processes
- Lists of employees, customers, contractors, and suppliers

Every business will have a different list, and will assign a different value to it. This is a core element of every cybersecurity program and what is at the heart of corporate risk.

The Board Reporting and Oversight process: By now, you should know that I'm a firm believer in a process for all critical activities, and this is no different. So, when we say that the Board must provide oversight, what does that actually mean? The intent is for the Board to provide management with guidance on the status of the cybersecurity program. As part of this, they must review the current program status, understand the current risks, and approve the new plans, policies, and programs.

Additionally, the Board is expected to provide management with expectations and requirements, and hold management accountable to specific actions. They must clearly charge the company management with the central oversight and coordination of the program. The Board should ensure that company management assign a person responsible for the program and the coordination of information security

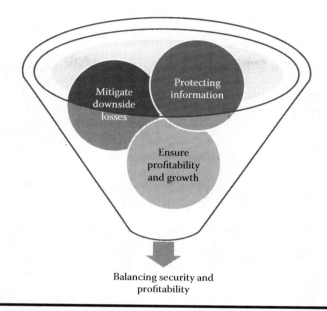

Figure B.1   Board engagement.

efforts. These duties should include but not be limited to risk assessment and measurement, monitoring, and testing and reporting.

The goal is to define a program to identify an information security program that balances the need to protect sensitive information and mitigate downside losses while ensuring profitability and steady growth for the company (Figure B.1). When done correctly, a program that balances profitability and security emerges. This should be presented to the Board for comment and eventual approval.

The Framework for Board Engagement

Let's look at the input side of developing a Board briefing (Figure B.2):

Top Cyber Risks Assessment

Ensure the Board understands the cybersecurity assessments performed by the organization. Without going into too much detail, include the type, frequency, and the population completing the risk assessment. Brief the Board on the top 10 risks identified by the assessment and report progress against the goal to remediate the risk. Your goal as CISO is to receive feedback, answer questions, and in general ensure that any oversight offered by the Board is acted upon and followed up at the next reporting period.

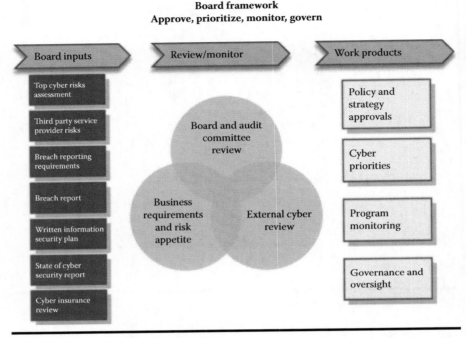

Figure B.2 Board framework.

Third-Party Service Provider Risks

Ensure the Board understands the cyber risks and regulatory obligations associated with third-party services including IT outsourcing (e.g., data center, application development, help desk), business process outsourcing (e.g., payroll, engineering design, logistics, accounts payable, accounts receivable), and Cloud solutions (Salesforce.com, Office 365, etc.). Review the status of your oversight for the business critical vendors.

Breaches and Breach Attempts

The Board should be aware of all major breach attempts made against the organization. Describe the vector of attack. Was the attack successful; if so, what was the root cause? If not, what control systems stopped the attack?

Discuss these events in terms of your remediation and incident response plan. If you don't yet have one, there is a sample plan with instructions included in Appendix C of this book. A standard set of data to be collected will facilitate root cause analysis and incident tracking. When dealing with regulators or auditors, you will find that keeping track of attempted data breaches proves that an organization has an effective intrusion detection and incident response program.

Identify and Report on Any Risks of State and Country Breach Reporting Obligations

Since almost every state and most countries have enacted data breach laws that require a notification in the event of a breach, you need a plan to identify your obligations and guide your response. Most have differing definitions and triggers, so a good source of quality information is needed to track proposed and enacted changes. Assuming you have a method of identifying higher-risk areas of concern, you must ensure that the Board understands how the organization assesses the risk of utilizing covered information in state and country jurisdictions. If there are any unique controls required for a jurisdiction, identify them in your briefing and ensure that they are supported by a process to remain current with changes.

Written Information Security Plan Approval and Yearly Update

In addition to being a formal record of the information security program for a company, the annual recertification of the plan serves as a verification of the Management's Commitment to Cybersecurity. Appendix A of this book contains a sample Written Information Security Plan (WISP) along with rationale and instructions for constructing you own.

Organization and Funding

The Board is ultimately responsible to ensure that the cybersecurity function is adequately funded to oversee the security of the organization. Additionally, they must ensure that an individual (not a department) is named to be responsible for the company's overall cybersecurity efforts.

The Board will typically utilize two methods to ensure that they are applying the right amount of governance. First is benchmarking with peer companies. What are similar firms doing, what risks are they assuming, and why? The second is to utilize the services of an external cybersecurity advisor who can bring the experiences of other organizations to the table. The key is to ensure that the Board uses all reasonable sources to ensure the span of control and the independence of the person in charge of cybersecurity efforts.

The Board Should Require an Annual "State of Cybersecurity" Report Delivered by the CISO or CIO

It is important that the report covers the whole scope of the cybersecurity program and documents the risk-related actions taken by the cybersecurity and executive management team.

Let's take a quick look at each of the sections:

The results of the risk assessment process: Was an enterprise-wide risk assessment performed and when? What risk assessment methodology was used, and was it consistently applied across the organization? This section should then list the prioritized risk assessment findings and the relative scoring, and list any pertinent comments collected during the process. Finally, is there an executive management consensus that the listed risks are actually the top risk for the company? In my career, I have seen where the risk function will issue a report that does not have agreement from the company management. If this happens, the whole report is in question.

The risk management and control decisions taken as a result of the risk assessment: It only makes sense that if a significant risk is identified to the executive management team, the company will take actions to mitigate or control the risk. This section should include any management responses to the identified risks, and any actions that have been taken to date to mitigate the risk.

Any specific service provider arrangements designed to control risk to the company: For example, a company may outsource part of its operations to a service provider. If such an arrangement is in place, what controls are implemented to ensure that any access to company-sensitive data is restricted to only those with a need to know? Has an onsite inspection taken place, and if so, what were the results? Does the company have a policy in place to manage third-party service provider relationships? If you look at all third-party relationships, which are the highest risk and what steps are being taken to reduce the risk? Remember, you can outsource your processing, but you can't abdicate your responsibility to protect your sensitive data, wherever it is. You, my friend, are on the hook. Remember the Target breach? Target was held liable even though the breach came from a third-party service provider network connection.

Specifically, related to third-party arrangements, you should include

■ Results of security monitoring and testing
■ Security breaches or violations and management's responses
■ Recommendations for changes to the information security program

Overall, the report to the Board should include the results of management assessments and reviews. Include any major gaps and comments and any high-level observations about the program or its organization. This is also the section in which you should include any internal and external audit activity related to information security. Be sure to list any management actions to which the company has committed. The information should also include the results of any third-party reviews of the information security program, or any other internal or external reviews designed to assess the adequacy of information security controls.

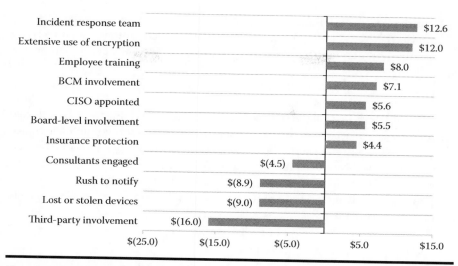

Figure B.3   Cost of a breach.

Cyber Insurance Oversight

The Board should receive an analysis that lets them verify that the cyber insurance coverage is sufficient to address the potential cyber risks. The information should include the projected cost per record of data breach as well as the total potential impact of a major data breach. An effective way to illustrate the effect of controls on the cost of the breach is shown in Figure B.3. The vertical axis represents the median cost per record of a breach. The bars represent the effect of a control (or lack thereof) on the median cost.

Board Actions from the Report and Briefings on Cybersecurity

There are several actions that should be on the Board agenda after it receives and reviews the cyber reports. Let's take a look at the primary activities:

Policy and Strategy Approvals: Annually, the Board should review and approve the policies, the WISP, and the Cybersecurity Strategic Plan that includes funding and staffing.

Cyber Priorities: Annually, the Board should review the Top 10 Cyber Risks for the company. These should be discussed in light of new and emerging threats and attack trends, and regulatory mandates. The Board should ensure that funding and staffing are earmarked to address the risks identified.

Program Monitoring: How is the program doing against the plan? The Board should review funding and staffing levels against plan and require explanation for any material changes in the plans they approved. This can be done at the Board level, but most organizations have the program reviews accomplished at the Audit Committee level. Since this committee usually receives audit results and mitigation plans, it is a natural fit for the cyber plan review.

Summary

It is generally accepted that cybersecurity will continue to pose a serious risk that the Board needs to actively measure and continuously monitor. For publicly traded companies, this means that the SEC will continue to mandate additional governance and oversight responsibilities for Boards. It is clear that in today's world, the onus is on the Board to take its strategic role seriously in providing oversight.

Cybersecurity is no longer simply another agenda item for IT; it is an agenda item for the Board as well.

Appendix C: Establishing an Incident Response Program

If you question the need for your company to develop an incident response program, just look in the news. As you look at the breaches that make the news, you will be able to separate the companies that had a response plan from those who don't. In your career with a company as well as your personal life, things will go wrong. You will find, however, that you will be judged by your response more than the original incident. Bad things happen every day to good companies and people. Your job as the CISO is to make sure the company responds in a professional, diligent matter.

NIST has great resources for developing an Incident Response program; in fact, a significant part of the framework I use is based on NIST Publication 800-61. It is easy to see why having a computer security incident response has become an important component of not just IT programs but company-wide response programs in general. Because cybersecurity-related attacks are increasing in voracity and pace, we must be prepared to act with precision and professionalism. This is not a place for luck; we make our luck through training and practice.

We don't have to "boil the ocean" with our plan. As I've stated throughout this book, the most important step is to start. Through risk analysis, we can define the areas that are the most likely targets for attack, and through preventative actions, we can hopefully limit the number of incidents. As we noted before, it is not just the voracity of attacks but also the speed at which they come at us. We must ensure that our plans enable us to respond rapidly and quickly. Just as with development and technology in general, agility is critical to our success.

Establishing clear procedures for prioritizing the handling of incidents is critical, as is implementing effective methods of collecting, analyzing, and reporting data. It is also vital to build relationships and establish suitable means of communication with other internal groups (e.g., human resources, legal) and with external groups (e.g., other incident response teams, law enforcement).

The NIST and other sources list a common set of activities that should be undertaken to build a complete incident response capability.

■ **Creating an incident response policy and plan:** The first step is to develop the foundation upon which the following activities are built. A good policy will set expectations and scope of the plan. Here is a sample, simple starting policy you can customize for your organization:

– *The purpose of this policy is to establish a protocol to guide a response to a computer incident or event affecting <COMPANY> computing equipment, data, or networks.*

– *This policy applies to all <COMPANY> employees, contractors, and others who process, store, transmit, or have access to information and computing equipment.*

– *Incidents are prioritized based on the following:*
  • *Criticality of the affected resources (e.g., public Web server, user workstation)*
  • *Current and potential technical effect of the incident (e.g., root compromise, data destruction)*
  • *Combining the criticality of the affected resources and the current and potential technical effect of the incident determines the business impact of the incident*

– *Incident reporting*
  • *All computer security incidents, including suspicious events, shall be reported immediately to your supervisor*

– *Mitigation and containment*
  • *Any system, network, or security administrator who observes an intruder on a network or system shall take appropriate action to terminate the intruder's access. (Intruder can mean a hacker, botnet, malware, etc.) Affected systems, such as those infected with malicious code or systems accessed by an intruder, shall be isolated from the network until the extent of the damage can be assessed. Any discovered vulnerabilities in the network or system will be rectified by appropriate means as soon as possible.*

– *Eradication and restoration*
  • *The extent of damage must be determined and course of action planned and communicated to the appropriate parties*

– *Information Dissemination*
  • *Any public release of information concerning a computer security incident shall be coordinated through the office of the CIO*

■ **Developing procedures for performing incident handling and reporting:** As in the example above, a clear set of expectations for an employee discovering suspicious activity is necessary. Escalation paths should be customized to match the hierarchy of the company.

- **Setting guidelines for communicating with outside parties regarding incidents:** This is a critical element as leaked or inaccurate information can cause significant damage to the reputation of a company. Rumors, once out in the public, can't be recalled.
- **Selecting a team structure and staffing model:** There are many models for consideration. Initially, build a core Emergency Management Team. Let that team define subsequent structures.
- **Establishing relationships and lines of communication between the incident response team and other groups, both internal (e.g., legal department) and external (e.g., law enforcement agencies):** *If you remember nothing else from this section, remember this: The worst time to meet your law enforcement liaison is the day you need them. Build a relationship in advance. Introduce them to your key executives and IT management. You will need a trusted partner: build that trust in advance. Call your local FBI or Secret Service office and ask for a liaison for your organization. You will be surprised how they will welcome the call.*
- **Determining what services the incident response team should provide:** When you start, keep it simple. As you mature and practice, you will add additional services. Initially focus on triage and isolation of the issue. Don't try to get overly complex out of the gate.
- **Staffing and training the incident response team:** Pick reliable, mature, experienced resources for your team. In this area, company knowledge is king; technical resources can be pulled in as necessary. A common mistake is to staff the initial response team with hard-core technicians who may not know how systems are supposed to work or function within the organization.

Preparation and Due Diligence

There are "common sense" actions that every organization should take as part of their efforts. NIST lists a few; let's take a closer look.

Organizations Should Reduce the Frequency of Incidents by Effectively Securing Networks, Systems, and Applications

The best incident is no incident. There is an old adage about the cost of quality called the rules of 10, which I mentioned previously. As a reminder: If you catch a product problem while it is being built, it may cost a dollar to fix. If you find the problem after the product is built, it may cost 10 dollars to disassemble and fix. If you have to recall the product from the store and fix it, it may cost 100 dollars to fix: You get the idea. As with product, preventing problems is often less costly and more effective than reacting to them after they occur. Thus, incident prevention is an important complement to an incident response capability. If security controls are insufficient, high volumes of incidents may occur. This could overwhelm the resources and capacity for response, which would result in delayed or incomplete recovery and possibly more extensive damage and longer periods of service and data unavailability. Incident handling can be performed more effectively if organizations complement their incident response capability with adequate resources to actively maintain the security of networks, systems, and applications. This includes training IT staff on complying with the organization's security standards and making users aware of policies and procedures regarding appropriate use of networks, systems, and applications.

Organizations Should Document Their Guidelines for Interactions with Other Organizations Regarding Incidents

The reason we do prior planning for emergencies is that clear thinking is difficult when, as we say, "our pants are on fire." If we do complete planning, we must also plan for the need to communicate with outside parties, such as other incident response teams, law enforcement, the media, vendors, and victim organizations. Because these communications often need to occur quickly, organizations should predetermine communication guidelines so that only the appropriate information is shared with the right parties.

Organizations Should Be Generally Prepared to Handle Any Incident but Should Focus on Being Prepared to Handle Incidents That Use Common Attack Vectors

As with any risk, some have a higher likelihood of occurrence. With your car, the incidence of a flat tire has a higher probability of occurrence than a major engine problem. That is why most cars have a spare tire and jack. Similarly, cyber incidents can occur in countless ways, so it is infeasible to develop step-by-step instructions for handling every incident. Different types of incidents merit different response strategies. According to NIST, common attack vectors are as follows:

- **External/Removable Media:** An attack executed from removable media (e.g., flash drive, CD) or a peripheral device
- **Attrition:** An attack that employs brute force methods to compromise, degrade, or destroy systems, networks, or services
- **Web:** An attack executed from a website or web-based application
- **E-mail:** An attack executed via an e-mail message or attachment
- **Improper Usage:** Any incident resulting from violation of an organization's acceptable usage policies by an authorized user, excluding the above categories
- **Loss or Theft of Equipment:** The loss or theft of a computing device or media used by the organization, such as a laptop or smartphone

In other words, these attack vectors have the highest probability of being the route by which a successful breach may take place. The lesson here is to plan in advance for these attack vectors and you will have a solid foundation for an incident response plan.

Organizations Should Emphasize the Importance of Incident Detection and Analysis throughout the Organization

Prior Planning and Monitoring. This is a common theme, particularly in Information Security. As CISO, it is your job to ensure that the organization is ready not just to respond to an attack but also to implement systems that give as much advance notice as possible. The earlier your organization gets notice of an ongoing incident, the higher your chance of a successful defense. As the NIST guideline states, "In an organization, millions of possible signs of incidents may occur each day, recorded mainly by logging and computer security software. Automation is needed to perform an initial analysis of the data and select events of interest for human review." However, you must remember that automation in itself is not a control. If you automate a bad process or one with inconsistent data, it will only allow you to make bad decisions faster. While event correlation software can be of great value in automating the analysis process, the effectiveness of the process depends on the quality of the data that go into it. Organizations should establish logging standards and procedures to ensure that adequate information is collected by logs and security software and that the data are reviewed regularly.

Organizations Should Create Written Guidelines for Prioritizing Incidents

Prioritizing the handling of individual incidents, or triage, is a critical element in the incident response process. Effective information sharing can help an organization identify situations that are of greater severity and demand immediate attention. Typically, there are multiple elements to an incident, so it is imperative that incidents be prioritized based on the relevant factors, such as the functional impact of the incident (e.g., current and likely future negative impact to business functions), the information impact of the incident (e.g., effect on the confidentiality, integrity, and availability of the organization's information), and the recoverability from the incident (e.g., the time and types of resources that must be spent on recovering from the incident).

Organizations Should Use the Lessons Learned Process to Gain Value from Incidents

After a major incident has been handled, the organization should hold a lessons learned meeting to review the effectiveness of the incident handling process and identify necessary improvements to existing security controls and practices. Lessons learned meetings can also be held periodically for lesser incidents as time and resources permit. The information accumulated from all lessons learned meetings should be used to identify and correct systemic weaknesses and deficiencies in policies and procedures. Follow-up reports generated for each resolved incident can be important not only for evidentiary purposes but also for reference in handling future incidents and in training new team members.

Data breaches and theft are reported daily, and hackers continue to find ways to attack data, despite tools and strategies to tighten data security. Every business should plan for the unexpected, including a data breach that can hurt your brand, customer confidence, reputation, and, ultimately, your business. It is important to develop an incident response plan to help you detect an attack and have procedures in place to minimize or contain the damage. Your plan can begin with being aware of the data security regulations that affect your business and assessing your company data security gaps. Once you have your plan in place, test it often. Early detection of a breach is a key benefit of an effective incident response plan.

Below is a sample of an Information Technology Incident Response Plan.

1. INTRODUCTION
1.1 Purpose and Scope
The purpose of the <COMPANY> Information Technology Incident Response plan for <COMPANY> is to clearly address computer security incidents and the appropriate response. This plan identifies the roles and responsibilities of the Computer Security Incident Response Team (CSIRT) and the roles of internal and external resources.

This plan seeks to assist <COMPANY> in addressing the risks associated with computer security incidents by providing guidance on appropriate response procedures. This plan concentrates on computer and data communications systems owned by or administered by <COMPANY>. This process does not include response to physical security incidents (i.e., stolen computer equipment, personal safety, etc.).

2. COMPUTER SECURITY INCIDENT RESPONSE CAPABILITY
This section describes the <COMPANY> Corporate Computer Security Incident Response Capability (CSIRC).

2.1 Events and Incidents
An event is an observable occurrence in a system or network. It is something that actually happened to an employee, company, system, or user that is shown to have actually happened by documentation in logs or audit files. Adverse events are events with a negative consequence, such as system crashes, network packet floods, unauthorized use of system privileges, and defacement of a Web page. A computer security incident results in harm or the significant threat of harm to <COMPANY> computer systems and data.

2.2 Computer Security Incident Response Team

A Computer Security Incident Response Team (CSIRT) provides a quick, effective response to computer security–related incidents such as computer security policy violations, denial of service attempts, hacking activities, improper disclosure of confidential information, breach of personal information, improper use of system or network, and other events with serious information security implications. The <COMPANY> CSIRT charter is located in Appendix <X>.

The CSIRT is authorized to take the steps deemed necessary to analyze, contain, mitigate, and resolve a computer security incident. The CSIRT is responsible for investigating digital security incidents and suspected intrusion attempts and for reporting findings to management and the appropriate authorities as necessary.

<COMPANY> CSIRT is led by a primary Incident Handler and has a secondary Incident Handler in the event of an emergency. The team is built from qualified, multidisciplinary personnel within <COMPANY>. This team is extensively trained and tested to ensure effective and efficient responses to incidents at <COMPANY>. An emergency communication plan has been developed with emergency conference bridge number and shared voice mailbox to ensure shared, uninterrupted communication between team members while addressing an incident.

2.3 Dependencies within the Organization

The CSIRT does not operate independently; instead, it relies on IT Support and teams throughout the organization for incident handling (Figure C.1).

IT Support Teams

IT technical experts (e.g., system administrators, network administrators, and software developers) provide the technical skills to assist in the response effort. Key resources include the following:

- Business application owners
- Client systems/server management
- Data management (database systems)

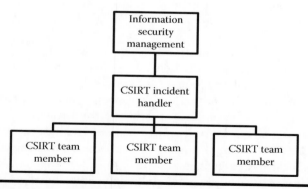

Figure C.1   CSIRT organization chart.

- Operation center (help desk)
- Network support

Corporate Teams

Various Corporate Teams play a role in incident response. Management is responsible for coordinating incident response among stakeholders in order to minimize damage, report, and authorize corrective actions. Key resources include the following:

- IT Leadership
- Business Leadership
- Corporate Security
- HR
- Legal
- Public Relations
- Functional IT partners

Computer Security Incident Response Notification Process

Following the identification of an incident, the Incident Handler is to contact the Corporate IT Security Manager (Figure C.2). It is upon the discretion of the IT Security Manager to notify key people within and outside of <COMPANY>.

3. INCIDENT ROLES AND RESPONSIBILITIES

Core team members

Support team resources would be drawn from the Information Security and Compliance Team.

Responsibilities

The primary responsibilities of the Core team would be to maintain the day-to-day operation of the CSIRT, provide advice, monitor for incident alerts and reports, manage incident investigations, and provide follow-up analysis and reports to the CSIRT management committee; in detail, the Core team would be responsible for the following support activities:

- Provide availability for contact and incident response
- Produce an incident classification scheme based on risk assessments for Information Technology resources
- Work with Computing Service central support teams to introduce proactive measures for incident avoidance or early incident detection
- Monitor external and internal sources for alerts and incident reports
- Notify and consult with IT support staff, network, and systems administrators
- Perform incident impact assessments
- Determine how incidents should be investigated and assign resources accordingly

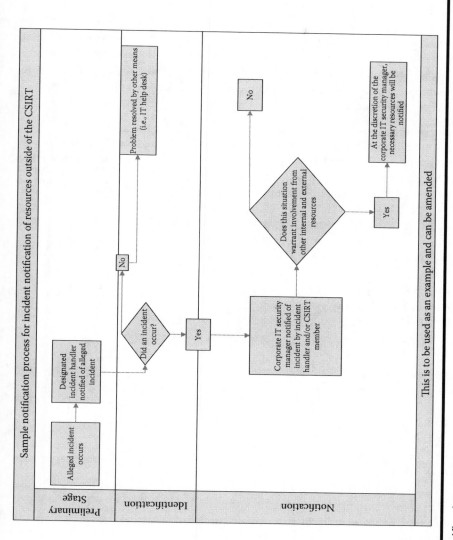

Figure C.2 Notification process.

- Manage, direct, or assist in incident control and containment
- Ensure that evidence is properly collected and documented
- Maintain chain of custody for all evidence

Support team members

Support team members would be ad hoc members, called upon to help the Core team as required. The Support team members would consist of systems, service, and applications specialists nominated by the various departments within the company. For incidents involving systems, services, or applications belonging to departments, at least one support team member would be a representative from the relevant department.

Responsibilities

The primary role of Support team members would be to assist the Core team during incident investigation and reporting. The Support team members would provide additional technical expertise in specialized subject, systems, or applications areas. The responsibilities of Support team members would include the following:

- Assist in incident impact assessment and damage
- Assist in incident control and containment
- Assist in evidence gathering and documentation
- Assist in interviews when required
- Assist in incident investigations and recommending courses of actions
- Assist in preparing incident reports
- Assist in incident eradication and recovery procedures
- Assist in incident recovery, where applicable

Extended team members

Some incidents may require resources from other Company constituencies:

- Legal
- Internal Audit
- Human Resources
- Marketing

These resources may be called upon under the direction of the CISO and CSIRT team leader as the severity of the incident under investigation dictates. Extended team members may be asked to provide assistance in specific cases.

CSIRT team leader

The CSIRT team leader would be chosen from the Core team membership. The team leader would be responsible for initiating incident investigations and all activities performed in support of those investigations, particularly the following:

- Convene IRT meetings
- Initiate and manage incident investigation
- Ensure that incident impact assessments are properly conducted
- Allocate resource for incident investigation—request support and extended team resources as required
- Liaise with external agencies and affiliations
- Consult with IT support staff, network, and systems administrators and senior managers for all incidents with a medium-/high-impact assessment
- Collate and archive all reports, documentation, and evidence
- Produce "follow-up analysis" report
- Report to management committee on operational issues, new incidents, and investigation status
- Coordinate IRT training and exercises
- Maintain list of local IT support staff, network, and systems administrators
- Recommend, acquire, and maintain operational resources—secure accommodation, hardware, software, and miscellaneous supplies

3.1 Incident Notification Roles and Responsibilities

- Data owners responsible for personal information play an active role in the discovery and reporting of any breach or suspected breach of information on an individual. In addition, they will serve as a liaison between the company and any third party involved with a privacy breach affecting the organization's data.
- All data owners must report any suspected or confirmed breach of personal information on individuals to the CISO immediately upon discovery. This includes notification received from any third-party service providers or other business partners with whom the organization shares personal information on individuals. The CISO will notify the appropriate administrator and data owners whenever a breach or suspected breach of personal information on individuals affects their business area.

3.2 Incidents Requiring Disclosure

The following incidents may require notification under contractual commitments or applicable laws and regulations:

- A user (employee, contractor, or third-party provider) has obtained unauthorized access to confidential information (PII, HIPAA, PCI, etc.) maintained in either paper or electronic form.
- An intruder has broken into database(s) that contain personal information on an individual or other confidential information.
- Computer equipment such as a workstation, laptop, CD-ROM, or other electronic media containing confidential information (PII, HIPAA, PCI, etc.) has been lost or stolen.

- A department or unit has not properly disposed of records containing confidential information (PII, HIPAA, PCI, etc.).
- A third-party service provider has experienced any of the incidents above, affecting the organization's data containing personal information.

4. COMPUTER SECURITY INCIDENT RESPONSE METHODOLOGY
Overview
Six Stages of Computer Security Incident Response

The phases of the Computer Security Incident Response are Preparation, Identification, Containment, Eradication, Recovery, and Post-Incident Activity. The Incident Response stages are generally executed in that order although overlap and reiteration may be required on some occasions. Figure C.3 illustrates the Six Stages of Computer Security Incident Response starting at Preparation and ending with the Post-Incident follow-up. The goal of <COMPANY> is to minimize the number of incidents that could occur by implementing controls based on risk assessments. Detection of security breaches is thus necessary to alert the

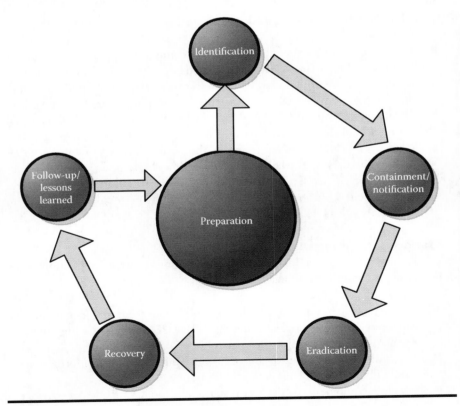

Figure C.3   Six stages of CSIR.

organization if an incident occurs. In keeping with the severity of the incident, the organization can act to mitigate the impact of the incident by containing it and ultimately recovering from it. After the incident is handled, <COMPANY> issues a report that details "lessons learned" from the incident: the cause cost of the incident and the steps for the organization to mitigate future incidents.

4.1 Explanation of the Six Stages of Computer Security Incident Response
Preparation
The preparation stage enables <COMPANY> to protect our company from the obvious threats posed by malicious or unintentional attacks.

Explanation: This stage requires the utmost vigilance as we establish policy and warning banners on system and make decisions with senior management before an incident happens to lay out responses. It is our goal to create relationships with law enforcement and CSIRTs to ensure cooperation should an incident require the notification of law enforcement.

Procedures: A CSIRT led by a primary Incident Handler has been built from qualified, multidisciplinary personnel. This team has identified a location for command post in the event of an incident and established visibility and a compensation plan. An emergency communication plan has been developed with emergency conference bridge number and shared voice mailbox to ensure efficient, uninterrupted communication between team members while addressing an incident.

Training is an integral part of the preparation stage as well as the success of the CSIRT. Therefore, meetings on scenarios, tools, and techniques occur often and are supplemented with white board exercises in which unannounced penetration tests are staged to evaluate team response. Training is not limited to the CSIRT, but extends to Help Desk personnel, system administrators, and network administrations. Cultivated relationship with and training these groups are <COMPANY> first-line defense as they are often the first targets of social engineering and in many situations the first to respond or receive notification of an incident.

Identification
In the event that an incident is reported, it must first be identified as an incident before progressing to further stages.

Explanation: In the identification stage, the previously appointed Incident Handler and the CSIRT will gather and analyze events to determine if there is or has been an incident.

Procedures: Extensive notes that can be later used as evidence are taken as a primary and secondary Incident Handler investigate the possible incident. Incidents can be identified through Network Perimeter Detection, Host Perimeter Detection, and/or System-level Detection. Unusual processes and services, files, network usage, scheduled tasks, accounts, and log entries are red flags and aid in identification of an incident.

Containment/Notification

Following the identification of suspicious activity as an incident, the CSIRT will begin the containment stage.

Explanation: The ultimate goal of the containment stage is to prevent the attacker from causing more damage by accessing more information or spreading to other systems.

Procedures: The three substages of the containment stage require short-term containment, system back-up, and long-term containment. This stage also includes notification of management and, at management's discretion, the notification of law enforcement and incident reporting agencies. During the short-term containment substage, the CSIRT will stop the advance of the attacker into the system while not destroying evidence on the compromised computer or server. Next, in the system backup substage, the initial backup of the affected system is created to be used for forensic analysis. Finally, the CSIRT will undertake long-term containment, in which the system is patched to allow the team to undertake the eradication stage and begin cleaning up the system.

Notification—The IT Manager will brief additional layers of management based on the severity of the incident and the potential for the disclosure of company confidential information. All contact with external media and press will be handled through the legal and/or communications department. Under no circumstances will an IT person grant a media interview.

Eradication

Explanation: The eradication stage is extremely difficult as it requires the complete and safe removal of any malicious code or other toxic remnants of the attack on the system, such as pirated software and pornography.

Procedures: The Incident Handler and the CSIRT will use information and evidence gathered during the previous stages to isolate the attack and determine the cause and symptoms of the incident. The team will improve system defenses and conduct a performance vulnerability analysis during this stage to ensure that the system will not be compromised in a similar way again.

Recovery

Explanation: When the threat and malicious material has been eradicated from the system, the CSIRT will restore the system to full operation.

Procedures: The system will be restored and monitored to ensure that the threat has been neutralized.

Post-Incident Follow-Up

The post-incident follow-up stage, commonly known as the "Lessons Learned" stage, requires the creation of a report to document the incident for feedback and constructive criticism to avoid future mistakes. A meeting to discuss the report and the incident will be held within two weeks of resuming production.

4.2 Explanation of Incident Severity Level Classification (Table C.1)

Table C.1   Security Level Classifications

Incident Severity Classification System		
Severity Level	*Description*	*Examples (Including, but Not Limited to)*
Low (Normal)	An incident with little or no impact to <COMPANY>. Procedures are already in place to handle the incident.	• Inappropriate use of e-mail, instant messaging, and other collaboration tools that threatens the security of the <COMPANY> system • Inappropriate usage of Internet access that threatens the security of the <COMPANY> system • Isolated virus or spyware infection (single computer or server)
Medium (Critical)	A threat potentially harmful to <COMPANY> has manifested itself. Some research required to determine possible impact and method of containment.	• A virus or worm affecting a <COMPANY> location • Suspected network intrusions • Notification by an external entity that a system within the network is the source of malicious traffic
High (Urgent)	A known threat is widespread and its impact is significant. Incident has broad impact implications on several operational groups, customers, and/or business units.	• <COMPANY> critical information has been compromised • <COMPANY> confidential information has been leaked in electronic form • Lost or stolen laptop • An Internet-facing website has been defaced • Denial-of-Service or Distributed Denial-of-Service attacks • Successful network/system intrusion/security breach • A virus or worm that has become widespread, propagating throughout the network, and/or is affecting a business unit • Breach of personal or credit card information • Any incidents requiring external disclosure

APPENDIX

Contents:

1. Contact Information (see Table C.2)
2. Sample Incident Roles and Responsibility Chart (see Figure C.4)

Table C.2   Contact Information

Position	Name	Title	Cell #	Office #	E-mail
CISO					
Primary handler					
CSIRT member					
CSIRT member					
CSIRT member					
Local law enforcement					
Federal law enforcement					
Legal contact					
Human resources contact					
Physical security contact					
Help desk contact					

<COMPANY>
Computer Incident Report for Medium- and High-Risk Incidents
Report Completion Date: _____ Time: _____
Incident Discovery Date: _____ Time: _____ Location: _____
Person who reported/discovered the incident: _____
Title: _____
Phone Number: _____ E-mail: _____
Incident Recovery Date: _____ Time: _____
Confidentiality Statement
Distribution of this document is limited to <COMPANY> Corporate IT Group. Access should only be granted to those with a business-related need-to-know. If you have any questions pertaining to the distribution of this document, please contact the Point of Contact listed below.

MUST BE COMPLETED WITHIN 15 DAYS OF REPORTED INCIDENT
Point of Contact (POC) Information
Name: _____
Title: _____
Telephone: _____
Fax: _____
E-mail: _____

Others who were involved in handling the incident (CSIRT, Management, etc.)

Name _____
Telephone _____
E-mail _____
Name _____
Telephone _____
E-mail _____
Name _____
Telephone _____
E-mail _____
Type of Incident: _____

Summary
The summary is at a high level, suitable for upper management. Elements include the following:

- Basic description of the incident
- Systems, services, and/or user communities affected by the incident
- Whether or not service was affected, degraded, or interrupted
- Duration of the incident (start to finish)

Sample incident roles and responsibilities

Phase	Action	Corporate IT	IT tech services	CSIRT	IT leadership	Human resources	Physical security	Legal
Prep	Security awareness training	Participant	Participant	Owner	Participant	Participant	Participant	Participant
Detect	Incident detection	Owner	May participate	None	May participate	None	None	Informed
Analysis	Incident classification and IT security notification	Participant	Updated	Owner	Informed	None	None	Informed
Contain	Evidence collection and initial defensive action	Participant	Updated	Owner	Informed	None	Informed	Informed
Eradicate	Digital investigation and permanent defensive action	Participant	Updated	Owner	Informed	Informed	Informed	Informed
Recover	Restoration of business service	Owner	Updated	Informed	Informed	Informed	Informed	Informed
Post-incident activities	"Lessons learned" review of incident	Participant	Participant	Owner	Participant	Participant	Participant	Participant

Figure C.4   Incident RACI.

Details of the Incident
Specifically, what caused the incident (who, what, where, when, how)?

The Notification Process

- Include every step in the notification process
- Automated monitoring notification
- Detail the flow of the incident response (i.e., John → Pam → Mike)
- Communication of resolution of the outage

Technical Details/Fix Actions

- Specific details of troubleshooting
- Specific changes (configuration, hardware, etc.)
- Steps to confirm the outage was resolved
- Ticket numbers

Conclusion

- What was the basic cause of the incident?
- What could have prevented this?
- Impact (none, degraded performance, downtime)
- Business criticality (revenue producing, business critical, low)
- Estimated cost (impact + business criticality)
- What prevents the incident from recurring?
- What additional actions or research need to happen?

Appendix D: Sample High-Level Risk Assessment Methodology

Introduction

A major theme throughout this book has been that we need to start simple. Start somewhere, get results, refine, and repeat. Doing nothing because the process seems too complex and expensive is not a wise approach. Besides leaving potential risks in place without a remediation plan, it will look like you aren't concerned with risk assessment to an entity like Internal Audit. The following is a simple approach to get started. It is adopted from a GAO document on risk assessment. Get started. Find the big risks. Document and remediate the risks, and repeat the process. As you repeat risk assessments, you will find that it gets easier and your organization will begin to see and appreciate the results.

Risk Assessment Objectives

The objective of the risk assessment is to determine the level of risk associated with a business function or process in order to determine the applicable security controls.

This is done by determining which of a predefined set of controls is appropriate for the business and comparing what is appropriate to controls already in place in order to identify and address gaps.

The key steps of the process are shown in Figure D.1 and discussed in greater detail on subsequent pages.

Initiating the Risk Assessment

Your organization's policy guidelines should require the business to conduct risk assessments at least once a year. Assessments are also required when a new business

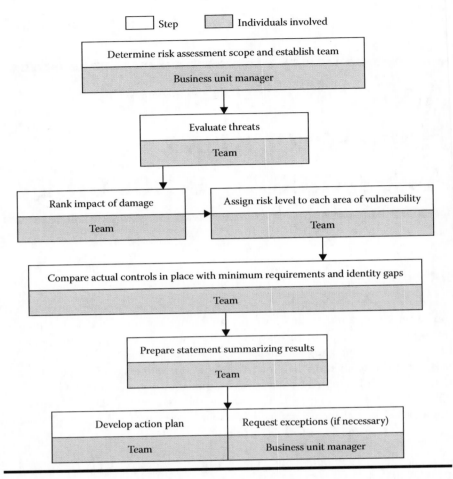

Figure D.1 Risk assessment.

operation is established or when significant operational changes occur. Responsibility for initiating the assessment lies with the business unit manager. The internal audit department should review compliance with the organization's risk assessment requirements through annual audits and report any noncompliance to business management.

Define the Scope

After identifying the need for a risk assessment, the business must determine the scope of the assessment and establish a risk assessment team. The assessment can cover an entire unit or a specific segment of operations depending on how information is accessed, processed, or disseminated. **In the early stages of risk assessment** maturity, avoid too broad of a scope. Bound the scope of an assessment in order to get meaningful results and provide some actionable insight and results to management.

Select the Assessment Team

The assessment team usually comprises five to seven individuals with expert knowledge of the business unit's assets and operations, and members from the information security office and audit department. After the team convenes, a representative from the information security office briefs team members on the risk assessment process and provides them with organizational guidance on conducting assessments. Ensure that all the members understand the process, the objectives, and the deliverables from the process.

Conducting and Documenting the Assessment

Risk assessment teams usually use predefined categories—developed by the information security and enterprise risk office—for ranking risk assessments. The categories cover specific elements that must be addressed for each assessment. This example includes five areas of potential vulnerabilities, four types of damage, and three possible consequences, as shown below. The purpose of predefined categories is to ensure a consistent approach throughout the organization.

Elements Considered in Ranking Risk

Areas of vulnerability
 Personnel
 Facilities and equipment
 Applications
 Communications
 Software and operating systems
Types of damage
 Unauthorized disclosure, modification, or destruction of information
 Inadvertent modification or destruction of information
 Nondelivery or misdelivery of service
 Denial or degradation of service
Potential consequences
 Monetary loss
 Productivity loss
 Loss of customer confidence

While there may be more elements to analyze in subsequent assessments, these are a solid starting point. They are easily understood across the organization and meaningful to business management. The first time you execute the assessment, document your processes to be used for future activities. Your eventual goal should be a documented step-by-step approach with associated training.

Determining Risk Level

The team's first step is to evaluate possible threats to information security that may affect the unit's operations and, based on its knowledge of the operation being assessed, consider the likelihood and consequences of the threat occurring.

The team should assign a risk level of high, moderate, or low for each area of vulnerability to show the possible effect of damage if the threat were to occur. In completing this step, the risk assessment team assumes that **no controls** are in place. (Later in the assessment, existing controls are compared to a set of control requirements to identify shortfalls.) The team uses a matrix to assist in its analysis of risk as shown in Figure D.2.

After completing the matrix, the team should summarize its findings by assigning a composite risk level to each of the five areas of vulnerability on the matrix. The team does this by considering the four potential types of damage identified under each area of vulnerability and judgmentally assigning a risk level of high, medium, or low to each area. The team then agrees on an overall risk level for each vulnerability in the last column of the table marked "Overall risk." Table D.1 is used to record this step.

Identifying Needed Controls Based on Predetermined Requirements

After determining the overall risk level for each area of vulnerability, the team identifies the minimum applicable controls that are prescribed in its organizational guidelines. The guidelines describe minimum requirements for each of three levels of risk—high, medium, and low. Guidelines require that each higher-risk category incorporate the controls of lower-risk categories. For example, a "high"-risk level incorporates controls from each of the three levels of risk—high, medium, and low. Similarly, "medium" risk includes controls for both medium- and low-risk levels.

Reporting and Ensuring That Agreed upon Actions Are Taken

After determining the minimum set of controls, the team compares those required controls with controls already in place and identifies any gaps. The team prepares

Risk assessment matrix									
Areas of vulnerability and possible effects of damage	Risk of monetary loss			Risk of productivity loss			Risk of loss of customer confidence		
	H	M	L	H	M	L	H	M	L
Personnel									
Unauthorized disclosure, modification, or destruction of information									
Inadvertent modification or destruction of information									
Nondelivery or misdelivery of service									
Denial or degradation of service									
Facilities and equipment									
Unauthorized disclosure, modification, or destruction of information									
Inadvertent modification or destruction of information									
Nondelivery or misdelivery of service									
Denial or degradation of service									
Applications									
Unauthorized disclosure, modification, or destruction of information									
Inadvertent modification or destruction of information									
Nondelivery or misdelivery of service									
Denial or degradation of service									
Communications									
Unauthorized disclosure, modification, or destruction of information									
Inadvertent modification or destruction of information									
Nondelivery or misdelivery of service									
Denial or degradation of service									
Software and operating systems									
Unauthorized disclosure, modification, or destruction of information									
Inadvertent modification or destruction of information									
Nondelivery or misdelivery of service									
Denial or degradation of service									

Figure D.2   Risk assessment matrix.

a short statement summarizing the outcome and documenting its decisions and decision-making process. It then provides the business a copy of the risk assessment table. Guidelines require the business unit being assessed to retain the completed matrix and documentation supporting the outcome, such as major threats considered, and major decision points, such as the team's rationale used in arriving at the appropriate level of risk.

Table D.1   Overall Risk

Risk Assessment Table				
	Risk Category			
Areas of Vulnerability	Monetary Loss	Productivity Loss	Loss of Customer Confidence	Overall Risk
Personnel				
Facilities and equipment				
Applications				
Communications				
Software and operating systems				

If there are areas where additional controls are needed to meet minimum requirements, management will develop an action plan and submit it for evaluation. The plan includes those controls management believes would provide the level of protection appropriate for the risk associated with the asset. Factors considered are security exposures, the level of risk associated with the business function or activity, the costs of implementing the controls, and the impact of noncompliance on other business units or operations within the organization.

If the business believes that the time needed to implement controls is too lengthy or the steps required are too costly, the business may request a waiver. The business manager must describe the rationale for the waiver and what compensating controls the unit has or will implement. The information and enterprise risk organizations must approve or deny requests that may affect the entire organization. If a waiver is approved, it should not to exceed one year.

While this process is very high level, it provides a solid starting point. It is easily understood and will not require an unreasonable amount of time investment from the business. Get started, kick the tires, and find out what works for your organization. Build the process with the involvement of the business. Be reasonable and show that you are a partner to the business, not just a "checker." You will find that done properly, this tool will be a valuable risk identification and remediation tool for the organization.

Index

A

Access control
  issues, 141
  lists, on network, 46
Accountability
  RACI matrix, 100
  for system, 27
Actions
  board, from report and briefings on
      cybersecurity, 251–252
  on objectives, phase of kill chain, 74
Adjustment, WISP, 239
Administration
  system and user account, 234
  user access and, 97–98
  WISP, 231–232
Adobe Flash, 42
Advanced Encryption Standard (AES), 235
Advanced persistent threat (APT)
  actors, 74
  prevention, 236
Advertisements, 193
AirCrack, 61
Alerts, 61, 73, 118, 235
American International Group, 223, 242
Analysis, incident, 257
Analysts, responsibilities, 87–89, 96
Androids, 62
Annual recertification, WISP, 249
Annual "state of cybersecurity" report, 249–250
Anonymizers, 53–54
Antivirus (AV) programs
  alternatives, 41–42
  companies, 46
  Linux servers, 42–43
  Mac users and, 42
  malware myths, 41–46

Reaper, 41
  security measures, 233–234
  up-to-date, 46
Apache, 43
Apple computers, 42
Applications
  architecture, 18
  DAM, 236
  deploying, 62
  layer, in OSI model, 25–26
  LDAP-capable, 234
  old/non-supported, 16
  public-facing, 43
  risk management, 27
  scanning, requirement, 23
  security, 35, 186, 255–256
Approval, WISP, 249
AppScan, 62
ARPAnet, government-created, 40–41
The Art of War, 124
Assessment
  cyber risks, 247
  high-level risk, methodology, 273–278
  risk, 121–125
  security strategy, 172–173
Asset(s)
  breach, 27–28
  management system, 26
  tracking IT, 26
  valuable, 189
Attacker(s)
  internal and external, 155–157
  running code, on your computer, 39–48
  smart and knowledgeable, 49–64
  think like, 65–81
Attacks
  forms, 49

frequency, 72
human based, 49
physical connection based, 49
protocol based, 49
SE, 47–48
software based, 49
state-sponsored, 53
types, 46–47, 49
Attack vectors, common, 256–257
Attendees, awareness seminars, 135–136
Audience, awareness, 135–136
Auditing tools, 46
Audit(s)
    internal, 125–127, 236
    logs, 46
    WISP, 235–236
Automation, 257
Awareness
    campaigns, 148–149
    defined, 151
    purpose, 151
    security, 130–131, 132, 144–150; *see also*
        Security awareness and training
    seminars, 135–143
    training *vs.*, 152
    WISP, 226–228

B

Backups, 42, 59–60, 103–104
Balance, maintaining, 86
Baudelaire, Charles, 166
BlackBerry, 170
Board engagement, framework for, 247–252
    actions from report and briefings on
        cybersecurity, 251–252
    annual "state of cybersecurity" report,
        249–250
    breaches and breach attempts, 248
    cyber insurance oversight, 251
    organization and funding, 249
    state and country breach reporting
        obligations, risks of, 249
    third-party service provider risks, 248
    top cyber risks assessment, 247
    WISP, approval and yearly update, 249
Botnets, 44–45, 53, 55, 57
Bots, 55
Breaches
    asset, 27–28
    attempts, board engagement and, 248
    cost, 30, 76, 156–157, 191, 251

document procedures, 245–246
Home Depot, example, 207–209, 245–246
penalties for, 52
reports, 5
state and country breach reporting
    obligations, risks of, 249
Bring Your Own Device (BYOD), 71, 189–190,
    200
Brown bag lunches, 147
Bugs, software, 40
Bulletins, 193
Business
    continuity plan, 237
    integration, 176
    knowledge, 83–102
BYOD (Bring Your Own Device), 71, 189–190,
    200

C

Cameras, security, 163–164, 198, 199
Campaigns, awareness, 137, 148–149
CapEx, 179
Capital expenditures, 179
Cardholder data, 160
Caremark International Derivative Litigation, 246
Cell phone cameras, 199
Certifications
    general, 155
    for security and compliance, 211–212
    stolen/forged certificates, 222
    types of, 155
Certified Ethical Hacker, 77
Certified Information Systems Security
    Professional (CISSP), 147
Charts
    Gantt, 178
    organization, risk management, 91–92
    RACI, 99–101
Chief Executive Officer, 92
Chief Information Officers (CIOs), 145
Chief Information Security Officer (CISO)
    advice, 98–101, 221–224
    first lesson, 9–12
    learning from history, 5–7
    overview, 3–4
    talking, to Board, 223–224, 241–252;
        see also Company boards
Chief Information Security Officer (CISO) Office
    basic components, 94–95
    compliance arm of, 96
Chief Risk Officer (CRO), 85, 92

Chief Security Officer (CSO), 92, 98
Chomsky, Noam, 197
Cisco, 187
CISSP (Certified Information Systems Security Professional), 147
Cloak-and-dagger approach, 200
Cloud-based providers, 63–64, 209
Cloud-based tools, use, 209–212
   certifications for security and compliance, 211–212
   compliance and security, 211
   data, storage, 212
   data encryption, 210
   physical security measures, at supplier's data centers, 212
   recovery plan for data, 210–211
Cloud security, 63–64
Code Spaces, 210
Command and control, phase of kill chain, 74
Common attack vectors, 256–257
Commonwealth of Massachusetts, 225–226
Communications
   central group and organizational units, 135
   guidelines, regarding incidents, 256
   issues, 31–32
   security-based culture, 192–194
   skills, 59
   WISP, 227
Company boards
   engagement, framework for, 247–252;
     see also Board engagement
   IT security awareness and training, 144
   liability, of Board Directors, 245–247
   talking to, 223–224, 241–252
Compartmentalization, of information, 56–58
Competitions, security-related, 184
Complexity
   avoiding, 120
   of modern software, 71
Compliance
   certifications for, 211–212
   CISO Office, 96
   program goals, 176
   risk management, legal, human resources and, 90–91
   security and, 211
Computer-aided design, 11
Computer Security Incident Response (CSIR)
   containment/notification, 266
   eradication, 266
   identification, 265
   methodology, 264–271

   notification process, 260, 261
   overview, 264
   phases of, 264
   post-incident follow-up, 266
   preparation, stages of, 265–266
   recovery, 266
   stages of, 264–265
   team (CSIRT), 258, 259, 260, 262–263, 265, 266
Conducting, risk assessment, 275
Conficker botnet, 55
Confidentiality, 80, 142, 158, 239
Con game, 138
Consulted roles, RACI matrix, 100
Containment stage, of CSIR, 266
Content management systems, 43
Contests, security-related, 184
Context-aware security, 63–64
Continuing education, 151
Continuing evaluation and adjustment, 239
Contracts, 52, 56, 58, 80, 213, 238, 239
Contractual training requirements, 149–150
Control(s)
   phase of kill chain, 74
   preventative, 109
   response, 110–112
   risk areas *vs.*, 113
Corporate Computer Security Incident Response Capability (CSIRC), 258–260
   CSIRT, 258, 259, 260
   dependencies within organization, 259–260
   events and incidents, 258
Corporate culture, 184, 196–197
Corporate governance, 213
Corporate teams, 260
Cost(s)
   awareness training, 131
   bots, 55
   breach, 30, 76, 156–157, 191, 251
   data breaches, prevention, 187
   data loss incidents, 158
   exploit kits, 165
   risk mitigation, strategies, 30–31
   switching, 32
   of systems, 32
   upgrade, 33–34
Country breach reporting obligations, risks of, 249
Creativity, 120, 184, 222
Credit card(s)
   botnets and, 45
   companies, 63

guidelines, PCI DSS, 158, 159–161
  processing procedures, 161–162
Creeper, 40–41
CSIR, *see* Computer Security Incident Response
    (CSIR)
Culture
  change, in organization, 130
  corporate, 184, 196–197
  security, *see* Security-based culture
Customer information
  defined, 229–230
  identification and assessment of risk to,
      230–231
Cybercrime, 53, 72, 166, 178
Cybercriminals, 42, 69, 166, 222
Cyber insurance oversight, 251
Cyber Resilience Review (CRR), 64
Cyber risks assessment, 247

D

Darknet, 53–54, 55
DarkWeb, 165
Data
  analyzing, 119
  backups, 42, 59–60
  breach, *see* Breaches
  cardholder, 160
  encryption, 36, 37, 74, 127, 210, 234, 235
  logging, 73
  loss, types, 158
  personal, 188
  recovery plan for, 210–211
  security, 10–11, 188–190
  sensitive, 25, 37, 156–157, 159, 165
  sharing, 192
  stealing, 156–157, 159, 162–167
  storage, 212
Data Access Management (DAM) technology,
    236–237
Database(s)
  encryption, 235
  security, 62
Data center(s)
  redundancy, 234
  of supplier, 212
Data loss prevention (DLP) tools, 157, 158,
    159–162, 195
Data Protection Directive, 105
Deliverables, 177–178
Delivery, phase of kill chain, 74
Dependencies, within organization, 259–260

Desktop security, 142
Detection
  incident, 257
  in risk management terms, 110
Disaster recovery plan, 238
Disclosure, incidents requiring, 263–264
Distributed denial-of-service (DDoS) attack,
    55, 166, 210
DLP (data loss prevention) tools, 157, 158,
    159–162, 195
Documentation, 28–29, 35–36, 245–246, 256,
    275
Domain servers, 73
Drafting, WISP, 228–239
Drozer, 62
Due diligence, 255–271
Duties, separation of, 86–90, 186

E

Earned certifications, for security and
    compliance, 211–212
Education
  on BYOD, 200
  continuing, 151
  example of, 152
  security-based culture, 200
  security skills, 152
  users, 57
  WISP, 226–228
Elements
  People, Process, and Technology model, 16–17
  in ranking risk, 275–276
E-mails, 43, 137–138, 142, 157, 195, 208, 234
Employee(s)
  compartmentalization of information,
      56–58
  incident response team, 255
  internal compromises, 157
  legal, 245–247
  loyalty, 162–167
  management, WISP, 232–233
  monitoring, 163–164
  morale, 196–197
  screenings, 162
  security concepts, 31–32
  stealing sensitive information, 156–157
  training, 5, 30, 32
  Use Cases, employment of, 31–32
Encryption
  connections, 54
  data, 36, 37, 74, 127, 210, 234, 235

database, 235
e-mail, 234
end point, 55, 124
file storage, 235
sensitive files, 37
use of, 140
End-user training, 130–131
EnerVest, 206–207
Engagement, Board, *see* Board engagement
Engineering
    SE, 47–48, 52, 138–139, 195, 200
    security operations and, 96–97
Enterprise, 75
Enterprise, risk management within, 84–86
Enterprise resource planning (ERP) system,
    20
Environment control, 26
Eradication stage, of CSIR, 266
European Union (EU), Data Protection
    Directive, 105–106
Evaluation, continuing, 239
Events, CSIRC, 258
Evolution, information security, 169–180
    assessment and measurement, 172–173
    capital expenditures, 179
    foundation/strategy, 172
    funding planning, 179–180
    key risk identification, 173–174
    operational expenses, 179–180
    overview, 169–171
    planning cycle, 172
    process inputs, 175–178
    strategic plan, development, 174–180
    strategic planning, 171–172
Executives, IT security awareness and training
    responsibilities, 144
Executive Steering Committee, 92, 93
Expenditures, capital, 179
Expenses, operational, 179–180
Exploitation, phase of kill chain, 74
Exploit kits, 165
Extended team members, 262–263

F

Facebook, 76
Federal Financial Institutions Examinations
    Council, 180
Federal Information Security Management Act,
    158
File servers, 73
File storage encryption, 235

Financial institutions, security breaches, 191–192
Firewalls, 72, 73
Flaws, security, 20–21
Forensics analysis, 59
Formal training, 147
Foundation
    security strategy, 172
    weak, risks and, 15–37
Framework
    for Board engagement, *see* Board engagement
    security culture, 196
Functions
    of information security group, 16–17
    outsourcing, 183, 209
Funding
    board engagement, 249
    cybercrimes, 166
    level of, 191
    security awareness and training program,
        144, 145, 149–150
    strategic planning, 179–180

G

Game of Thrones, 184
Gantt chart, 178
General certification, 155
General users, security awareness education,
    135–136
Gerstner, Louis, V., Jr., 182
Glass–Steagall Act, 105
Goals
    awareness material, 136
    company, 101–102
    security, 101
Golden Rule, 79
Gorbachev, Mikhail, 204
Governance, corporate, 213
Gramm–Leach–Bliley Act (GLBA), 105, 158
Guidelines
    document, for interactions with other
        organizations regarding incidents, 256
    PCI DSS credit card, 158, 159–161
    written, for prioritizing incidents, 257

H

Habermas, Jurgen, 197
Hackers
    ethical, 62
    penetration test and, 24
    vulnerabilities, focus on, 21

Health Insurance Portability and
    Accountability Act, 158
Hidden Service URLs, 54
High-level risk assessment methodology,
    sample, 273–278
    assessment team, selection, 275
    conducting and documenting, 275
    elements, in ranking risk, 275–276
    initiating, 273–274
    matrix, 276–278
    needed controls, based on predetermined
        requirements, 276
    objectives, 273
    overall risk, 278
    overview, 273
    risk level, determining, 276
    scope, defining, 274–275
Hire
    new hire training, 133–135
    outsiders, 80
    reputable firms, 79, 80–81
    skilled people, 78–79
Home Depot, 207–209, 245–246
Honeypots, 72
Human resources, 90–91
Hybrid Clouds, 64

I

Identification
    key risk, 173–174
    stage, of CSIR, 265
Identity theft, 158
Incident response program, establishing,
    253–271
    common attack vectors, 256–257
    CSIRC, 258
    detection and analysis, importance, 257
    document guidelines for interactions with
        other organizations, 256
    effectively securing networks, systems, and
        applications, 255–256
    handling and reporting, developing
        procedures, 254
    Information Technology Incident Response
        Plan, sample, 258–271
    lessons learned process to gain value from
        incidents, 257–258
    NIST, 253, 254
    policy and plan, creating, 254
    preparation and due diligence, 255–271
    services, determining, 255

    setting guidelines, 255
    staffing and training, 255
    team structure and staffing model, selecting,
        255
    written guidelines for prioritizing incidents,
        257
Information
    absorbing, filtering, and processing, 119
    compartmentalization of, 56–58
    customer, 229–231
    disclosure of, 158
    owners, 146
    protection, 142
    reducing uncertainty, 119
Information Risk Officers (IROs), 94
Information security
    computer-aided design, 11–12
    endless possibilities, 10–11
    evolution, *see* Evolution
    goals and objectives, 101
    primary functions, 16, 17
    rules, 12
    WISP, *see* Written Information Security
        Plan (WISP)
Information Security Department Staffing,
    94–96
Information Security Executive Council, 93
Information Security Officer Committee, 92,
    93–94
Information Security Officers (ISO),
    responsibilities, 95
Information Sharing and Analysis Centers
    (ISACs), 192
Information Sharing and Analysis
    Organizations (ISAOs), 192, 193
Information systems, WISP, 233–238
    APT appliances, 236
    business continuity and disaster recovery,
        237–238
    DAM technology, 236–237
    data center redundancy, 234
    encryption, 235
    general security measures, 233–234
    monitoring and audits, 235–236
    system and user account administration and
        management, 234
Information technology (IT)
    owner, 27
    security awareness and training, 144–150
Information Technology Incident Response
    Plan, sample, 258–271
    contact information, 268

corporate teams, 260
CSIRC, 258–260
CSIR methodology, 264–266
CSIR notification process, 260
CSIRT, 258, 259, 260, 262–263, 265, 266
dependencies within organization,
    259–260
incident roles and responsibilities,
    260–264
overview, 258
purpose and scope, 258
requiring disclosure, 263–264
security level classifications, 267–271
support teams, 259–260
Informed person/position, RACI matrix, 100
Initiating, risk assessment, 273–274
Inputs, process, 175–178
Insider threat, 52
Installation, phase of kill chain, 74
Insurance, cyber, 80, 191–192, 251
Integrated Risk Management (IRM) strategies,
    93, 94
Integration, business, 176
Internal audit
    dealing with, 125–127
    WISP, 235–236
Internal trust, 213–217
International Business Machines Corporation
    (IBM), 182
International Organized Crime Threat
    Assessment (IOCTA), 53
Internet
    computer crime and, 105
    drawback, 54
    government-created ARPAnet, 40–41
    international law, 53
    packet filters, 11
    proxies and controls, 43–44
    war, 53
Internet Security Alliance, 223, 242
Intrusion detection, approach to, 156
Intrusion Detection Systems (IDS), 235
Intrusion Prevention System (IPS) devices, 73
Investment priorities, 177
iPhone, 170
ISACA.org, 174

J

Jacek, Rick, 6
Java, 42
JBoss, 43

K

Keep it simple, stupid (KISS) principle, 120
Key risk identification, 173–174
Kill chain, 73–78
    defined, 73
    examples, 75
    phases, 74
    process, 74–75
KISS (keep it simple, stupid) principle, 120

L

Laptop security
    with cable locks, 186
    while on travel, 140–141
Leadership, 191
Leakage, 158
Learning, from history, 5–7
Legality, 90–91
Legal staff, 245–247
Lessons learned process, to gain value from
    incidents, 257–258
Liability, of Board Directors, 245–247
Life cycle, support, 19
Line managers, awareness education for, 135
LinkedIn, 48
Linux servers, 42–43, 128
Lloyd, Timothy, 204–206
Lockheed SR-71 Blackbird, 34
Log files, 60
Logical access, to systems, 139
Loss
    consequences of, 158
    types, 158
Los Zetas, 166
Loyalty, employee, 162–167

M

Mac users, AV and, 42
Madoff, Bernie, 204
Mail Gateways, 233
Malware
    category, 40
    infection, production networks and, 25
    myths, 41–46
    overview, 40
Management
    employee, WISP, 232–233
    organizational, 92–94
    password, 137, 185

risk, *see* Risk management
system and user account, 234
of system failures, 238
Managers, IT security awareness and training
responsibilities, 145–146
Marketing folks, communications, 194
McAfee, 187, 222
Means (resources), risk *vs.*, 117, 118–119
Measurement
general security, 233–234
physical security, at supplier's data centers, 212
security-based culture, 197–198
security strategy, 172–173
Medical transcription, 208–209
Message Gateway, 234
Methodology
CSIR, 264–271
training, 132–133
Metrics, security-based culture, 197–198
Microsoft, 19, 58, 71, 128
Misconceptions, scanning, 23–26
Misuse, company resources, 130–131
Mobile devices, 36, 55, 62, 189–190
Model structure, risk management, 91–92
Modems, 62–63
Monitoring
around-the-clock, 60
DAM technology for, 236–237
employees, 163–164
Internet and phone communications, 198
networks, 73–78
ongoing risk, 213
system, 60
WISP, 235–236
Morale, employee, 196–197
Multilayered defense, 60
Myths
malware, 41–46
patching, 21–22

N

Name recognition, 80
National Association of Corporate Directors,
223, 242
National Cyber Security Awareness Month, 184
National Institute of Standards and Technology
(NIST), 151–152, 180, 253, 254
Network Attached Storage (NAS), 235
Networks
another business, penetration, 40
monitoring, 73–78

of other countries, penetration, 40
production, containing sensitive data, 25
securing, effectively, 255–256
security alerts, 73
segregating, 72
social network sites, 57
vigilance, 72–73
VPNs, 54, 63
wireless, 61–63
New CISO, advice for, 98–101, 221–224
New hire training, 133–135
Newsletters, organizational, 148
Notification process, CSIR, 260, 261, 263, 266

O

Objectives
risk assessment, 273
risk management, 107
security, 101
Office of Management and Budget (OMB), 229
Offshore providers, 52–53
Omega Engineering, 204–206
Onshore outsourced services, 52
Open System Interconnection (OSI) layers,
25–26
OpenVAS, 62
Operating systems
malware, attack, 43
new versions, 19
obsolete, 18
Operational expenses, 179–180
OpEx, 179
Opportunity, preparation and, *see* Preparation
Organizational management, risk management
and, 92–94
Organizational newsletters, 148
Organizational pressures, risk *vs.*, 87
Organization chart, risk management, 91–92
Organization(s)
board engagement, 249
dependencies within, 259–260
document guidelines for interactions with
others, 256
effectively securing networks, systems, and
applications, 255–256
incident detection and analysis, importance,
257
kinds of, 155–168
lessons learned process to gain value from
incidents, 257–258
preparation, to handle any incident, 256–257

security-based culture, *see* Security-based
culture
security policies, 46
written guidelines for prioritizing incidents,
creating, 257
Outside intelligence, 175–176
Outsourcing
benefits, 209
business process, 248
data storage and processing, 209, 212, 250
functions, 183, 209
services, 52, 208
Owners
data, 263
information, 146
IT, 27

P

Packet filters, 11
Paper shredder, 199
Password
change interval, 139–140
cracking, 49
default, 21, 24
expiration, 127
management, 185
protection, 36, 133, 139–140
selection, 139–140, 233
sharing, 133, 138, 139
usage and management, 137
Patching, 19–22
breaking custom programs/applications,
70–71
implement, 186
MS Server 12, 32
myths, 21–22
overview, 19–21
Patton, George S., 75, 76, 77
Payment Card Industry Data Security
Standards (PCI DSS)
credit card guidelines, 158, 159–161
regulations, 43
PCI compliance, defined, 211
PCI DSS (Payment Card Industry Data
Security Standards)
credit card guidelines, 158, 159–161
regulations, 43
Penalties, for breaches, 52
Penetration
another business' network, 40
networks of other countries, 40

Penetration tests
application, 79–80
scanning and, 23–25
vendor, picking, 79
People, Process, and Technology model, 6,
16–18, 104–106, 107–108, 112–113,
120, 214–215
Personal data, 188
Personally identifiable information (PII),
229–230
Phishing, 57–58, 195, 208
Physical access, to spaces, 141
Physical security
measures, at supplier's data centers, 212
of protected information, 238
Picking, right penetration test vendor, 79
"Plan, Do, Check, Act" loop, 172
Planning
attack and breach, 167–168
business continuity, 237
cycle, 172
disaster recovery, 238
project, 121–125
recovery, for data, 210–211
risk, 121–125
WISP, *see* Written Information Security
Plan (WISP)
for worst, 58–61
Planning, strategic
capital expenditures, 179
development, 174–180
funding, 179–180
operational expenses, 179–180
process inputs, 175–178
security, 171–172
Policies, security, 143–144
Polymorphism, 222
Ponemon Institute, 163
Poor economy, employee loyalty, 162–167
Porn, visiting, 43–44
Portable Document Format (PDF), 74
Posters, security, 193
Post-incident follow-up stage, CSIR, 266
Powers, Francis Gary, 34
Predetermined requirements, needed controls
based on, 276
Preparation
CSIR, stages, 265
incident response program, 255–271
Preparation, opportunity and, 129–153
awareness campaigns, 148–149
awareness seminars, 135–143

brown bag lunches, 147
CIOs, 145
company board and executives, 144
end-user training and security awareness,
        130–131, 132
formal training, 147
funding, 149–150
high school memories, 132
IT security program manager, 145
managers, 145–146
new hire training, 133–135
organizational newsletters, 148
roles and responsibilities, 144–147
security policy, 143–144
tests and quizzes, 149
training methods, 132–133
users, 146–147
Pretext calling, 232
Prevention
    approach, DLP systems, 159–162
    APT, 236
    in risk management terms, 109
Principles
    KISS, 120
    Safe Harbor, 106–113
Prioritizing incidents, written guidelines for, 257
Privacy Act, 158
Procedures
    credit card processing, 161–162
    developing, for performing incident
        handling and reporting, 254
    documenting, for data breaches, 245–246
Process inputs, 175–178
Production networks, containing sensitive data, 25
Productivity, security-based culture, 190–192
Professional development, 153
Professionalization, 153
Program manager, IT security awareness and
        training, 145
Project planning, 121–125
Protection
    from attacks, 46–47, 137
    information, 142
    whistleblower, 163
Providers
    cloud-based, 63–64, 209
    offshore, 52–53
    service, 238–239, 248
Provision/de-provision users, 97
Purpose, Information Technology Incident
        Response Plan, 258
PWN Pad, 62

Q

Questionable sites, 43–44
Quizzes, 149

R

Ranking risk, elements in, 275–276
Ransomware, types, 41–42
Reagan, Ronald, 204
Reaper, 41
Reconnaissance, phase of kill chain, 74
Recording Industry Artist Association (RIAA),
        51
Recording Industry Association of America
        (RIAA), 156
Recovery
    plan, for data, 210–211
    processes, 112–113
    stage, of CSIR, 266
Redundancy, data center, 234
Regulatory drivers, 175
Relays, Tor server, 54
Replacing, systems, 33–34, 35
Reports
    annual "state of cybersecurity" report,
        249–250
    board actions from report and briefings on
        cybersecurity, 251–252
    penetration-testing vendor, selection, 80
    risk of state and country breach reporting
        obligations, 249
    vendor risk management program, 213
Requirements
    contractual training, 149–150
    funding, 149–150
    predetermined, needed controls based on, 276
    scanning, 23–37
Resiliency, risk controls and, 109
Resources (means), risk *vs.*, 117, 118–119
Response controls, 110–112
Response program, incident, *see* Incident
        response program
Responsibilities
    analysts, 87–89, 96
    core team members, 260, 262
    CSIRT, 258, 260, 262–263
    incident, 260–264
    ISO, 95
    RACI matrix, 99
    support team members, 262
    for system, 27

Responsibilities, IT security awareness and
        training, 144–147
    CIOs, 145
    company board and executives, 144
    managers, 145–146
    program manager, 145
    users, 146–147
Responsible, accountable, consulted, and
        informed (RACI) matrix, 99–101
Responsible Disclosure Policy, Facebook, 76
Reviewing
    test documentation, 28–29
    vendor risk management program, 213
    WISP, 227–228
Rework, 85
Risk management
    detection, activity, 110
    legal, compliance, and human resources,
        90–91
    model structure, 91–92
    objective of, 107
    organizational management, interaction,
        92–94
    people, process, and technology
        methodology and, 104–106
    prevention, activity, 109
    recovery processes, 112–113
    response controls, 110–112
    role, within enterprise, 84–86
    scanning and, 27–33
Risk(s)
    assumption, 115–128
    cyber risks assessment, 247
    defined, 117
    high-level, assessment methodology,
        273–278
    identification and assessment, to customer
        information, 230–231
    internal audit, dealing with, 125–127
    key risk identification, 173–174
    level, determining, 276
    matrix, 29–30
    means *vs.*, 117, 118–119
    mitigation plans, 177
    mitigation strategies, 30, 36
    organizational pressures *vs.*, 87
    planning, 121–125
    ranking, elements in, 275–276
    simplicity, strive for, 120–121
    state and country breach reporting
        obligations, 249
    third-party service provider, 248

too many alerts, 118
    types, 108
    uncertainty and, 118–119, 244, 245
    weak foundation and, 15–37
Roles
    CSIRT, 258, 260, 262–263
    incident, 260–264
    WISP, 231–232
Roles, IT security awareness and training,
        144–147
    CIOs, 145
    company board and executives, 144
    managers, 145–146
    program manager, 145
    users, 146–147
Rules, of Information Security, 12

S

Safe Harbor principles, 106–113
Scanning
    environment control, 26
    misconceptions, 23–26
    penetration test and, 23–25
    requirement, 23–37
    risk management, 27–33
    tracking IT assets, 26
    vulnerabilities, 23–24
Scope
    Information Technology Incident Response
        Plan, 258
    risk assessment, 274–275
Screenings, employee, 162
SCUBA, 62
SE (social engineering), 47–48, 52, 138–139,
        195, 200
Secret police, 7
Security
    awareness, 130–131, 132
    certifications for, 211–212
    compliance and, 211
    context-aware, 63–64
    data, 10–11, 188–190
    desktop, 142
    fixes, 31
    flaws, 20–21
    laptop, while on travel, 140–141
    measures, general, 233–234
    operations and engineering, 96–97
    physical, 212, 238
    policies, 46, 143–144
    system, process of testing, 127–128

Security awareness and training, 144–150
  brown bag lunches, 147
  campaigns, 148–149
  CIOs, 145
  company board and executives, 144
  formal training, 147
  IT security program manager, 145
  managers, 145–146
  organizational newsletters, 148
  roles and responsibilities, 144–147
  users, 146–147
Security-based culture, 181–201
  basics, 185–187
  communications, 192–194
  data security, 188–190
  e-mails, 195
  employee morale, 196–197
  framework, 196
  metrics and measures, 197–198
  overview, 181–183
  productivity, 190–192
  technology, 187–188
  training, 183–185
  workplace, 198–200
Security Basics and Literacy, 152
Security Event Information Management
    system, 117–118
Security Information and Event Management
    (SIEM) systems, 73
Security SHell Daemon, 43
Segregating networks, 72
Selection
  password, 139–140, 233
  risk assessment team, 275
  service providers, 238–239
  vendor, 80–81
Self-assessments, risk, 121, 236
Self-examination, 197
Self-replicating program, 40
Self-reproducing automata, 40
Seminars, awareness, 135–143
Senior and executive management, security
    awareness education, 135
Sensitive data, 25, 37, 156–157, 159, 165
Separation, of duties, 86–90, 186
Service-Level Agreements (SLAs), 96–97
Service providers
  selection, 238–239
  third-party, risks, 248
Shadow IT, 188
Sharing, data, 192
Shredder, paper, 199

Simplicity, strive for, 120–121
Social engineering (SE), 47–48, 52, 138–139,
    195, 200
Social media, 200
Social network sites, 57
Society of Human Resources Management, 209
Software
  license restriction issues, 141
  new versions, 18–19, 21
Sony, 166
Source code, access to, 58
Spam, 43, 138, 157
Spyware, 40
Staff/staffing
  compartmentalization of information,
      56–58
  incident response team, 255
  internal compromises, 157
  legal, 245–247
  loyalty, 162–167
  management, WISP, 232–233
  monitoring, 163–164
  morale, 196–197
  screenings, 162
  security concepts, 31–32
  stealing sensitive information, 156–157
  training, 5, 30, 32
  Use Cases, employment of, 31–32
Star Trek series, 75
State breach reporting obligations, risks of,
    249
State-sponsored attacks, 53
Stealing
  data, 156–157, 159, 162–167
  e-mail addresses, 208
Strategic planning
  capital expenditures, 179
  development, 174–180
  funding, 179–180
  operational expenses, 179–180
  process inputs, 175–178
  security, 171–172
Supplier's data centers, physical security
    measures, 212
Support life cycle, 19
Support teams, IT, 259–260
Switching, 32
Symantec, 187
Systems
  administration and management, 234
  failures, management, 238
  securing, effectively, 255–256

T

Talking, to Boards, 223–224, 241–252
Target, 208, 211, 245
Team leader, CSIRT, 262–263
Teams
    core team members, 260, 262
    corporate, 260
    CSIRT, 258, 259, 260, 262–263, 265, 266
    extended team members, 262–263
    IT support, 259–260
    risk assessment, selection, 275
    support team members, 262
Technical certification, 155
Technical debt, 16
Technical experts, IT, 259–260
Technical staff, awareness education for, 135
Technology, 103–113
    backups, 103–104
    creativity and, 120
    DAM, 236–237
    risk management for, 104–106
    Safe Harbor principles, 106–113
    security-based culture, 187–188
Test documentation, reviewing, 28–29
Testing
    penetration, *see* Penetration tests
    security awareness training, 149
    system's security, 127–128
The Onion Router (Tor), 54
Third-party service provider risks, 248
Thomas, Bob, 40
Threat cycle, 3, 4
Tinba, bot, 55
Tiny Banker, bot, 55
Titanic, 35
TomCat, 43
Top cyber risks assessment, 247
Tor (The Onion Router), 54
Tor Hidden Services, 54
Tracking IT assets, 26
Training
    awareness, 130–131, 132, 152
    awareness *vs.*, 152
    Certified Ethical Hacker, 77
    CSIRT, 265
    end-user, 130–131
    formal, 147
    incident response team, 255
    methods, 132–133
    new hire, 133–135
    plan, 178

    risk, reducing, 30
    security, 144–150; *see also* Security
        awareness and training
    security-based culture, 183–185, 200
    staff, 5, 30
    tests and quizzes, 149
    uncertainty and, 118
    user, 46
    WISP, 232–233
Transparency, defined, 92
Trojan Horses, 40, 41–46, 137, 214
Trust, 203–217
    cloud-based tools, 209–212
    internal, 213–217
    overview, 203–207
    with value, 215
    Vendor Oversight Program, 212–213
    vendors, 207–209
Tuning, 118
Tzu, Sun, 77, 78, 124

U

Uncertainty, risks and, 118–119, 244, 245
Update, WISP, 227–228, 249
Upgrading, systems, 16, 18, 21, 24, 25, 30, 31,
        32, 33–34, 35, 36
Up-to-date AV programs, 46
Use Cases, 31–32
User access, administration and, 97–98
User(s)
    account, administration and management, 234
    education, on BYOD, 200
    general, security awareness education,
        135–136
    IT security awareness and training
        responsibilities, 146–147
    training, 46
U-2 spy plane, 34

V

Vega, 62
Vendor, penetration-testing
    picking, 79
    selecting, 80–81
Vendor Oversight Program, 212–213
Vendors
    contracts and review, 213
    earned certifications for security and
        compliance, 211–212
    trust your, 207–209

Verification, 203–217
Vigilance, network, 72–73
Virtual private networks (VPNs), 54, 63
Virus(es), 41–46
    Creeper, 40–41
    defined, 41
    protection, 108–113, 137
    security myths, 41–46
Visitor control, 141
Von Clausewitz, Carl, 53, 77, 78
Von Neumann, John, 40
Vulnerabilities
    configuration management tool, 27
    Darknet, 54
    discovering, 28, 29, 31, 76
    exploit kits, 165
    Microsoft, looking for, 71
    obsolete operating systems, 18
    OSI layers, 25–26
    patching and, 18, 19–20, 21, 31
    scanning, 23–24
    sharing, 10
    upgrading existing system, 32

W

Weaponization, phase of kill chain, 74
Web usage, 138
Whistleblower protection, 163
White Hat Responsible Disclosure Policy,
        Facebook, 76
White hats, 62, 76
Wifite, 61
Windows Active Directory, 234
Wireless network, 61–63
Wireshark, 61
WISP, *see* Written Information Security Plan
        (WISP)
Word Press, 43
Workplace, security-based culture, 198–200
Worms, 40, 41–46, 137

Wright, Wilbur, 119, 120
Written guidelines, for prioritizing incidents,
        257
Written Information Security Plan (WISP),
        225–239
    appropriate service providers, selection,
        238–239
    approval and yearly update, 249
    APT, 236
    business continuity plan, 237
    communications, 227
    comprehensive, writing, 226
    continuing evaluation and adjustment,
        239
    customer information, identification and
        assessment of risk to, 230–231
    DAM technology, 236–237
    data center redundancy, 234
    disaster recovery plan, 238
    drafting, 228–239
    education and awareness, 226–228
    employee management and training,
        232–233
    encryption, 235
    general security measures, 233–234
    information systems, 233–238
    management of system failures, 238
    monitoring and audits, 235–236
    overview, 225–226
    physical security of protected information,
        238
    PII, 229–230
    review and update, 227–228
    roles and plan administration, 231–232
    sample, 228–239
    system and user account administration and
        management, 234

Z

Zap, 62